THE MEDICAL ACCIDENTS HANDBOOK

Action for Victims of Medical Accidents
1st–4th Floor
44 High Street
Croydon
Surrey CR0 1YB
Tel: 0181–688 9555 Fax: 0181–667 9065
DX: 84207 Croydon

Action for Victims of Medical Accidents (AVMA) was set up in 1982 as a direct result of a television play, 'Minor Complications' by the author and playwright, Peter Ransley. This play was based on the true story of a woman who suffered disabling injuries as a result of a failure to diagnose complications following a routine operation. Faced with a wall of silence, she embarked on a long and difficult journey to find out why her treatment had gone wrong and to seek reparation. There was an overwhelming public response to the play which led to the establishment of Action for Victims of Medical Accidents, a charity specialising in providing independent advice and support to patients injured during the course of medical treatment.

Advice for patients

AVMA provides a range of services for medical accident victims and their advisers. There is a free advisory service for patients and relatives seeking advice and information following a medical accident. This includes both medical information to assist people to investigate their care, and legal advice in the event that they are seeking compensation. If appropriate, AVMA can arrange a referral to an experienced medical negligence solicitor from AVMA's specialist panel.

Support network

An integral part of AVMA's work with medical accident victims is the Support Network which coordinates a range of support services including support meetings, newsletters, local contacts, and an annual conference.

Medico-legal services

AVMA also provides medico-legal services for lawyers specialising in this field through its subscription based Lawyers Service including the recommendation of appropriate medical experts, information on medical and procedural issues, and critical analysis of expert medical reports. AVMA runs a series of training courses and conferences for lawyers and healthcare workers and jointly produces a medico-legal journal, 'Clinical Risk'.

Campaigning

In addition to helping individuals, AVMA is actively campaigning both for improved regulation of standards within the health service to reduce the number of avoidable accidents as well as working towards a fairer, more effective system for meeting the needs of accident victims.

For further details, telephone 0181–686 8333 AVMA for an information pack.

Charity Registration No. 299123

THE MEDICAL ACCIDENTS HANDBOOK

A Practical Guide for Patients and their Advisers

Edited by

Liz Thomas
AVMA

Paul McNeil LL B
Solicitor of the Supreme Court

JOHN WILEY & SONS

Chichester • New York • Weinheim • Brisbane • Singapore • Toronto

Published by John Wiley & Sons Ltd,
Baffins Lane, Chichester,
West Sussex PO19 1UD, England

National 01243 779777
International (+44) 1243 779777
e-mail (for orders and customer service enquiries): cs-books@wiley.co.uk
Visit our Home Page on http://www.wiley.co.uk
or http://www.wiley.com

Other Wiley Editorial Offices

John Wiley & Sons, Inc, 605 Third Avenue,
New York, NY 10158–0012, USA

WILEY-VCH Verlag GmbH, Pappelallee 3,
D-69469 Weinheim, Germany

Jacaranda Wiley Ltd, 33 Park Road, Milton,
Queensland 4064, Australia

John Wiley & Sons (Asia) Pte Ltd, 2 Clementi Loop #02–01,
Jin Xing Distripark, Singapore 129809

John Wiley & Sons (Canada) Ltd, 22 Worcester Road,
Rexdale, Ontario M9W 1L1, Canada

British Library Cataloguing in Publication Data

A catalogue record for this book is available from the British Library

ISBN 0-471-96642-8

Typeset in 11/13 pt Sabon by The Midlands Book Typesetting Company, Loughborough, Leicestershire.
Printed and bound in Great Britain by Biddles Ltd, Guildford and King's Lynn.
This book is printed on acid-free paper responsibly manufactured from sustainable forestry, in which at least two trees are planted for each one used for paper production.

CONTENTS

FOREWORD

Rt Hon. Lord Ashley of Stoke, CH

House of Lords
London
SW1A 0PW

The principle of the David and Goliath legend is rooted in many conflicts; none more so than in disputes about medical accidents. The victims not only face massive odds, but they are often disorientated before battle commences.

As if these disadvantages were not enough, people seeking explanation or redress face a maze so complex as to defy analysis, let alone negotiation. Unaware of their rights, unable to comprehend the rules and faced with legal jargon, it is no surprise that victims can be beaten before they start.

In recent years, a beacon for them has been Action for Victims of Medical Accidents. Now that fine organisation has published this comprehensive book. Its contents are described in the introduction and the pages themselves are illuminating. From beacon to bible is a hazardous step, but AVMA has accomplished it successfully.

Jack Ashley   8 April 1998

CONTRIBUTORS

Mr Patrick Allen
Hodge Jones & Allen
148–150 Camden High Street
London ED2N 2AA

DX 57050
CAMDEN TOWN

Mr Frank Burton QC
12 King's Bench Walk
Temple
London EC4Y 7EL

DX1037
CHANCERY LANE

Mr Richard Ennals
7 Turpin Way
Wallington
SM6 0SN

Ms Claire Fazan
Bindman & Partners
275 Gray's Inn Road
London WC1X 8QF

DX 37904
KINGS CROSS

Ms Nina Fletcher
Department of Law
University of Staffordshire
College Road
Stoke on Trent
SP4 2DE

Mr Graham Girvan
Darlington Community Health Council
9 Northgate
Darlington
DL1 1TL

Ms Caroline Hallisey
Hardwicke Building
New Square
Lincoln's Inn
London WC2A 2SB

Ms Caroline Jenkins
Parlett Kent & Co
Signet House
49/51 Farringdon Road
London EC1M 3JB

DX 53308
CLERKENWELL

Ms Sarah Leigh
Leigh Day & Co
Priory House
25 St John's Lane
London EC1M 4LB

DX 53326
CLERKENWELL

Mr Paul McNeil
Field Fisher Waterhouse
41 Vine Street
London EC3N 2AA

DX 823
LONDON

Simeon Maskrey QC
9 Bedford Row
London WC1R 4A2

DX 347
CHANCERY LANE

Mr Keith Miles
Action for Victims of Medical Accidents
1st–4th Floor
44 High Street
Croydon CR0 1YB

DX 84207
CROYDON

Mr Rodney Nelson-Jones
Field Fisher Waterhouse
41 Vine Street
London EC3N 2AA

DX823
LONDON

Mr Tom Osborne
Osborne Morris & Morgan
Danbury House
West Street
Leighton Buzzard LU7 7DD

DX 90804
LEIGHTON BUZZARD

Mr Richard A Oswald
The Orchard Cottage
Cripplegate Lane
Southwater RH13 7HN

Ms Susan Polywka
The Stable Block
Manor House
Headley Way
Oxford OX3 9DZ

Mr Arnold Simanowitz
Action for Victims of Medical Accidents
1st–4th Floor
44 High Street
Croydon CR0 1YB

DX 84207
CROYDON

Ms Paula Sparks
Action for Victims of Medical Accidents
1st–4th Floor
44 High Street
Croydon CR0 1YB

DX 84207
CROYDON

Mr Robin Stewart QC
2nd Floor
199 Strand
London WC2R 1DR

DX322
CHANCERY LANE

Ms Liz Thomas
Action for Victims of Medical Accidents
1st–4th Floor
44 High Street
Croydon CR0 1YB

DX 84207
CROYDON

Dr Charles Vincent
Department of Psychology
Torrington Place
London WC1E 6BT

INTRODUCTION

Arnold Simanowitz

THE REASON FOR A GUIDE

When AVMA was founded, in 1982, medical accidents were not even recognised as a problem. Indeed, one of AVMA's primary aims, set out in their very first press release, was 'to bring medical accidents onto the agenda'.

It has to be acknowledged that in this aim AVMA has been hugely successful. Great strides have been made in raising the awareness of members of the public of their rights, both to be fairly treated if something does go wrong in the course of medical treatment and to compensation when what goes wrong causes damage as a result of negligence[1]. Similarly, awareness has been raised among healthcare providers of their obligations to patients in those circumstances.

During that time AVMA has been the only organisation dedicated to dealing with medical accidents. Many lawyers have become expert on the legal side of the problem and many books have since been written for lawyers on the subject of medical negligence. But AVMA has remained the only resource able to advise across the board on the many complex and interwoven issues involved in the subject.

It is not possible for one small charity to advise everyone who needs assistance in this area. Besides, many people do not require anything more than to be given the right guidelines on how to approach the problem themselves, whilst many agencies, such as Community Health Councils and Citizens Advice Bureaux would be quite capable of giving the basic advice such people need if they had a reference work which covered the whole field in a comprehensive and user-friendly manner.

Help for individuals and agencies

This handbook is intended to meet the needs of those who wish or need to have an understanding of the issues involved: of those individuals who want to help themselves when they believe they

[1]For an explanation of negligence in the medical context see Chapter 16

have been the victim of a medical accident, both up to the point where the technical assistance of a lawyer experienced in the field becomes necessary, as well as by monitoring the performance of their lawyers to ensure they are receiving an adequate service. It is also intended to meet the needs of the advice agencies which not only need a guide to enter into the world of medical accidents but may also wish to monitor the progress of any legal action upon which their consultees may embark.

Lawyers

It will also help those lawyers entering the field for the first time. They may well have a good grasp of the law and practice of medical negligence but will from time to time need to know much more about the context in which such accidents occur, and the resources available to their clients for whom compensation may not be the only, or even the most important, need.

HOW TO USE THE GUIDE

General education

Whilst it is hoped that the guide will be of benefit to those simply interested in the subject of medical accidents who wish to read it in order to have a greater understanding, most people who turn to it will be either those who have suffered a medical accident or are advising someone who has, and want to know what to do.

The sections have therefore been carefully designed to enable readers to follow step by step the procedure which is necessary to give them the satisfaction they require. Each section stands alone but they follow on in such a way that readers are taken carefully through all the stages involved in seeking appropriate redress.

What is vitally important, however, is that those seeking redress should have an understanding of what is involved when they set out on what could be quite a tortuous path.

Complaints

If, for example you simply wish to make a complaint about the care you received while being treated under the National Health Service, the chapter on that subject will show exactly what you have to do.

It would be helpful, however, for you first to understand the structure of that service and the division of responsibility within it. Similarly, you should have an idea of what the purpose of the complaints procedures is and the limitations on what can be achieved in order to avoid unreal expectations. Accordingly a reading of the chapters describing the National Health Service and introducing the complaints procedures, if not compulsory, would be worthwhile.

Legal action

Similarly, the majority of you who do consult the guide will do so because you believe that you or your relative have suffered a medical accident and may be seeking compensation. As the main way to obtain compensation is through the courts, you may be contemplating consulting a lawyer. Before you do so you need to understand what is involved in proving a claim, what a lawyer can and cannot do for you and what you are likely to receive by way of compensation.

The section on medical negligence and legal action is carefully divided into chapters which should answer all those questions and it is advisable to read them all before embarking on litigation.

Step-by-step guide

At the same time, however, most of the specific questions about all the detailed matters which so concern those who are seeking redress can be answered by turning to the particular topic in the guide. By looking up the particular procedure which you have decided to select you should be able to follow that procedure yourself without too much outside assistance insofar as the complaint side is concerned.

As importantly, where legal action is involved, you will be able to understand all the steps your lawyer is taking on your behalf and you should carefully monitor that she is taking those steps at the correct time and in the right way. If that is not happening you should use the guide to challenge them and ask for explanations.

Using the guide you should be able to deal with most situations yourself. If you do need help, however, there are a number of agencies who can assist with specific problems or generally and they are referred to in appendix 1. Even when consulting others *you* should use the guide to identify what questions you should ask and check the advice you were given.

Most importantly, however, you should be clear about what you actually want to achieve as well as how to achieve it. There are many options open to those who believe they have suffered a medical accident and this guide will help you to identify the option which is most likely to give you the satisfaction you are seeking.

THE AVAILABLE OPTIONS

Notwithstanding the attempt by the Government to rationalise and simplify the system by the setting up of the Wilson inquiry[2], there remains a bewildering number of procedures for anyone who is unhappy about the medical care (or lack of it) he or she has received.

It is essential that you are clear in your own mind what you want to achieve before you start on one of the procedures available. That is because the option you choose will decide what you do in fact achieve.

The options

- Complaint
- Disciplinary inquiry
- Legal action
- Mediation
- Criminal prosecution

COMPLAINT

Most people who feel that something has gone wrong simply want an explanation and, if appropriate, an apology. Many also want to ensure that what happened to them does not happen to anyone else. If that is what you wish to achieve then you should make a complaint using the procedures which must be set up in all hospitals and for all general practitioners[2]. The result of those procedures may be to secure a satisfactory explanation and apology for you and may lead to a change in systems to try and ensure that the problem does not arise again.

[2]An inquiry under Professor Alan Wilson into the handling of complaints within the NHS. For further details, see Chapter 5

DISCIPLINARY INQUIRY

The complaints procedures will not however concern themselves with disciplinary matters. Indeed, they are specifically prevented from doing so. If, therefore your main concern is the fitness of a healthcare practitioner to practise or you consider that he or she has been guilty of serious professional misconduct then you must make a complaint to the relevant professional body. (See Chapter 10)

LEGAL ACTION

The complaints procedures do not make provision for the awarding of compensation save in very limited circumstances and for very limited sums. If you are clear that it is compensation that you are after then in most situations you will have no option *but* to take legal action.

WARNING The only purpose of the courts is to award compensation if it is appropriate. They are not concerned with ensuring that 'the truth comes out' nor with disciplinary matters. Often a legal case will be settled with the payment of compensation without a hearing and the person responsible for the damage will never appear. This can lead to great dissatisfaction on the part of the person complaining.

On the other hand, if you indicate at the outset that what you want is compensation and you will be taking legal action to obtain it, then it is not possible for the complaints procedures, which might give you the explanation you are seeking, to be used. Part 3 will explain how to approach this difficult topic but it can be seen that a lawyer is probably not the best person to consult for advice at this stage, although some lawyers have a clear understanding of this dilemma.

The role of the client

Once a decision has been taken to litigate it is important that you are aware of the part you can and should play in the proceedings. It has traditionally been the role of the client of a solicitor to accept the advice given and to let the solicitor get on with the case. However long the procedure lasted and whatever concerns the client had about the way in which the case was being conducted, most people felt that the law and legal procedure was so complicated that they could not and should not intervene in any way. They were usually encouraged in this feeling by the attitude of the solicitor.

Any good medical negligence solicitor today will accept that the relationship is much more one of partnership and that the client can actually assist with the successful prosecution of the case. It is essential that clients should no longer see themselves as 'sleeping partners'. At every stage you have an important part to play:

- when the solicitor first takes instructions, you should ensure that what you consider is important is recorded;
- you should always see your medical records, preferably with your lawyer who should be able to help you understand what they say;
- you should also insist on regular reporting; when you receive the report, if there is anything you do not understand, you should ask the solicitor to explain.

All this will enable you to play an active rather than a passive part in the case and will keep your solicitor up to the mark. Clients should understand that even the best solicitors can delay cases unnecessarily, often for the very reason that they are good and are therefore too busy. You can do a lot to ensure that your case is kept on track.

It is also important that you seek support if you feel the case is getting you down. Medical negligence cases can take a long time and can cause considerable distress. For example, the defence to the claim may say that the accident was nobody's fault, or the doctor acted in an exemplary manner or that you had not really suffered as alleged. This can be extremely distressing.

Further, to have to go through the story time and again – to the solicitor, to the medical expert, and to the barrister, often on more than one occasion, and then again in court so that you often recount the same story seven or eight times – can impose an enormous strain. Add to that the length of time the case takes and the uncertainty about the result and you have an extremely tortuous process. Many patients ask themselves during that process, and even after a successful result, whether it is worth it. Two things can help to make it so. Firstly, if the case is handled properly by your solicitor much of the pain can be eased. Secondly, you should seek support while the case is proceeding. Such support can be available from friends and family or even a professional counsellor. However, AVMA's Support Network has been established to meet that particular need and it is a resource you should not overlook.

MEDIATION

The one procedure that may be able to give you much of the satisfaction you require is mediation. The outcome of such a procedure is intended to be the resolution of the differences between the parties. It could help you to obtain a full explanation and an apology, to meet the healthcare professional face-to-face if that is what you want and to receive compensation.

Mediation has proved to be very successful in many disputes other than healthcare treatment. It deals with disputes in a less adversarial way, takes far less time and is considerably less costly and as a result it is becoming increasingly popular. Indeed, Family Mediation has become an accepted procedure for dealing with matrimonial disputes, particularly those involving custody of children.

Insofar as clinical disputes are concerned, it is by no means clear that it will always be of advantage to patients. That is because the parties do not start on a level playing field. The dispute is about medicine and the healthcare providers will hold all the cards. On the other hand there is much to gain, apart from reducing the cost and delay, in removing the adversarial element from an area where it least belongs. In order to try and ascertain whether mediation is appropriate to the dispute the Department of Health set up a pilot scheme in 1995 in two Regions. That pilot will be academically evaluated and it is hoped that the full result will be known during 1998.

As a result a number of disputes have already been mediated and lawyers on both sides are urged to consider their cases for submission to the pilot. If you think it may work for you, you should raise the possibility with your lawyers. There are a few disputes being mediated outside the pilot but that is not recommended because, with the potential problem involved in mediation in this area, it is desirable that all mediation takes place within the controlled conditions of the pilot.

CRIMINAL PROSECUTION

There are certain extreme situations in which the actions of a healthcare provider can amount to a criminal act. For example, operating without consent would amount to an assault. It is not desirable, however, that every act which would amount to a criminal act should be presented as a crime. If failure to obtain consent is deliberate or reckless and if the damage caused is very serious it may be appropriate. The main criterion in this and other possible criminal action is whether the healthcare provider is likely to be appropriately brought to account in other ways – for example by disciplinary action.

If you feel very strongly about the behaviour of a healthcare provider, you should at least raise this question with your lay or legal adviser.

Section I

ACCESS TO HEALTH CARE AND PATIENTS' RIGHTS

Chapter 1

MEDICAL ACCIDENTS AND RISK MANAGEMENT

Charles Vincent

This chapter explains the background to medical accidents in the context of the NHS today. It discusses the causes and consequences of accidents and the development of a risk management strategy.

Patients may be harmed, disturbed or disappointed by treatment, even when treatment is entirely appropriate. Admission to intensive care for instance may be frightening even when staff do their utmost to be sympathetic and reassuring. Some treatment is disappointing because it does not have the effects that the patient expects or hopes for. In such cases complaints may be made because patients have not understood or have not been warned that the treatment's effect is uncertain. Treatment for serious illness may necessarily involve disfiguring and harmful operations because this is the only way to arrest the progress of the disease.

Medical accidents are incidents in which patients are unintentionally injured by medical treatment. Alternatively the failure to diagnose or institute the proper treatment may lead to harm that could have been averted. Some people find the term accidents unsatisfactory, because it implies an unpredictable, chance occurrence, and so the more general term "adverse events" is often used. In some cases there may have been no physical damage, but the patient has been unnecessarily traumatised by the process of treatment or the attitude and behaviour of staff. Many complaints arise through a combination of an unsatisfactory, or harmful, outcome of treatment combined with poor communication or upsetting comments from staff.

ADVERSE EVENTS ARE MORE COMMON THAN IS GENERALLY REALISED

American studies have found that approximately 4% of admissions involve an adverse event. These include death, increased length of stay, readmission to the hospital and unplanned transfer to the intensive care unit. In one study errors in management were identified in over half the cases and in 1% of admissions care was judged to be negligent. In 70% of the adverse events the resulting disability was slight or short-lived, but in 7% it was permanent and 14% of patients died in part as a result of their treatment. (Many of the patients who died would already have been seriously ill and might not have recovered in any case.) If we extrapolate these results to a British context it appears probable that a considerable number of people each year are harmed in some way by their treatment, though many of these will be quite minor problems.

THE COSTS OF ADVERSE EVENTS

The occasional large sums awarded to patients, sometimes over £1 million, attract much media attention. However the overall current cost of litigation to the NHS is still relatively small, currently about £250 million per annum, when compared with the total budget of £37 billion. Since 1990 the cost of litigation has been borne by the hospital, though many hospitals have elected to become members of the new Central Negligence Scheme for Trusts (CNST) which in effect insures them against large claims. Litigation is increasing however and the eventual cost to hospitals may amount to a significant part of their budgets.

The cost of adverse events generally is very much higher, in both human and financial terms, than the cost of litigation. There are, to begin with, many more adverse events than claims. Many adverse events involve a huge personal cost to the people involved. Patients may suffer increased pain, disability and psychological trauma. They and their relatives may become depressed, angry and bitter and experience their treatment as a terrible betrayal of trust. Their problems are often compounded by a protracted adversarial legal process. Staff may experience shame, guilt and depression after making a mistake. Feeling responsible for injuring a patient appears to be one of the main sources of stress for young doctors. Litigation imposes an additional burden, in that staff may feel unfairly attacked and blamed. Injury to patients also means increased use of hospital resources and additional time with staff. The financial costs in terms of use of resources and reduced efficiency are unknown, but probably vastly greater than the immediate costs of litigation.

UNDERSTANDING ADVERSE EVENTS

Why do things go wrong? With a few exceptions, as in any profession, doctors, nurses and other clinical staff are hardworking, caring people who have the interests of their patients at heart. On occasions of course even the most highly skilled and dedicated persons make a mistake, and this becomes more likely if they are tired, over-stretched or have other problems in their lives. Less forgivably some staff may act rashly at times, attempting procedures for which they do not have sufficient training, or they may fail to seek advice when facing a difficult or dangerous situation. Junior staff may experience particular difficulty in that they may not have the experience to recognise when a patient's condition has become serious.

The actions of individual staff are only part of the picture – hospitals, general practice and community services are extremely complex organisations. Many delays and difficulties occur which cannot be controlled by the staff who are actually caring for the patient. It is hard for a team of people to unravel the often complex series of events that leads to a bad outcome. Worrying cases are routinely reviewed in audit meetings in many specialities, but there is not always sufficient time to analyse the cases in detail. There may also be a tendency to simply attribute blame rather than try to understand what has happened.

Formal studies of the quality of care are relatively recent in Britain. The first formal studies of adverse outcomes began in the 1950s with the confidential enquiry into maternal deaths.

However clinical audit, in which aspects of care are systematically reviewed, did not really become established in most medical specialities until the late 1980s.

Confidential enquiries into maternal and postoperative deaths have revealed problems with supervision of junior staff and a higher mortality from surgeons operating outside their own speciality. Critical incident studies in anaesthetics have pointed to a repeated failure to check equipment and unfamiliarity with the way the equipment works. An analysis of major obstetric claims identified three major areas of concern: inadequate fetal monitoring – staff were often unable to recognise abnormal fetal heart traces; mismanagement of forceps – undue traction, too many attempts; lack of involvement of senior staff – inexperienced doctors were left alone and without help.

Serious medical accidents occur against a background of more frequent minor incidents and errors. A British study found that over half of admissions included an adverse occurrence, an occasion on which treatment did not go according to plan. Many were trivial but over a third were clinically relevant. Adverse occurrences include such incidents as unplanned return to operating theatre, cardiac or respiratory arrest and abnormal results not accessed by the physician. Studies of the accuracy of tests and clinical procedures also suggest that errors are common. High rates of error have been found in detecting the clinical signs of cyanosis, interpreting electrocardiograms and radiographs, taking a history and assessing biopsy specimens in the laboratory. Even basic skills such as resuscitation have been found to fall short of the expected standard.

ACCIDENTS, RISK AND SAFETY

Analyses of accidents in industry, transport and military spheres, whose methods are beginning to be applied to medicine, give us further clues as to how such complex questions can be approached. Such studies have led to a much broader understanding of accident causation, with less focus on the individual who makes the error and more on pre-existing organisational factors. Human decisions and actions play a major part in nearly all accidents contributing to two main types of failure.

Active failures are committed by those at the "sharp end" of the system (pilots, air-traffic controllers, anaesthetists, surgeons, nurses etc) whose actions can have immediate adverse consequences. They include memory lapses, slips during actions, mistakes due to ignorance or mis-reading a situation. In medicine most attention has been paid to the active failures.

Latent failures arise from fallible decisions often taken by people not directly involved in the workplace. They provide the conditions in which unsafe acts occur: high workload and fatigue; inadequate knowledge, ability or experience; poor equipment design; inadequate supervision or instruction; a stressful environment, or rapid change within an organisation. Behind these error-producing conditions may lie a further set of wider organisational problems such as a conflict between profit and safety, inadequate communications and deficient training.

The analysis of an adverse event often reveals a series of errors combined with a set of unusual circumstances which together lead to an adverse outcome. Consider the range of factors involved in medicine. Training is often informal and based on observation only; the learning of key skills may not be assessed. Combine trial and error learning with a lack of supervision and the risks become apparent. Add work overload, lack of sleep, lack of awareness of hazardous situations, a degree of over-confidence stemming perhaps from a desire to prove oneself and the potential for major disasters becomes apparent. Looking at the problems in this way, one can also see that sometimes staff are caught up in a web of circumstances over which they may have little control.

PREVENTING INJURY TO PATIENTS

In the last ten years there have been a considerable number of initiatives, such as clinical audit, aimed at improving the overall quality of care in the health service. All of these have the potential to reduce adverse events. Risk management, a very recent development in Britain, is another method of improving the quality of care but one particularly aimed at preventing harm to patients.

Risk management programmes aim primarily to:

- reduce the frequency of preventable adverse events;

- minimise the trauma to those involved in adverse events; and
- reduce the frequency and cost of litigation.

At the heart of most programmes are methods for early identification of adverse events, usually from staff reports. This requires establishing a culture in which staff feel able to report dangerous or worrying incidents without fear of immediate censure or blame. The reports are used to create a database to identify common patterns and prevent future incidents. Individual cases that may lead to claims can be investigated while memories are still fresh, instead of years later from medical records as so often happens in litigation as currently practised. The immediate investigation of serious incidents should greatly assist the resolution of claims and complaints. The analysis of these incidents can have important implications for the organisation of care. Patients and relatives should be informed about adverse incidents and immediate action taken where necessary to minimise both the physical and psychological trauma. Patients with justified claims can be swiftly compensated, and the organisation and its staff are more effectively defended against unjustified claims.

Formal risk management programmes are desirable but more specific changes are also needed. Improvements in training and supervision are clearly important. Senior doctors and hospital management may be unaware of the extent to which junior doctors are called upon to act beyond their competence. Poor communication between professions is another source of errors and lost information.

Low staffing levels, fatigue and stress are clear examples of error-producing working conditions, particularly the absurd hours that some junior staff are still required to work in Britain. It is a curious paradox that it is illegal to drive a coachload of healthy passengers without regular rest, yet it is considered acceptable to care for a ward full of desperately sick patients when close to exhaustion. Another important development is the increased use of formal guidelines in the management of many conditions. Guidelines can be perceived as limiting clinical freedom or restricting innovation, but when properly used they can allow necessary clinical flexibility while still setting limits on safe practice.

WHEN ACCIDENTS DO OCCUR: CARING FOR PATIENTS AND STAFF

Compensation, although very important in many cases, is not the only motive for legal action. Patients may blame doctors not so much for the original mistakes, as for a lack of openness or willingness to explain them after the event. A valuable feature of the legal system, much appreciated by patients, is that each case is reviewed by a truly independent expert instructed by a lawyer. Many patients find that a clear and sympathetic report or interview is a relief, whether or not it suggests that care was actually negligent. Simply knowing the truth brings some peace of mind. Risk management will hopefully encourage a greater openness and willingness to explain when treatment has not gone as planned.

Many injured patients wish to ensure that their experience is not repeated and this is often one of their reasons for taking legal action. If useful changes are made they may feel that at least some good has come of their experiences which may also help them cope with the trauma involved. In a few cases they may decide not to initiate litigation.

Counselling for patients may be valuable. After major incidents staff too may need help and signs of stress in such situations should not be taken as weakness. For staff to attempt to cope regardless of the consequences to themselves and their patients is dangerously irresponsible.

CONCLUSION: HOPE FOR THE FUTURE

The negative aspects of complaints and litigation are clear to everyone involved. Nevertheless, a positive side is emerging. Complaints and litigation have continued to draw attention to the immense problems faced by patients who are harmed or disturbed by their treatment. To begin to use complaints as a form of feedback and to focus on adverse events as revealing deeper problems in an organisation requires a fundamental shift in attitude in many hospitals and practices, but there are now many clinical staff who support such a change. Risk management and other associated approaches offer the chance to turn a potentially disastrous downward spiral of litigation and mistrust into a focused quality initiative targeted at the avoidable injuries that do so much harm to patients and staff alike.

FURTHER READING

More detailed discussions of work on medical accidents and risk management by senior doctors and academics, and references to many other books and articles on the subject, can be found in *Clinical Risk Management*, edited by Charles Vincent, British Medical Journal Publications, 1995.

Chapter 2

THE ORGANISATION OF THE NHS

Caroline Hallisey

This chapter traces the origins of the NHS from its inception in 1946 and describes the present structure of the NHS and the role of the health professional within the components of the NHS.

The NHS and Community Care Act 1990 radically altered the organisation of the NHS, introducing commercial concepts to the previously solely publicly financed and managed health system.

The reforms introduced by the Act were the culmination of the reorganisations of the NHS which had continually taken place since the date of its creation. In some respects the changes mirrored reforms in other national healthcare systems.

THE ORIGINS OF THE NHS

The idea of public responsibility for health originated in the nineteenth century.

However it was not until 1942 and the Beveridge report that the Government accepted the need for a nationally organised comprehensive health service. The aim of the National Health Service Act 1946 (which came into effect on 5th July 1948) was to establish a 'comprehensive health service designed to secure improvement in the physical and mental health of the people of England and Wales and the prevention, diagnosis and treatment of illness.'

Free health care was to be available to all, based on clinical need.

THE ORGANISATION OF THE NHS IN 1948

The NHS created by the 1946 Act was administered in three parts. Regional Health Boards (at first 14, and later 15) were set up based around university medical schools, Local Health Authorities which administered community health services, such as vaccination and immunisation, and Executive Councils which were established to administer the family practitioner service (GPs, dentists etc).

The three parts were separately funded which resulted in a lack of cohesion and the failure to establish a satisfactory standard across the NHS.

THE 1974 REORGANISATION

The 1974 reorganisation was motivated by the desire to create a more integrated and unified NHS.

Regional Health Authorities (RHA) were to concentrate on national and strategic planning. Ninety Area Health Authorities (AHAs) were set up to prepare strategic plans for each district. These were responsible not only for providing but also planning services by deciding how best to use the resources allocated by the RHA.

District management teams were established to deal with the day to day running of health care in their area (formerly run by local authorities such as community and school health services).

However, notwithstanding the reorganisation, there remained general dissatisfaction with the reformed system, in particular with the confusion created by the dual responsibility of Area Health Authorities for both planning and providing services.

THE ROYAL COMMISSION ON THE NHS 1976

The Secretary of State for Health acknowledged that the 1974 organisation had failed by establishing a Royal Commission to investigate and report on the NHS.

The Commission took three years to report, by which time the Conservative Party had won the 1979 General Election. The Commission was critical of some aspects of the management of the NHS, primarily that:

- there were too many administrators;
- there were too many tiers of authority; and
- decision making was too slow.

These criticisms struck a chord with the incoming administration who published its own views in 'Patient First', a consultative paper published in 1979 on the structural changes it thought the NHS needed to be an effective provider of health services.

The Government felt that decision making should take place closer to the patient at district level by district health authorities and that the Area Health Authorities should be abolished.

Districts were to be based around district general hospitals.

This formed the basis for the 1982 reorganisation of the NHS.

1982 REORGANISATION

District Health Authorities became responsible for hospitals and community health services. Family practitioner committees administered the contracts of GPs. Both were supervised by Regional Health Authorities and the Department of Health and Social Security.

FUNDING PROBLEMS AND THE INTRODUCTION OF MANAGERIALISM 1982–1990

The 1982 reorganisation did not solve the administrative problems within the NHS. The Government was concerned about rising costs; NHS funding continued to grow in real terms but at a slow rate. There was an increasingly large gap between Government funding and the money needed to meet the needs of an ageing population and advances in medical technology.

The way that the NHS was funded did not encourage greater efficiency. Resources were allocated globally regardless of how many patients a hospital was treating. This created what was termed the "efficiency trap" where a hospital was in effect penalised for being more efficient and treating more patients, because there was no corresponding increase in their funds.

The Government reacted by trying to ease the pressure on the NHS by encouraging patients to use private sector health services and by contracting out some NHS support work such as laundry services which was then extended to non-clinical areas such as pathology and diagnostic services.

Marketing ideas were introduced into the NHS with the Health and Medicines Act 1988 and the Department of Health's guidelines on schemes for income generation. This resulted in shops being opened in hospital corridors, land being sold for car parks and hospital wall space being sold for advertising.

This took place against a backdrop of increasing financial crisis. Ward closures, long waiting lists and tales of underfunding became the norm. The BMA called for better funding and the Presidents of the Royal Colleges of Physicians, Obstetricians and Gynaecologists and Surgeons called on the Government to save the health service.

The Government reacted by injecting cash and announcing in 1988 a Ministerial Review of the future of the NHS.

MINISTERIAL INQUIRY 1988

The inquiry concentrated on an efficient use of resources and in this climate, the concept of an internal market began to catch on.

THE INTERNAL MARKET

The idea was originally developed by Professor Enthoven in the 1980s[1]; in 1985 he devised an internal market for the NHS in which district general managers were able to purchase medical services for the residents of their districts from private hospitals and NHS hospitals in other districts.

Its central theme was the theory of separating out the functions of the purchasing and providing of services. In the internal market, money would follow the patient thus avoiding the efficiency trap and promoting economy with decreased administrative costs.

[1] Reflections on the Management of the NHS, London 1995

The legislation

The Government Inquiry reported a year later with the publication of 'Working for Patients' as a White Paper on 31st January 1989. This was then incorporated into the NHS and Community Care Act 1990.

The Government announced that the basic principles of the NHS would not be changed. The service was to remain funded primarily from taxation. Access to care was to be based on clinical need. More autonomy was to be given to the providers of health care, and there were to be incentives for efficiency. Internal NHS finance was to be organised to relate hospital incomes more directly to their activities and hospitals were to be allowed to behave more entrepreneurially to respond to new opportunities.

Main changes

Separation of purchaser and provider roles and creation of internal market

On the purchasing side were the District Health Authorities (DHA), Family Health Service Authorities (FHSA) and fund-holding GP practices. The main providers included the new self-governing hospitals (NHS Trusts), directly managed hospitals, general practitioners, private hospitals and other specialist provider units. These would be competing with one another for the custom of the purchasers' demand led by patients.

DHAs were allocated funds to provide services for the people in their area and had to use the allotted funds to bring the most benefits to the patients. It was believed that this would promote efficiency and improve the quality of services. In the past, hospitals were not rewarded for the number of patients treated; productivity was not rewarded by increased funding. In the new NHS, money would follow the patient, and inefficient providers would be penalised by no custom in they did not provide the requisite standard of services.

The Purchasers

GP fundholders

The idea of GP fundholders was not central to 'Working for Patients' and in many ways was seen as something of a late addition, surfacing half way through the Ministerial Review. Giving GPs their own budget was thought to bring the decision making closer to the patient or consumer who could change GPs if they were not satisfied with the GP's handling of resources.

Main features of fundholding

Fundholding practices receive a budget allocation from Central Government to be spent only on specified areas (not for example on increasing doctors' salaries) although any surplus can be spent on the practice's premises. The money was held by the Family Health Services Authority, which had replaced The Family Practitioner Committee, to pay the providers (hospitals) when the practice told them to. The budget was set by assessing what use had been made of services in the past and their cost.

Initially the fundholder could only spend money on:–

- hospital inpatient care for a specified type of operation;
- outpatient care, including diagnostic tests;
- practice's drug budgets.

From April 1993 the range of services covered was broadened to include community health services like district nursing.

Fundholding practices were also given greater freedom over personnel matters. In the past, the FHSA would have had a say in staff employment.

Reactions to fundholding

At first the BMA and most GPs were fiercely opposed to the concept of fundholding which they felt had been imposed without consultation or negotiation.

Three hundred and six GP fundholders were established on 1st April 1991. The first fundholders were seen by other (non-fundholding) GPs as betraying their colleagues. Soon, however,

GPs realised that there were benefits to the changes. In the first year, the average income exceeded the intended target by £6000 a head[2]. Largely as a result of this profitability fundholding numbers grew rapidly until by April 1994 there were 2000 fundholding practices – 'Militancy was doused by prosperity'[3].

GPs were no longer merely referring their patients to the local hospital; their role as purchasers of services gave them greater freedom. Fundholding practices could negotiate shorter waiting times for hospital services and switch contracts between providers if better services were available.

In addition there was the possibility of greater service development with, for example, fundholding practices providing on-site services, such as physiotherapy and counselling.

Understandably, patients of non-fundholding practices became concerned as a two tier system of general practice (with fundholders getting a better service from providers) developed.

In 1993, the BMA reported that patients of fundholders *were* getting preferential treatment. However in the face of the scheme's popularity (by then) with GPs there was little the BMA could do. By 1994 over a third of the country's population were in fundholding practices[1], rising to 50% following the sixth wave of fundholding applications.

District Health Authorities (DHA)

Before the 1990 legislation, DHAs received a budget from Regional Health Authorities to manage the hospital and community health services in its area. Under the new legislation DHAs became purchasers as well as providers of services.

They were allocated funds to purchase medical services for the people living in their area. The amount paid was calculated on the local population, their age and sex.

At first the change was difficult because DHAs were providing services as well as purchasing them. This dual role had to be separated by leaving the purchasing decisions to DHA headquarters and the providing decisions to the directly managed units who would eventually become NHS Trusts.

In April 1996, the Health Authorities Act 1995 led to DHAs

---

[2] Review Body on Doctors' & Nurses' Remuneration (22nd Report)
[3] The New Politics of the NHS (3rd Ed.) : R. Klein

being merged with Family Health Service Authorities to create 100 unified Health Authorities. This enabled a more integrated approach to purchasing at local level. At the same time, Regional Health Authorities were abolished, their main functions being taken over by eight regional offices whose responsibilities include managing the performance of purchasers and providers, arbitrating in contractual disputes, and approving GP fundholding applications. The regional offices are headed by regional directors, directly accountable to the Chief Executive of the NHS.

The Providers

NHS Trusts

Fifty seven NHS Trusts came into existence on 1 April 1991 covering a wide range of services, from hospitals to ambulance services. This number increased over the next few years until by April 1994 there were almost 500 Trusts.

NHS Trusts are independent organisations providing secondary and community health care services. When a hospital becomes a Trust, its assets are transferred from the government to its trustees, while the government holds a debt of equal value.

Trusts are directly accountable to the Secretary of State for Health. NHS Management Executive outposts were established regionally to monitor the financial performance of the Trusts, and on an annual basis to approve their Annual Business Plans and agree an external financial limit.

Trusts are given greater freedoms than directly managed units in both personnel and financial matters. Trusts are not constrained by national pay rates but are able to negotiate locally with employees.

Financially, Trusts have more powers to borrow money than Health Authorities. They are able to raise capital from private sources as well as the Treasury.

Other providers

In addition to NHS Trusts, the other main providers include Family Health Service Practitioners, directly managed hospitals, special

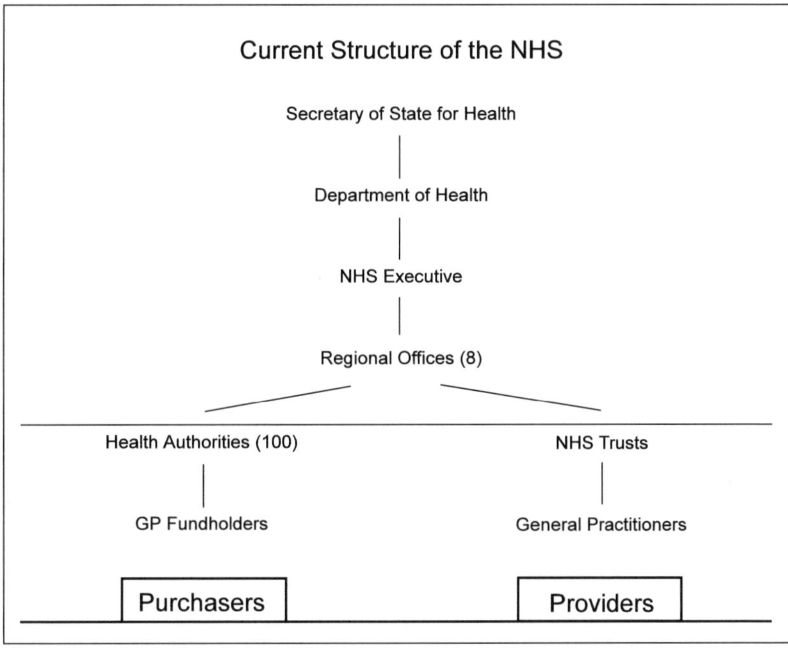

health authorities e.g. National Blood Authority, and independent contractors e.g. private hospitals. Services are purchased through a variety of contractual and funding arrangements.

THE LINK BETWEEN PURCHASER AND PROVIDER – THE CONTRACT

NHS contracts are not agreements in a legal sense – neither party can enforce the contract through the courts. They are *service agreements* which set out the cost, quality and care that the provider has agreed to deliver. At the beginning most contracts were block contracts with purchasers paying providers a fixed sum over a period of a year to deliver a defined range of services. The contract was usually based on previous patterns of treatment.

Cost and volume contracts involved purchasers paying an agreed price to deliver a specified volume of work. The contract could be adjusted, if for example extra work was done, by more payments being made for the extra work or less, for less work.

There are also cost per case contracts to cover types of service not covered by other contracts.

Extra-contractual referrals occur where a patient is referred to a hospital which does not have a contract with the District Health Authority where the GP practises. In these cases, the DHA is responsible for paying for the service.

In practice this requires Health Authorities to have procedures for dealing with extra-contractual services. This may mean determining whether or not the referral is really necessary, or refusing to pay for the referral until the following financial year.

Emphasis is placed by purchasers on quality standards such as waiting times and patient satisfaction. This was reinforced with the publication of the Patients' Charter in 1991 in which one of the patient's rights was specified as 'to be given detailed information on local health services, including quality standards and maximum waiting times' and the publication of league tables of the performance of providers.

Critics of the reforms pointed out that no reference was made to the need to assess or raise clinical standards.

But the Patients' Charter signalled the shift of power away from the providers of health care towards the patients or consumers of it.

COMMUNITY CARE

Changes to the delivery and financing of community care for the vulnerable, the old and the mentally ill, were planned in parallel to the core changes to the NHS. The changes stemmed from the White Paper 'Caring for People' which was incorporated into the NHS and Community Care Act 1990.

The main changes were:

- local authorities were given the responsibility for community care by preparing plans for community care in conjunction with health authorities;
- community care services were funded out of the social security budget; (the Government's expressed intention was for local authorities to purchase services from the private sector rather than directly providing the services themselves.)
- care managers were appointed by the local authorities to assess an individual's need for community care, liaising with GPs and Health Authorities where appropriate.

Before the 1990 Act, eligibility for community care was assessed on the patient's income with income support paying for the cost of residential care. After the Act, a local authority with a fixed budget had the responsibility of determining who obtained access to services.

In practice, this could mean that where an elderly patient was in hospital ready to be discharged, the absence of appropriate services in the community might mean that the patient had to remain in the bed.

In a situation of limited funding and an ageing population, the danger was that Health Authorities and local authorities might evade responsibility by passing the buck from one to the other.

To avoid this, some authorities entered into joint commissioning arrangements with local authorities for the commissioning of health services and social services, with joint planning and joint pooling of resources. This development could become more common in the future.

MANAGING THE NEW NHS

The cost of implementing the NHS reforms was seen in the sharp increase in managers from 6,091 in 1989/90 to 20,478 in 1992/3.

The Functions and Manpower Review was set up with the overall aim of reducing management costs and central intervention in the NHS and creating a more streamlined command structure.

CONCLUSION

At the time of writing there remains a political economic and administrative crisis in the NHS which has yet to be resolved by the incoming Labour Government. Whether this will be tackled by administrative reform remains to be seen.

Chapter 3

PATIENTS' RIGHTS

Nina Fletcher

This chapter explores patients' rights both in terms of obtaining treatment and the manner in which that treatment is provided.

INTRODUCTION

Individuals have few positive, enforceable, legal rights. Legal rights to and in health care derive from the duties owed by the state in relation to the provision and running of the NHS (and these are generally governed by statute) and which health professionals owe in their relationships with patients (mostly governed by the common law).

PROVISION OF HEALTH CARE – THE STATUTORY DUTY TO PROVIDE

Two main statutes, the National Health Service Act (NHSA) 1977 and the National Health Service and Community Care Act (NHSCCA) 1990 govern the provision of health care in the NHS including hospital, GP and other services, thereby creating statutory duties.

Section 1 of the 1977 Act charges the Secretary of State for Health with a duty to continue to promote a comprehensive health service which is designed to secure improvement in:

- physical and mental health;
- the prevention, diagnosis and treatment of illness.

Section 3 of the 1977 Act imposes a duty to provide a range of services to the extent that he considers necessary to meet all reasonable requirements.

The Secretary of State delegates these duties to Health Authorities while fund-holding practices and NHS Trusts have responsibilities conferred on them by the NHSCCA 1990.

PATIENTS' RIGHTS TO TREATMENT

Patients have tried to argue that the duties imposed on the Secretary of State and Health Authorities by the NHSA 1977 create 'a right to treatment'. In the case of *R* v *Secretary of State for Social Services, ex p. Hincks* ((1992) 1 B.M.L.R. 93) four patients had been on a waiting list for hip-replacement surgery for some years. They sought a declaration from the court stating that the Health Authority was in breach of its duty and asked the court for an order compelling the Health Authority to provide the surgery and for compensation for their pain and suffering. The patients argued that they had waited longer than was medically advisable and that the delay resulted from a failure to allocate the funds necessary to build an orthopaedic unit – the need for which had been acknowledged by the Minister for Health.

The Court of Appeal dismissed their action holding that:

- the lack of financial resources, to which the Minister was subject, had to be considered in assessing reasonable requirements for hospital and medical services; and
- it was for the Minister to decide what was required and the court could intervene only where he acted so unreasonably as to frustrate the policy of the 1977 Act. No unreasonableness was found in this case and the patients had no right to demand that the treatment be provided.

Subsequent cases involving patients have been equally unsuccessful. This effectively has meant that patients have no right to make particular demands on limited resources and have no right to demand treatment which is against the clinical judgment of a practitioner.

For a court to intervene on the patient's behalf, the decision-maker must act unreasonably. The courts have been very reluctant to say when a Health Authority's decision would be so unreasonable as to attract court intervention. The good news is that the publicity raised by some of the cases has occasionally resulted in money being found or donated and the operation going ahead.

THE PATIENTS' CHARTER

The Patients' Charter (DoH, London, 1995) provides a statement of the rights and expectations which patients may claim in receiving health care. The Patients' Charter is not legally enforceable although most of the rights it contains are recognised either in statutes or by the common law. It may also be used as evidence for or against a breach of duty of care.

The Patients' Charter originated as a programme to improve and modernise the delivery of the NHS to the public and to reaffirm the fundamental principles of a service which was designed to provide health care on the basis of clinical need which is free at the point of delivery. It aims to clarify the standards which ought to be achieved and to make more information available to the public about the health service.

The National Charter sets out ten general rights of patients and nine standards of service which should be achieved by those involved in the management and delivery of health care. It also provides specific statements relating to services provided by GPs, hospitals, community care, ambulances, dentists, opticians and pharmacists. In addition to the National Charter Standards, many Health Authorities and hospitals set and publicise local Charter Standards which may add to and improve on national standards.

In order to publicise information, hospitals are required to display information on their Charter performance in public places. Health Authorities produce annual reports on local hospitals' performance and NHS Comparative Performance ('League') Tables are published to show how local hospitals and ambulance services are performing against some of the national standards. In theory patients should be able to use this information to 'shop around' but inequalities in the health system have been exposed and not all patients have the desired or intended freedom or means of making that choice.

RIGHTS UNDER THE PATIENTS' CHARTER

The following rights form the basis of the Charter:

- to receive health care on the basis of clinical need regardless of the ability to pay;

- to be registered with a GP;
- to receive emergency treatment (from GPs, ambulances, accident and emergency departments);
- to be referred to a consultant who is acceptable and to be referred for a second opinion;
- to choose whether to participate in research or medical teaching (at present privacy, dignity and religious and cultural beliefs are expectations only, not rights);
- to have any proposed treatment, including any risks involved in that treatment and any alternatives, clearly explained before deciding whether to agree to it;
- to have access to health records and to know that there is a legal duty of confidentiality;
- to have any complaint about NHS services investigated;
- to receive detailed information on local health services;
- to be guaranteed admission for virtually all treatments by a specific date no later than two years from the day the consultant places the patient on a waiting list.

THE RIGHT TO HAVE RISKS AND ALTERNATIVES EXPLAINED – THE RIGHT TO BE INFORMED

In law, any right that patients have to information about risks, side-effects and alternatives to proposed procedures, rests on the requirements that health professionals must obtain consent to any procedures or treatment which they propose.

How is consent given?

The consent renders the treatment lawful. It is standard practice before surgery for a written consent form to be signed but consent may be given orally or may even be implied from the circumstances (such as when a patient rolls up his sleeve and holds his arm out for a vaccination). The standard hospital forms usually provide authority for any additional surgery which is necessary in order to save the life of the patient but they may be amended to suit the particular circumstances. Patients can and should make deletions or additions and request more information and may improve their situation by stating levels of risk they would want to know about.

Right to alter consent form

Such forms do not constitute consent in themselves but merely provide evidence of the patient's consent. If a patient can prove that despite signing the form, he did not understand the implications of its terms, then it is irrelevant.

Information required to be given by the doctor

The practitioner's duty is to explain in broad terms only and this is not necessarily the same as having to provide full information. The amount of information given to the patient as to the potential risks of the treatment will depend upon the circumstances in which that treatment is given. For example in an emergency situation it may be acceptable to omit informing the patient of the risks of treatment. If a patient asks directly about potential risks then that patient must receive complete and truthful answers to her inquiries. Where the risk of a very serious complication is very slight, the doctor is still under a duty to communicate such slight risk to the patient.

In *Sidaway* v *Royal Bethlem Hospital* [1985] 1 All ER 643 the highest court in the land decided that a practitioner fulfils his duty to warn of inherent risks if he acts in accordance with a practice which is 'accepted at the time as proper by a responsible body of professional opinion'.

RECORD KEEPING

Records are a necessary part of patient care and both GPs and hospital doctors are under a legal obligation to maintain medical records.

Ownership of medical records

Medical records do not belong to the patient: NHS hospital records (including X-rays and videos) are the property of the Health Authority or Trust concerned, ownership being vested in them by the Secretary of State. General practice notes are owned by the relevant Health Authority and/or Department of Health. NHS dental records are the property of the practice but the Secretary of State, Dental Practice Board and Health Authorities have a right of access.

The records of private patients may belong to the private consultant or the private hospital. However, items such as X-rays paid for by the patient are generally considered to be the property of the patient.

Responsibility to keep records for a set time

A health service circular HC(89)20 outlines the responsibilities of Health Authorities in relation to the preservation and retention of health records. This recommends that the following *minimum* retention periods should be observed:

- obstetric records: 25 years (or if the child dies, 8 years after the death of the child);
- records relating to treatment given to a child: until patient's 25th birthday or 26th if record was made when patient was 17;
- records relating to a person under a mental disability within the meaning of the Mental Health Act 1959: 20 years from the date that the doctor considers that the patient no longer requires treatment;
- records relating to a patient of any age (i.e. child or adult) who has died: 8 years after the death; and
- all other health records: 8 years after the conclusion of treatment.

THE RIGHT TO CONFIDENTIALITY

Health professionals are under a legal duty not to disclose information about their patients. This right to confidentiality is, however, not absolute. Confidential information may be disclosed if a patient has expressly or impliedly consented to the disclosure and there are also circumstances in which disclosure of information is compulsory. Where information is required by a court order, or where there is a statutory obligation to answer questions or provide health care information and statistics, health professionals are obliged to break the duty of confidentiality. The Road Traffic Act 1988, for instance, requires health professionals to answer questions posed by police officers about traffic accidents and doctors are required to report cases of infectious diseases under the Public Health (Infectious Diseases) Regulations 1988, SI 1988/1546.

Where a health professional discloses confidential information without consent in circumstances where he is not obliged to do so, all the patient can do at present is to bring a legal action for breach of confidence. The problem for patients here is that the right to confidentiality is classed as a public interest which must be weighed against other competing public interests. If the court decides that the breach of confidence is in the public interest, the disclosure may be justified and the patient will have no redress.

It has long been recognised that the common law does not adequately protect the patient's right to confidentiality. The issue of confidentiality remains on the agenda. A European Communities Directive on confidentiality will require the UK to enact specific legislation. The Disclosure and Use of Personal Health Information Bill was introduced into the House of Lords in January 1996, and received a second reading in March 1996. The Bill has failed to progress any further. The Bill attempted to give the right of confidentiality statutory backing, making it a criminal offence to disclose confidential, personal, health information without the patient's consent. There were, however, exceptions to the right which were similar to those recognised by the current law.

ACCESS TO MEDICAL RECORDS

• Access to Health Records Act 1990

Before the Access to Health Records Act 1990 came into force, patients had no right of access to manual records held by health professionals. The Access to Health Records Act 1990 gives patients the right to see and copy information recorded on their health records made on or after 1st November 1991 (see Chapter 18 and Appendix 6). The NHSE has issued guidance encouraging health bodies to take a more flexible approach towards access which means that some health providers may be willing to voluntarily disclose earlier records not covered by the 1990 Act.

• Inaccurate records

The applicant may apply in writing to have the record corrected if she believes it is inaccurate, misleading or incomplete. If the holder is satisfied that the information in the records is inaccurate, the necessary corrections should be made to the records. If the holder does not agree with the applicant's corrections, she must add a note recording the applicant's views. The applicant should be supplied with a copy of the correction or note free of charge.

- **What if the holder refuses to allow access in accordance with the Act?**

If patients think the 1990 Act has not been complied with, they may complain using the NHS Complaints Procedures (see Chapters 5–8). Alternatively, if the applicant believes there has been an unreasonable delay in providing access or access has been wrongly denied, he or she can apply to the local county court for an order to produce the relevant records. The applicant may have to bear the costs of any such application (possibly including those of the holder of the record) if unsuccessful or if the court considers that the delay was not unreasonable.

- **Data Protection Act 1984**

The Data Protection Act 1984 gives individuals the right to ask whether any personal data is held on computer and, if so, to be supplied with a copy of any such information. This includes computerised health records but not, for example, records on microfilm. To apply for access, the applicant must write to the holder of the record. Access should be given within 40 days although, as with manual records, there are a number of situations where access may be denied e.g. if it is likely to cause serious harm to the patient. A fee of £10 may be charged. Applicants have a right to have inaccurate or misleading data corrected or erased. If the holder fails to comply with the Data Protection Act 1984, the applicant should contact the Data Protection Registrar's office. Computerised information about someone who has died is exempt from the Act.

- **Access to Medical Reports Act 1988**

Patients have a right of access to reports provided by medical practitioners for employment or insurance purposes. Only reports prepared by a doctor who is or has been responsible for the patient's medical treatment are covered by the Act. Therefore reports prepared by independent medical practitioners would be exempt under the Act. However, it may be possible in certain circumstances to obtain exempt reports under the Access to Health Records Act 1990. If a medical report has been prepared for a social services department, the report becomes part of the individual's personal file and an individual may seek access under the provisions of the Access to Personal Files (Social Services) Regulations 1989.

- **The Code of Openness**

The NHS Executive's Code of Practice on Openness in the NHS sets out the principles underlying public access to information about the NHS and indicates the sort of information that NHS Trusts and Health Authorities should, as a matter of good practice, publish or make available.

The information that Trusts and Health Authorities should publish or make available as a matter of good practice includes:

- information about provision of services, the targets and standards set and results achieved, and the cost and effectiveness of those services;
- details about health policy proposals or proposed changes in the way services are delivered, including reasons;
- details about important decisions on health policies and on changes to the delivery of services;
- information about the management and provision of health services and who is responsible;
- information about how to contact Community Health Councils and the Ombudsman; and
- information about gaining access to personal health records.

CONCLUSION

Documents like the Charter and the Code of Openness serve a purpose in increasing awareness of what patients may expect but neither of these documents fully advances patients' rights. Awareness may help to empower patients and may discourage attempts to restrict or infringe their rights. Few rights are absolute but the provisions of the Access to Health Records Act 1990 have improved patients' rights of access considerably. It is proposed to revise the Patients' Charter to include patients' responsibilities as well as rights.

Chapter 4

PRIVATE HEALTH CARE

Richard Ennals and Liz Thomas

The independent sector now plays an increasingly important role in the provision of health and social care in the United Kingdom, providing a diverse range of services from long-stay residential care to acute surgical procedures. This chapter provides an overview of the private healthcare sector, its relationship with the public sector and its regulation.

The private healthcare sector encompasses a wide range of services and providers, from complementary therapies at one end to in-patient care in the private unit of an NHS hospital at the other. It has experienced major growth over the past twenty years, a significant player in more recent years being the NHS itself. The boom years of the 1980s, concerns over the future of the NHS and the growth in company health insurance all combined to fuel the private healthcare market. From a relatively small industry in the late 70s, it now has revenue in excess of £13 billion. There is a close interplay between the independent and public healthcare sectors, the existence of the NHS acting to limit growth in the private sector. However, where there are shortfalls within public sector provision, the private sector is increasingly ready to fill the gap, which has in turn led to concerns about the creeping privatisation of NHS services.

In order to understand how the private sector fits into the overall provision of health care in this country, it is first necessary to briefly discuss the current organisation of state provision. Public sector health and social care is broadly divided into 'health' services funded by the NHS which is generally free at the point of delivery and 'social' care funded by local authorities which is subject to means testing. Over the past 20 years, there has been a substantial shift in the boundary between health and social care with many patients who were previously cared for under the NHS now coming under local authority care. In practice, this often means patients being cared for within the independent sector. This shift has been brought about by a number of factors including the closure of long-stay institutions, the move towards community care and increasing financial pressures both within the NHS as well as throughout the public sector in terms of the present and future costs of caring for an ageing population.

The divide between health and social care

Needless to say there continues to be considerable argument about the divide between health and social care in terms of what constitutes health care and what constitutes social care, the demarcation frequently being far from clear. This is highlighted in relation to disputes over responsibility for long-term care, the concern often expressed being that the pendulum has swung too far with the result that increasing numbers of people who should be receiving 'continuing care' within the NHS are instead being placed in means tested local authority care. From the patients' perspective, the concern is not just a financial one, but whether the care received is appropriate to their needs, particularly given the restricted budgets of local authorities.

Services operated by the independent sector

The services operated by the independent sector span the divide between health and social care, ranging from long-stay residential care to acute medical services (see below). Many of these services are provided under contract to the NHS/social services to form part of state provision, as well as to individual private patients.

Health Care Provided by the Private Sector

- Acute hospital services – surgical and medical treatment
- Psychiatric and substance abuse services
- Community Care – nursing homes, residential homes, dual registered homes, domiciliary services
- Specialist services: fertility treatment, abortions, rehabilitation services, screening
- Other healthcare services: dentistry, ophthalmic services, medical equipment, pharmaceuticals, complementary medicine

Independent provision of social care services

The independent sector provides a wide range of 'social care' services from care of the elderly to rehabilitation of brain injured patients. Three quarters of all community care beds – in residential and nursing homes – are now provided by the independent sector. The rapid expansion of the independent sector has followed both the closure of long-stay NHS institutions, as well as a dramatic and sometimes controversial reduction in local authority residential homes; there have been a number of well-publicised cases where elderly long-stay residents have died very shortly after being transferred, often at short notice, out of local authority homes. The independent sector has also begun to make inroads into the community care market providing, for example, domiciliary and respite services.

Independent acute healthcare sector

The acute private healthcare market comprises services provided by independent hospitals and clinics, individual private practitioners, and by the NHS in the form of private paybeds/ units within NHS Trust hospitals as well as some joint ventures with the independent sector. In 1996, the value of the private acute market including independent hospitals, NHS private facilities, and specialist fees, was in the region of £2350 million.[1]

Whilst there has been a significant change towards purchasing 'social' care from the independent sector, this has not been mirrored in relation to the provision of acute health services.

ACUTE HEALTHCARE PROVISION

Independent Hospitals

Acute hospital services

In 1996, there were 221 independent acute hospitals in the UK providing in the region of 11,100 beds. Approximately two thirds are commercial, 'for profit' hospitals, and of these about a quarter are owned by overseas concerns. The remaining third are hospitals registered as charities. Most independent hospitals now belong to one of the three major groups: British Medical International

[1] Laing & Buisson Review of Private Healthcare, 1997

(BMI), British United Provident Association (BUPA) and Nuffield Hospitals.

Revenue earned by independent acute hospitals and clinics makes up the largest part of the total acute healthcare market (£2350 in 1996), at an estimated £1446 million in 1996, £56 million of which was provided under contract to the NHS. The bulk of private hospital revenue is earned from medical and surgical inpatient and outpatient work, and this amounted to approximately £1267 million in 1996. The remaining £179 million represents psychiatric and substance abuse services. Fees to surgeons, anaesthetists and physicians undertaking private treatment during the same year came to an additional £652 million.[2]

The private sector now carries out approximately 20% of all elective surgery[2]; this includes both major and minor surgical procedures. For example, 30% of all hip replacements and 20% of all coronary bypass operations are now carried out in the private sector.

Psychiatric hospitals

With the closures of large psychiatric institutions and the move towards care in the community, many psychiatric patients and patients suffering from substance abuse are now treated within the independent sector under contract with the NHS and/or local authority.

Staffing

Private hospitals generally employ full/part-time nursing staff and usually have at least one doctor on the staff – referred to as the resident medical officer (RMO). A doctor should be on duty or on call in the hospital at all times unless special circumstances apply and this has been agreed with the registering authority.

Medical Advisory Committee

Most hospitals have a Medical Advisory Committee (MAC) which managers can consult on all medical matters e.g. clinical care evaluation, admission rights. It may also review the performance and conduct of individual consultants as well as having a role in audit.

---

[2] Williams B, Nichols J. Various papers, IHA market audit

NHS PRIVATE FACILITIES

In 1996, private patient revenue earned the NHS in the region of £250 million. To put this in context, public spending on health is currently in excess of £37 billion. Private facilities within NHS Trusts range from amenity beds and paybeds to dedicated private units which will only treat private patients. The NHS is expected to continue to increase its share of the private market, possibly with more joint ventures with the independent sector and a move towards PFI (Private Finance Initiative) private units.

THE PRIVATE DOCTOR

Private medical care is provided by contract (usually unwritten) between the patient and the private consultant. Private consultants can treat patients in private rooms in an independent hospital, in private facilities within an NHS hospital, in their own private consulting rooms or where appropriate, within part of their own home. A doctor wishing to carry out private work must be fully registered with the GMC, i.e. not on provisional or limited registration.

The consultant carries overall clinical responsibility for his patients subject to arrangements with the particular private facility. Very few private consultants have salaried posts within the independent sector being independent contractors. The main exception to this is psychiatrists in private psychiatric units/ hospitals.

Admission rights

In order to practise in an independent hospital, the consultant will have to obtain 'admission rights'. This is usually a matter for the hospital's Medical Advisory Committee to decide. The admission rights granted to a consultant will include what rights the consultant has in terms of admitting patients and the facilities available to him or her. A hospital can terminate admission rights if, for example, the doctor's name is removed from the GMC register or he or she fails to subscribe to an appropriate medical defence organisation. Admission rights are also generally withdrawn once a doctor reaches the age of 70. There is nothing to prevent a hospital's withdrawing admission rights without giving a reason.

Independent hospitals to a greater or lesser extent rely on consultants to bring in patients and are therefore having to compete to attract consultants' 'business'. This might in turn be an influential factor when it comes to the handling of complaints within independent hospitals; it is possible, from the hospital's viewpoint, that it may be more of a priority to keep the consultant happy than the aggrieved patient. Hospitals cannot pay consultants for bringing in patients nor can consultants pay private hospitals for allowing them to treat patients.

The majority of consultants carrying out private work are employed by the NHS and are permitted under their NHS contracts to carry out a certain amount of private work within their contracted NHS hours. Traditionally, a full-time NHS consultant was allowed to earn up to 10% of his salary doing private work whilst one with a part-time contract was not subject to a financial limit. With the introduction of Trust status, hospitals have however started to introduce new contracts which have enabled them to place greater restrictions on the rights of consultants to carry out private work. This could include anything from limiting the amount of private work permitted to prohibiting all private work except that carried out within the Trust. In some cases, treating private patients within the private facility of a Trust may form part of their NHS contractual duties.

Junior doctors are not normally allowed to treat private patients within the NHS and can only do private practice outside their contracted NHS hours. However, they often assist their consultant with private patients being treated within the Trust.

PRIVATE HEALTH INSURERS

There are in the region of 140 different health insurance policies offering a wide range of benefits. Private consultants must normally be 'recognised as of specialist status' by insurers in order for their subscribers to be reimbursed for the cost of treatment and private hospitals will normally be subject to some form of vetting. The larger insurance companies are moving towards having more tightly controlled lists of approved hospitals, steering their subscribers towards hospitals on their named list. Insurers are also imposing tighter restrictions on the standards required for a consultant to be recognised as of specialist status. In many cases, this means a consultant must have been appointed to a substantive consultant post within the NHS or be appropriately accredited by, for example, his or her Royal College or the Joint Committee for Higher Specialist Training.

Health insurers potentially have a considerable influence over the standards operating within the private sector. In addition to tightening their criteria for recognising a particular hospital or consultant, there are also moves towards monitoring treatment to ensure it conforms to agreed protocols. Insurers are also encouraging, and in some cases requiring, regular audits to be carried out. However, their role in improving standards has not as yet been reflected in their willingness to become directly involved in clinical complaints. Given the importance of complaints in monitoring and maintaining standards, this must be something that health insurers are going to have to address in the near future.

PRIVATE MEDICAL RECORDS

In practical terms, the private consultant's clinical notes belong to the consultant, nursing notes etc. prepared by the private hospital's staff belong to the hospital and items such as x-rays which the patient has specifically paid for belong to the patient. Patients can in any event obtain copies of their records under the Access to Health Records Act 1990 (see Chapter 18 and Appendix 6).

Whilst there is no statutory requirement to retain medical records for a minimum period, it is recommended that private records should be retained by the holder for an equivalent period to that recommended within the NHS (see Chapter 3).

THE PRIVATE PATIENT

Research suggests that a significant factor for people opting for private treatment relates to concerns about waiting lists within the NHS. Other factors include the convenience of being able to choose where and when to have treatment, the guarantee that a particular doctor will carry out any treatment, the comforts and facilities available to private patients and also the popular belief, if not necessarily always borne out in practice, that private treatment will be of a higher clinical standard.

Quality of care in private hospitals

As regards the quality of care in private hospitals, whilst there are some undoubted advantages in 'going private' (for those who can afford to do so), these can sometimes be offset by what could be perceived as a number of serious disadvantages. For example, if a patient has complications, it is not always the case that the patient's private consultant will be at hand to provide the specialist expertise to deal with the situation, as much of his/her time will be taken up with NHS commitments. If a patient has complications during the night or on a Sunday, it is possible that there will be no other consultants or even a Resident Medical Officer (RMO) available. An RMO is a doctor employed by the private hospital to provide medical care in the absence of the patient's consultant. A number of private hospitals still fail to provide 24-hour resident medical cover. Even if an RMO is available, this is often only a junior doctor who may not have the requisite experience or specialist knowledge to cope. Where complications are spotted in time, the hospital may not have the appropriate facilities or equipment available. Although many private hospitals now have intensive care units, these are intended primarily for post-operative patients following major surgery and beds may not always be available for emergencies. Accordingly, patients in such situations may sometimes have to be transferred to the nearest NHS hospital.

Few private hospitals employ resident anaesthetists, and it is possible that a patient requiring resuscitation during the hours when a visiting anaesthetist is not available (i.e. when operations are not being carried out) may not always receive the optimum care.

In the light of this, patients considering private treatment may wish to consider drawing up a check list of facilities offered by hospitals in order to establish what safeguards are in place should complications, minor or major, occur. Where a patient has concerns about the service on offer from a private hospital, an alternative would be to opt for treatment in the private wing of a large NHS Trust hospital.

REGULATION OF PRIVATE HOSPITALS

The Registered Homes Act 1984

Private hospitals are regulated by the Registered Homes Act 1984 and the accompanying rules and regulations (S.I. 1578 of 1984). Under the terms of the Act, all residential care homes and nursing homes (which includes private hospitals) must be registered either by the local authority or the Health Authority, depending on the type of care provided, and be subject to regular inspection.

Residential care homes

Part I of the Registered Homes Act 1984 deals with 'residential care homes'. These are defined as establishments providing residential accommodation and care for 'persons in need of personal care by reason of old age, disablement, past or present dependence on alcohol or drugs, or past or present mental disorder'. All independent residential homes must be registered and subject to inspection, but establishments with less than four residents are subject to less stringent requirements[3]. The registration authority responsible for registering and inspecting residential care homes is generally the local authority. Local authority homes are exempt from registration but are subject to inspection.

Nursing homes

Part II of the Registered Homes Act 1984, which deals with nursing homes and mental nursing homes, contains the legislation covering the registration of private hospitals. Private hospitals are dealt with as nursing homes that undertake surgical or invasive procedures. The body responsible for registering and inspecting nursing homes, and therefore private hospitals, is the local Health Authority.

Dual registration

An establishment may be registered both as a nursing home and a residential home. A dual registered home will be subject to the registration/inspection requirements of both the Health Authority and the social services department of the local authority.

Regulation and inspection of private hospitals

Under the terms of the Act, the types of premises which must be registered under Part II would include any independent acute hospital, clinic or acute service in which any of the following procedures are carried out:

[3] Registered Homes (Amendment) Act 1991

- surgical procedures under anaesthesia;
- termination of pregnancies;
- endoscopy;
- haemodialysis or peritoneal dialysis;
- treatment by specifically controlled techniques;
- invasive procedures e.g. laser treatment (class 3B and 4);
- invasive investigations or treatments e.g. colposcopy, hair transplants, in-vitro fertilisation, x-ray procedures involving injection of dyes/radio opaque substances;
- lithotripsy;
- vasectomy;
- hyperbaric oxygen therapy.

Some of these procedures are also subject to additional legal requirements stemming from specific legislation. This includes organ transplantation which is subject to the provisions of the Human Organ Transplant Act 1989, in-vitro fertilisation which is subject to the Human Fertilisation and Embryology Act 1990 and terminations of pregnancy where the premises must be approved by the Department of Health and reviewed every two years under the provisions of the Abortion Act 1967.

Inspection of premises

Inspections of acute independent hospitals registered by the Health Authority often amount to no more than the statutory minimum of two visits a year, one unannounced. The visits are carried out by Registration and Inspection Officers who may be accompanied by a doctor or pharmacist. Under current legislation this evaluation relates largely to the non-clinical or 'hotel' aspects of the care. Significantly, there is no legal requirement on the hospital or registering authority to seek to ensure that there is quality of care, whether clinical or non-clinical.

The 1994 RCN report 'An Inspector Calls?' identified a number of further problems in the regulation of private hospitals including the following:

- checks on registered operators and persons in charge of private hospitals and homes were not adequate and were often conducted in an *ad hoc* manner;
- some Health Authorities undertaking only the statutory minimum of two inspections a year were announcing both visits – in breach of the legislation – with the effect that the adequacy of standards was not being properly assessed;
- inspections in a quarter of the authorities surveyed were

carried out by just one inspector, with the inherent risks of individual bias affecting objectivity and of intimidation from less co-operative operators; and

- there was the danger of objectivity being further compromised in situations where private hospitals or homes inspected by the authority were also at the same time contracted by the authority to treat some of its NHS patients.

THE NEED FOR CHANGE

The current legislation, the Registered Homes Act 1984, and the legislation which preceded it, was not designed for, and is inadequate for, monitoring of standards in private hospitals. Consequently, it is for the most part the day-to-day needs of long stay nursing home patients that are addressed in this legislation, rather than those of hospital patients having operations or medical treatment.

The legislation has also been subject to criticism by the independent sector, in particular that the public sector is effectively immune to the provisions of the legislation. Whilst local authority residential homes are subject to inspection, there are no powers to enforce minimum standards. NHS hospitals are not subject to an equivalent inspection and many would question how many NHS facilities would in fact be able to meet the regulatory requirements if these were imposed.

There can be little doubt that there is a need for improved regulation of private hospitals. With something as important as health care, a twice yearly visit to assess the adequacy of the secondary, largely non-clinical aspects of a hospital's facilities is wholly insufficient. The Registered Homes Act should be replaced by new legislation that properly addresses the more important issue, from the patient's point of view, of the quality of clinical care including the level of cover at night and at weekends. Such registration should also incorporate a complaints procedure for aggrieved or injured patients. The present voluntary, internal procedures or codes of practice for complaints – when patients are advised of their existence – are insufficient and may not always be impartial.

Ideally, there should be a fully resourced independent national inspectorate which could set, monitor and enforce standards, especially clinical standards, and which would have the powers to fully investigate untoward incidents.

INFORMATION ON PRIVATE HOSPITALS

Little independent information is available about standards of care in private hospitals. Whilst some hospitals may publicise the fact that they have successfully undergone quality audits resulting in accreditation, it should be noted that these are for the most part organisational audits i.e. evaluations of the organisation of delivery of care (and also based to a large extent on self-assessment). Moreover, specific details of the findings of such audits are confidential and as such are not publicly available.

For the private patient seeking to make an informed choice about the hospital that he or she may use, information concerning the hospital's performance in clinical matters would probably be of more value, such as for example information concerning patient outcomes or post-operative mortality rates in relation to other private hospitals. Unfortunately no such data is available as, surprisingly, no central healthcare body appears to be collating this.

Following a recently upheld complaint by the Health Service Ombudsman about the failure of a Health Authority to release information about its inspection of a nursing home, patients or relatives wishing to find out more about a private hospital will be able under the Code of Openness in the NHS to obtain from the registering Authority reports of previous inspections.[4] Reports of inspections dating from 1 April 1998 onwards are published and should be available at public libraries.

INFORMATION ON DOCTORS

Private patients have the option to choose the consultant or surgeon who will carry out their treatment although in practice this is often done by the referring GP. Patients wishing to find out more about their prospective private consultant may find the following publications of assistance:

[4] Health Service Commissioner: 1st Report for Session (1996–7) Selected Investigations Access to Official Information in the NHS

The Medical Directory and *The Medical Register*: available in most larger libraries. Between them these set out doctors' dates of registration, qualifications, positions and publications.

The Good Doctor Guide: available in most libraries. This is a listing of 1000 doctors in England, Scotland and Wales, covering 37 areas of medical expertise.

Directory of Surgical Specialists (published in December 1997). This list declared specialisms of 2–3000 surgeons.

CONCLUSION

Privately funded health care will become even more prevalent as the NHS lurches from crisis to crisis. Regulation of private hospitals and private nursing homes is less than perfect. Nevertheless there are a number of avenues of complaint available to an aggrieved or injured patient which can bring satisfaction.

Sources
NHS Handbook 1997/98 published by the NHS Confederation
British Journal of Health Care Management, 1996, Vol 2, No 2
The Fitzhugh Directory 1997/8
Laing & Buisson Review of Private Healthcare 1997

Section II

COMPLAINTS ABOUT HEALTH CARE

Chapter 5

AN INTRODUCTION TO COMPLAINTS WITHIN THE NHS

Susan Polywka

This chapter provides an introduction to complaints within the NHS together with an overview of the NHS Complaints Procedure introduced in April 1996.

INTRODUCTION

> *'Complaining is one of several ways in which patients, their families, friends and carers, make their views known to the NHS. . . . The response they get when they make a complaint is a fundamental test of the NHS as a public service.'*
>
> 'Being Heard', Wilson Review Committee, May 1994

Complaints about services provided by the NHS necessarily cover a very wide range, from complaints about hospital food, lost property and cancelled appointments, right through to complaints about professional misconduct and medical accidents. Most patients complain because they want the cause of their complaint to be acknowledged and for it to be recognised that there is a justified grievance. Patients also need information: for someone to explain what if anything went wrong and why. If a mistake was made, an apology is an important part of acknowledging what has happened. It is clear from this that essentially much of what patients and other users of the service are seeking is better communication.

Where a grievance has been acknowledged, many complainants may want no more than the cause of their complaint to be corrected – for their spectacles to be replaced, for a new appointment to be made, for their taxi fare to be refunded. However, where the complaint is about failed treatment, where it may not be possible to put right what has happened, then other issues become much more important. If a baby dies as a result of a mismanaged delivery, the parents not only want an explanation as to why this was allowed to happen, they also want some form of accountability and, more particularly, an assurance that appropriate steps will be taken to prevent such an incident ever happening again.

The impact of a medical accident, coupled with the realisation that professional and organisational concerns can sometimes appear to outweigh the needs of the patient, can leave individuals feeling very vulnerable and mistrustful. Some will not take the matter further. However, for the remainder, establishing some form of accountability is fundamental to coming to terms with what has happened.

Patients can sometimes feel, particularly if an explanation has not been forthcoming when initially requested, that their only recourse is to the law. However, legal action is essentially about compensation and will rarely bring about the sort of investigation and resolution that the patient is seeking. It is therefore important that patients do have access to an effective complaints procedure.

There are a number of options for investigating complaints about health care which are outlined below:

OPTIONS FOR INVESTIGATION

Health Provider	Options for Investigation	Time Limit	Further Details
NHS Treatment	1. NHS Complaints Procedure	6 months *	Chapters 5–8
	2. Health Service Ombudsman	1 year	Chapter 9
	3. Professional body e.g. GMC, UKCC	none	Chapter 10
Private Treatment	1. Complain to hospital/clinic/ doctor	Refer to their literature	Chapter 12
	2. Request Health Authority investigation	none	Chapter 12
	3. Professional body e.g. GMC, UKCC	none	Chapter 10

Health Provider	Options for Investigation	Time Limit	Further Details
Following a death	1. Contact the Coroner 2. Complain as above	As soon as possible	Chapter 13
Patients detained in hospital under the Mental Health Act 1983	1. Complain as above 2. Mental Health Act Commission 3. Mental Health Review Tribunal		Chapters 5–8

*This may be extended up to one year if a patient was not initially aware that he or she had cause for complaint.

WHAT MAKES AN EFFECTIVE COMPLAINTS PROCEDURE?

A complaints procedure cannot be truly effective if it is perceived simply as a method of appeasing dissatisfied users. Complaints can offer one of the most accurate indicators of the quality of the service and offer the opportunity for health providers to identify problems at an early stage and, where appropriate, to review and improve procedures for the benefits of other patients. Developing a good complaints procedure represents only half the battle; for it to be effective it has to be implemented with the full cooperation of all concerned. This can only be achieved through training and changing attitudes towards complaints and, more particularly, complainants.

COMPLAINTS PROCEDURES PRE-1996

In the past, inconsistencies between the various complaints procedures which applied to different parts of the health service contributed to an overall perception (and, all too often, the reality) of inaccessibility. Only since the Hospital Complaints Act of 1985 was there any legal requirement for all hospitals to have a formalised procedure for dealing with complaints, with separate procedures existing for clinical and non-clinical complaints. In general practice, the complaints procedure was inextricably linked to disciplinary procedures. This effectively meant that a complaint could only achieve vindication where the practitioner was found to be in breach of his/her terms of service.

It was not unusual for it to take two years or even longer for a complaint to reach a conclusion and even after this length of time complainants were frequently left dissatisfied with the outcome. Both complainants and the NHS staff involved felt a high degree of dissatisfaction and frustration with the system, in its operation and its results.

THE WILSON REVIEW – *BEING HEARD*

It was against this background that Professor Alan Wilson was asked to lead a review of NHS complaints procedures, and his committee published its report, *Being Heard*, in May 1994. This identified the principles that should be incorporated into any NHS complaints procedure and then went on to say how these principles could be developed into particular features of a complaints system including:

- separation of disciplinary elements;
- publicity;
- use of informal responses;
- well-trained staff;
- support for complainants and respondents;
- investigation;
- use of conciliation;
- time limits;
- confidentiality;
- recording;
- monitoring;
- impartiality.

NHS COMPLAINTS PROCEDURE

The NHS Complaints Procedure came into effect on 1st April 1996. This replaced all existing hospital, Community Health

Service and Family Health Service complaints procedures with a single two-stage procedure.

Two stage procedure

It was decided to use self-contained titles for each part of the complaints procedure to avoid the inference that complaints would automatically progress through the different stages. The two stages of the procedure are:

- Local Resolution; and
- Independent Review.

The main emphasis underlying the new procedure is that wherever possible complaints should be resolved locally by the health provider using its own Local Resolution procedures. It is only where these procedures have been exhausted and the complainant is still dissatisfied that the complaint would then be considered for an investigation by an Independent Review Panel.

Changes in the role of the Health Service Ombudsman

In tandem with the changes in the NHS Complaints Procedure, the jurisdiction of the Health Service Ombudsman was extended in April 1996 to include complaints wholly or partly about the exercise of clinical judgment and complaints about Family Health Service Practitioners.

Before complaints will be considered by the Health Service Ombudsman, the complainant must have exhausted local complaints procedures. For further information on the Health Service Ombudsman, see Chapter 9.

Time Limit for Complaints

The Wilson Committee made recommendations on time limits for making complaints as well as time limits for responding to complaints. Normally a complaint should be made:

- within six months from the incident that caused the problem, or
- within six months of the date of discovering the problem, provided that it is within twelve months of the incident.

There is a discretion to extend this time limit where it would be considered unreasonable in the circumstances of a particular case for the complaint to have been made earlier, (for example, where the individual was suffering distress or trauma), and where it is still possible to investigate the facts of the case. If a complaint is outside the time limit, it is the responsibility of the Complaints Manager to consider an extension of the time limit. If a complaint is rejected on the basis that it is out of time, the complainant can complain about this and if unsuccessful, can request an Independent Review. If this is refused, the complainant can then refer the matter to the Health Service Ombudsman.

Disciplinary Action

One of the fundamental principles of the new complaints procedure is that disciplinary action should be dealt with quite separately by the employing Trust or Health Authority and will not form part of the complaint. This represents a significant change with regard to Family Health Service complaints.

LOCAL RESOLUTION

Local Resolution

Each Trust, Health Authority and Family Health Services practice is expected to develop and have in place its own Local Resolution procedure for the resolution of complaints.

In accordance with the recommendations of the Wilson Review Committee any Local Resolution procedure must be designed to be:

- accessible for patients and complainants;
- simple;
- completely separate from disciplinary procedures;
- amenable to the extraction of lessons to be learned about the quality of service delivery;
- fair to staff and complainants alike;
- rapid and open;
- honest and thorough, with the prime aim of resolving the problems and satisfying the concerns of the complainant.

Complaints Manager

In order to try and avoid complaints procedures becoming too rigid and bureaucratic, each NHS body is encouraged to provide a flexible Local Resolution procedure, offering a range of different options for responding to complaints from which the most appropriate may be employed depending on the nature and circumstances of the complaint.

Trusts and Health Authorities must have a designated Complaints Manager who is readily accessible to the public. The main role of the Complaints Manager is to oversee the complaints procedure. Family Health Services practices must nominate an appropriate person to be responsible for their complaints procedure.

WHAT SHOULD CHARACTERISE THE RESPONSE TO ANY COMPLAINT BROUGHT?

The role of 'front-line' staff

Considerable emphasis has been placed on the role of 'front-line' staff – nurses, receptionists, doctors, administrative staff, etc – in responding to complaints. It is expected that a significant proportion of the complaints received will be capable of being resolved by an immediate, and often informal, response by staff in the front line.

All members of staff should therefore be empowered to:

- respond openly and in a non-defensive way to any complaint which they hear;
- resolve it where they can; and
- recognise where further action should be initiated *(e.g. a referral to the Chief Executive or Complaints Manager where the complainant requires a more detailed investigation).*

The availability of other options under Local Resolution

Some complaints will require a more formal investigation, for example, if it involves possible errors in treatment or where a patient has been harmed. The range of options available for complainants could include e.g. a formal investigation headed by the Chief Executive or Complaints Manager, and/or an opportunity for the complainant to meet with them and/or the NHS staff complained against. Within Family Health Services, complaints can be referred for conciliation where a lay conciliator will try and help the complainant and the Family Health Service practice to reach agreement. It is suggested that Trusts and Health Authorities should also consider providing conciliation services and some may already have this service in place.

It is the responsibility of the healthcare provider to endeavour to resolve the complaint as quickly as is possible. Recommendations for response times for dealing with complaints are included in the guidance but are meant as a guide rather than absolute deadlines. Where a healthcare provider fails to respond within a reasonable period of time, the complainant may have recourse to the Health Service Ombudsman.

CONCLUSION OF LOCAL RESOLUTION

Clear communication of the outcome

Whichever option – or combination of options – is deployed, the healthcare provider should clearly communicate the outcome of any Local Resolution investigation to the complainant. Where the complaint was made in writing, this should be by letter from the Chief Executive of the Trust or Health Authority; or the nominated person within any FHS practice.

The healthcare provider must advise all complainants of their right to seek an Independent Review in the event that they are not satisfied with the outcome of the Local Resolution procedure. It must also be made clear to the complainant that any such request must be made within 28 calendar days of completion of Local Resolution.

A difficulty that some complainants have experienced is a reluctance on the part of some healthcare providers to bring the Local Resolution stage to a close. Where complainants find themselves in this situation, then it may be helpful to refer to the NHSE's guidance on the handling of complaints and, in particular, the recommended time scale for responding. They could also seek advice from the 'convener' (see below) and, if necessary, the Health Service Ombudsman.

INDEPENDENT REVIEW

Stage Two – Independent Review

Where a complainant is dissatisfied with the outcome of Local Resolution procedures he or she can request an Independent Review. For full details of the Independent Review Procedure see Chapter 8.

COMPLAINTS COVERED BY THE NHS COMPLAINTS PROCEDURE

The new procedure applies to all services provided under the NHS including:

- hospitals/Trusts;
- community health services;
- Family Health Services;
- Health Authorities;
- ambulance services.

In addition to complaints about NHS treatment, the NHS Complaints procedure can also be used for:

- complaints about the staff or facilities in a Trust providing private pay bed facilities but not including the care provided by the private consultant;
- failure to comply with an application under the Access to Health Records Act 1990;
- complaints by, or on behalf of, individual patients about purchasing decisions by Health Authorities and GP fundholders;
- complaints about services purchased from the independent sector for NHS patients by Trusts, Health Authorities and GP fundholders;
- complaints about the administrative function of Health Authorities, e.g. provision of Family Health Services.

COMPLAINTS NOT COVERED BY THE NHS COMPLAINTS PROCEDURE

Matters which are *not* covered by the NHS Complaints Procedure include:

- failure to disclose information under the Code of Openness in the NHS; these complaints should be dealt with under that Code. Complainants also have the option of taking such complaints to the Health Service Ombudsman.

- private health care provided in an independent (private) hospital or clinic;
- treatment provided by a private consultant within an NHS facility (see above).

COMPENSATION

Ex-gratia payments

If a patient has incurred costs as a result of a mistake made by the healthcare provider, for example transport costs or lost property, the healthcare provider may be willing to compensate the complainant for his or her losses. If a patient has been harmed or injured as a result of a poor standard of clinical or nursing care, and wishes to claim compensation, then normally the patient would need to seek advice from a solicitor with a view to pursuing a legal claim for compensation. Some healthcare providers may be willing to offer compensation, possibly on an 'ex gratia' basis (i.e. a payment made on the basis that the healthcare provider is not acknowledging any legal duty to compensate), without the complainant having to pursue legal action or involve legal advisers. Such payments are generally, but certainly not always, offered in relation to relatively minor injuries but complainants would be advised to seek independent advice from an agency such as AVMA or a specialist medical negligence solicitor before accepting any such payment. This is in order to ensure that any offer of compensation is fair and reasonable as acceptance may preclude a subsequent legal claim.

IS IT POSSIBLE TO COMMENCE A LEGAL CLAIM WHILST A COMPLAINT IS UNDER INVESTIGATION?

As soon as a complainant indicates that he or she intends to take legal action the complaints procedure will be brought to a close.

WILL THE PATIENT'S CONSENT BE OBTAINED BEFORE HIS OR HER RECORDS ARE EXAMINED?

Under "Complaints: Listening . . . Acting . . . Improving" (Guidance on implementation of the NHS Complaints Procedure NHSE March 1996) it is not necessary to obtain the patient's consent before accessing personal information about the patient in order to investigate a complaint. However, any information disclosed in this way should be relevant to the investigation and should only be disclosed to those people who need to know it for the purposes of investigating the complaint. If a complaint is being made by someone other than the patient, then care must be taken not to breach the patient's rights of confidentiality. Those investigating the complaint must also respect the confidentiality of third parties who may have given information on a confidential basis.

WHAT HAPPENS IF A COMPLAINT INVOLVES MORE THAN ONE NHS SERVICE?

If a complaint involves more than one NHS service, for example, a general practitioner and a Trust, there should be full cooperation between the various bodies where it will help to resolve the complaint. If the complainant wishes to pursue the matter to Independent Review, with the complainant's agreement, the conveners should liaise with the aim of establishing close cooperation between the respective bodies. Separate panels would need to be set up but it would be possible for the panels to share the same chairman, in some cases the same third panel member and where appropriate, the same clinical assessors. The panels would still be required to produce separate reports. However, the complainant does not have to agree to this arrangement and can request that entirely separate panels are set up.

WHAT HAPPENS IF A COMPLAINT INVOLVES BOTH HEALTH AND SOCIAL SERVICES?

There are an increasing number of complaints which involve both Health and Social Services. At present, these complaints are dealt with separately by the two services although both bodies should try and ensure that the complainant is made aware of what aspects of his or her complaint will be dealt with under which procedure. Health and Social Services departments should work together where a complaint does involve both services. Similar cooperation should exist where a complaint involves Health Services and also comes under the remit of the Mental Health Act Commission.

WHAT HAPPENS IF A COMPLAINT IS ALSO SUBJECT TO INVESTIGATION BY THE CORONER'S OFFICE?

It is recommended that even if a matter is under investigation by the Coroner, the healthcare provider should continue to investigate the complaint.

CONCLUSION

The reforms are an attempt to fundamentally change the way the NHS deals with complaints so that patients' views are considered and that the appropriate responses can be provided. The test is now whether the practices can match the theory.

THE NHS COMPLAINTS PROCEDURE : A FLOW CHART

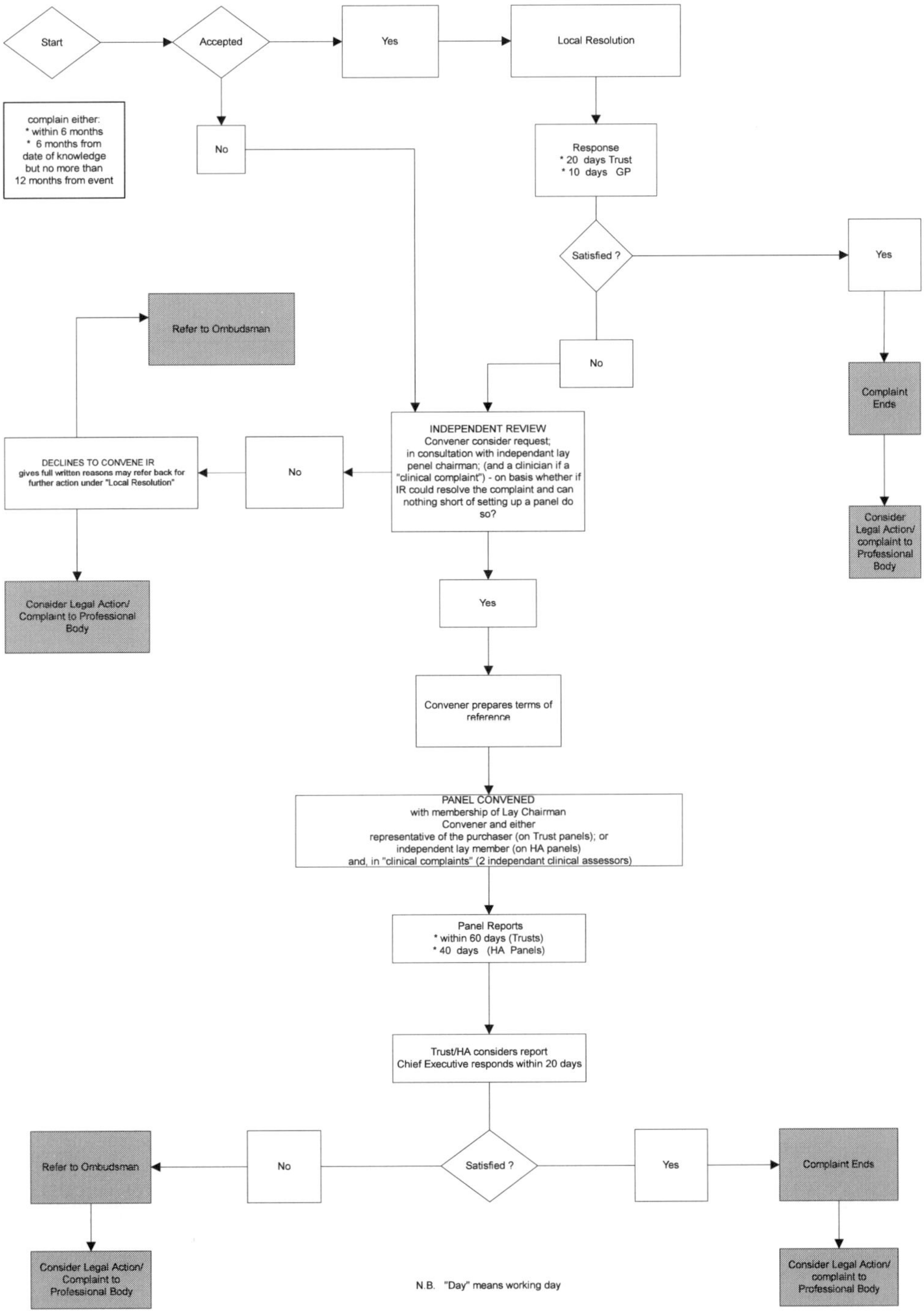

N.B. "Day" means working day

Chapter 6

COMPLAINTS ABOUT CARE BY HOSPITAL OR COMMUNITY NHS TRUSTS

Graham Girvan

This chapter will explain how Local Resolution procedures operate within NHS hospitals and community health service trusts with particular reference to clinical complaints.

INTRODUCTION

Whenever patients experience problems whilst receiving treatment in hospital or care from a community Trust, the first step would be to talk about their concerns with those directly responsible for their care. If a patient does not feel able to do this or does not receive a satisfactory response, he or she may then need to consider making a more formal request for an explanation in the form of a complaint using the NHS Complaints Procedure. The NHS Complaints Procedure is intended to provide patients with the means to have their treatment investigated and to obtain the explanation they are seeking.

As described in Chapter 5, the NHS Complaints Procedure is divided as follows:

- Local Resolution; and
- Independent Review.

LOCAL RESOLUTION OF HOSPITAL COMPLAINTS

Following the introduction of the NHS Complaints Procedure in April 1996, all NHS Trusts must have in place 'Local Resolution' procedures for responding to complaints. Each Trust is responsible for developing its own complaints procedures in accordance with guidelines laid down by the National Health Service Executive (NHSE).[1]

All complaints, whether they are made directly to staff or members of the Trust Board, whether in writing or made verbally, will be investigated using the Trust's Local Resolution (complaints) procedures. This applies equally to complaints which are judged to be serious, and those that are less serious.

WHAT SORTS OF COMPLAINTS CAN BE INVESTIGATED?

Types of complaints

The NHS Complaints Procedure can be used for all types of complaints about any service provided by an NHS Trust hospital or community Trust. This could include, for example, complaints about:

- medical treatment e.g. delays, mismanagement or errors;
- poor nursing care;
- surgery e.g. unexpected injury or side-effects;
- medical equipment/prosthetics e.g. faulty equipment;
- facilities e.g. access, catering, accommodation, parking, cleaning or transport;
- administration e.g. appointments, referrals, waiting times or medical records;
- communication e.g. inadequate explanations/information or difficulty in accessing information;
- personnel e.g. attitude of individual staff members, competence or rudeness;
- security e.g. lost property or personal safety;
- management of services e.g. communication between departments or policy.

---

[1] "Complaints: Listening . . . Acting . . . Improving . . . " Guidance on the implementation of the NHS Complaints Procedure NHSE March 1996

Community Trusts

NHS Trusts include both hospital Trusts and community Trusts. Community NHS Trusts may be responsible for providing a range of different health services within the community. For example, this could include mental health services, child health services, speech therapy, occupational therapy, district nursing, services for the elderly or learning disability services.

WHAT IS THE TIME LIMIT FOR COMPLAINTS?

A complaint about a Trust or Health Authority should normally be made:

- within six months of the incident that gave rise to the complaint; or
- within six months of the date of discovering the problem, provided that it is within twelve months of the incident.

There is discretion to extend the time limit where it would be unreasonable in the circumstances for the complaint to have been made earlier and where it is still possible to investigate the facts of the case. If a complaint is rejected as being out of time the complainant can complain to the convener about the refusal to investigate his or her complaint. The convener may decide to take no further action in which case the complainant may refer the matter to the Ombudsman, refer the complaint back for Local Resolution or set up a panel to investigate the complaint.

WHO SHOULD THE COMPLAINT BE MADE TO?

Front-line staff

The main emphasis underlying the NHS Complaints Procedure is that patients or relatives should feel able to raise concerns with any member of staff, but particularly with front-line staff i.e. those in direct contact with patients. This might, for example, be the named nurse, the ward sister, the clinic clerk or the doctor treating the patient. The individual receiving the complaint should assess whether it is a matter which he or she can respond to without the need to refer the matter on or whether the nature or seriousness of the complaint indicates the need for a more independent investigation, in which case, he or she should refer it to the Complaints Manager. In practice, some front-line staff may not have the time or be appropriately trained to deal with complaints and in this situation it may be necessary to go direct to the Complaints Manager.

Complaints Manager

All Trusts have to have a designated Complaints Manager, who should be readily accessible to the public. The Complaints Manager should be a senior member of the Trust's staff, and if not the Chief Executive, should report directly to her or him, or to another Director who has personal access to the Chief Executive.

If complainants do not want to raise their concerns with the front-line staff they can contact the Complaints Manager, or if they prefer, the Trust's Chief Executive.

Oral complaints

Within an NHS Trust it is the Complaints Manager who is responsible for investigating written complaints. However, some oral complaints may also need to be recorded in writing by the Complaints Manager and followed up or investigated as appropriate.

WHEN SHOULD A COMPLAINT BE PUT IN WRITING?

- if the complainant wants a written reply;
- if they feel that they may want to take it further than Local Resolution;
- if the complaint is serious;
- when the complaint is against different people or about differing parts of the Trust.

The Patients' Charter gives complainants the right to a written reply from the Chief Executive in response to a written complaint. This might be a full personally signed response or a shorter letter covering a fuller report from another member of staff.

Any letter which refers to matters of clinical judgment must be agreed by the clinician concerned and, in the case of medical care, by the consultant responsible for the care of the patient.

HOW WILL COMPLAINTS BE INVESTIGATED?

Less serious complaints

If a patient complains to a member of the front-line staff about a relatively minor matter, not requiring a formal investigation, then the member of staff should endeavour to respond to the complaint immediately, e.g. by ensuring appropriate action is taken to remedy the problem. In other words, it is possible that some complaints will be resolved without the need for a written response or the need to call on more formal procedures.

Serious or complicated complaints

If the matter is more serious, perhaps requiring a more in-depth investigation, the member of staff should refer the matter to the Complaints Manager. Each Trust will have developed its own protocol for investigating complaints and different Trusts will therefore adopt different approaches for investigating complaints. This could range from a relatively informal investigation where the Complaints Manager would discuss the problem with the members of staff and then write to the complainant with the outcome of such enquiries, to a far more formal investigation, where reports would be obtained from the staff involved in the complaint and, where relevant, senior clinicians or department heads. If it is a serious clinical complaint there might be a detailed review of the medical records and the Trust may suggest obtaining an independent assessment of the treatment from an outside clinician. The complainant may be invited to attend a meeting(s) with those directly involved in the incident and/or senior clinical staff such as the consultant or clinical director.

The aim is to ensure the procedures are flexible and appropriate to the needs of the individual complainant. If a complainant is not happy with the way in which the complaint is being investigated then it is important for the Complaints Manager to allow the complainant to set out how she thinks the complaint would be best resolved.

HOW QUICKLY SHOULD THE TRUST RESPOND TO A COMPLAINT?

If the complaint is not one that can be resolved immediately the complainant should receive an acknowledgement of his or her complaint within 2 working days and a full response within 20 working days. Alternatively, instead of an acknowledgement, the complainant may receive a full reply within 5 working days if it is feasible to complete the investigation within this time. These are recommended target times rather than absolute deadlines.

INVESTIGATION OF DISCIPLINARY MATTERS

Disciplinary matters cannot be investigated under the NHS complaints procedure. This is a matter for the employing Trust. Where a complaint raises disciplinary issues this should immediately be referred to the appropriate manager where it will be subject to a separate disciplinary investigation. Any part of the complaint which relates to the disciplinary investigation will cease to be investigated under the complaints procedure. The complainant should be informed of this, especially if he or she is likely to be asked to give evidence for the disciplinary inquiry. Where appropriate, complainants should be advised of the outcome of any disciplinary investigation.

HOW DOES THE LOCAL RESOLUTION STAGE END?

It is recommended that Trusts should complete the Local Resolution procedure with a letter to the complainant. This letter should provide the complainant with a full response to his or her complaint and an apology with an explanation of actions taken to prevent a recurrence. It should explain the right to request an independent review and that the request has to be made within 28 days of the date of the letter.

Some Trusts do try very hard to provide a full response. However, complainants have found that some responses are often little more than a repetition of the facts with no explanation and whilst some Trusts are willing to apologise, this is often for matters which are not relevant to the main areas of complaint. Complainants do not have to accept this as this goes against all the principles underlying the NHS Complaints Procedure. If they have not already done so, they should seek advice from their local Community Health Council and/or AVMA.

SOME EXAMPLES OF COMPLAINTS:

- Mrs Horrobin wants to complain that her elderly mother on Ward 21 is not eating. She goes to the ward receptionist who suggests that she speak to the charge nurse. He assures her that he will look into it. He tells her the next day that her mother had been having problems with her dentures and that he has arranged for her mother to be seen by a dentist the next day.
- Mr Patel is upset by the attitude of the clerk in his local child health clinic. He does not want to say anything at the clinic, so takes one of the Trust's complaints leaflets which explains the role of the CHC. He telephones the CHC and asks them for advice. The CHC suggests that he write to the Trust's Complaints Manager, and help him with the letter. The Complaints Manager replies and interviews the clerk and hears her comments. Finally, he writes to Mr Patel and explains that the clerk had not intended to upset him and is most apologetic. The letter also informs Mr Patel of his right to seek an independent review and the need to make the request within 28 calendar days.

WHAT IF THE COMPLAINANT IS NOT SATISFIED WITH THE OUTCOME OF LOCAL RESOLUTION?

There are a number of reasons why a complainant might be unhappy with the outcome of Local Resolution. For example, the complainant may feel that:

- the Trust did not respond satisfactorily to the specific issues raised by the complainant;
- there was a failure to acknowledge possible errors or misjudgments;
- the Trust failed to take appropriate action as a result of the complaint;
- the investigation of the complaint was inadequate.

Having received the letter concluding Local Resolution the complainant has 28 calendar days to request an independent review. This can be done orally or in writing. The request should then be passed to the 'convener', the person responsible for considering requests for Independent Reviews. (See Chapter 8 for details of the Independent Review procedure).

COMPLAINTS ABOUT NHS CONTINUING CARE

Following growing concerns about the failure of the NHS to meet the needs of patients requiring continuing medical or nursing care and the premature discharge of patients following treatment, the NHS Continuing Care Guidance was published in February 1995: LAC (95)5 HSG 95/8. This Guidance introduced a right of patients, their families and carers to request a review of a hospital's decision to discharge a patient from inpatient NHS care whether in a hospital or a NHS funded placement in a hospice, nursing home or other establishment. If a patient or his or her family believes that the patient should be receiving NHS continuing care, they can ask the designated officer at the Health Authority to review the decision. A response should be given within two weeks. The designated officer within the Health Authority, in reaching his or her decision, will normally consult with an independent panel unless it is believed that the patient clearly falls outside the criteria for receiving continuing care. The panel will comprise a chairman appointed by the Health Authority and representatives from the Health Authority and local authority, and will be advised by appropriate clinical advisers. Detailed guidance on the operation of the panel is contained within LCA (95)17. If the patient and/or family are not happy with the decision of the Health Authority and/or panel, they should complain to the Health Service Ombudsman.

COMPLAINTS ABOUT PSYCHIATRIC CARE

The majority of complaints about psychiatric care will be dealt with under the NHS Complaints Procedure. If a patient has been detained in hospital under the provisions of the Mental Health Act 1983 there are additional procedures set up specifically to protect the rights of detained patients. There are two independent bodies responsible for protecting the rights of detained patients, each having quite separate functions:

- Mental Health Act Commission (investigation of complaints);
- Mental Health Review Tribunal (applications for discharge from hospital).

Mental Health Act Commission

The Mental Health Act Commission is concerned with protecting the rights of patients who are (or have been) detained in hospital ('involuntary patients') under the Mental Health Act 1983. The Mental Health Act Commission is a special Health Authority appointed by the Secretary of State which has a number of responsibilities including:

- visiting and interviewing detained patients in hospitals and mental nursing homes;
- investigating complaints by and about detained patients;
- appointing doctors to provide a second opinion on a detained patient before treatment is given where this is required under the Mental Health Act 1983, and subsequently reviewing any treatment given.

In other words, the Commission is there to ensure that involuntary patients have been lawfully detained under the Mental Health Act 1983, that their rights are protected and that any treatment is lawfully given.

The Mental Health Act Commission also has more general responsibilities in relation to ensuring that the powers and duties which various bodies have under the Mental Health Act 1983 are appropriately exercised and for setting up a code of practice.

Complaints to the Mental Health Act Commission

The Mental Health Act Commission will normally only investigate a complaint after it has first been subject to investigation by the healthcare provider using the NHS Complaints Procedure. The Mental Health Act Commission can investigate complaints from existing and former patients and/or their relatives. The sorts of complaints the Commission will look into will generally relate to a failure by a healthcare provider to comply with the Mental Health Act 1983 (and Code of Practice 1993).

Complaints about detention under the Mental Health Act 1983

Patients (and their relatives) who believe they have been wrongly detained under the Mental Health Act 1983 can make an application for discharge to:

- the 'detaining authority'; and/or
- Mental Health Review Tribunal.

The managers of the hospital or clinic where the person is detained are termed the 'detaining authority'. A patient may apply to the managers for discharge from hospital. If the patient is unsuccessful in his or her application to the detaining authority or if he or she does not wish to apply to the detaining authority, he or she can apply to the Mental Health Review Tribunal for the detention to be reviewed.

Mental Health Review Tribunals

Patients (or their relatives) who believe they have been wrongly detained under the Mental Health Act 1983 can apply to the Mental Health Review Tribunal for a review of the detention and to be discharged from hospital. A detaining hospital may also request a Mental Health Review Tribunal to review/reassess the appropriateness of a detention under the Mental Health Act 1983, for example, where patients have been detained for six months or more and have not themselves requested a review.

The tribunal consists of a panel of three people: a legal chairman, a medical person (psychiatrist) and a lay person. The patient may have legal representation for which legal aid is available. The tribunal may either order or refuse discharge.

The important addresses are as follows

Mental Health Act Commission
Maid Marian House
56 Houndsgate
Nottingham NG1 6BG
Tel: 0115 943 7100

Mental Health Review Tribunals
Area: Northern Yorkshire & Trent
Address: Spur A. Block 5
Government Buildings
Chalfont Drive
Western Boulevard
Nottingham NG8 3RZ
Tel: 0115 929 4222

Area: Northern, Western, Mersey & West Midlands
Address: Cressington House (3rd floor)
249 St Mary's Road
Garston
Liverpool Ll9 0NF
Tel: 0151 494 0095

Area: NE, NW Thames, East Anglia & Oxford (except Broadmoor)
Address: Canons Park
Government Buildings
Honeypot Lane
Stanmore
Middlesex HA7 1AY
Tel: 0171 972 3734

Area: SW, SE Thames, Wessex & South Western (and Broadmoor),
Address: Hinchley Wood Block 3, Crown Offices
Kingston By-Pass Road, Surbiton
Surrey KT6 5QN
Tel: 0181 268 4520

CONCLUSION

A good Health Service should provide a good complaints procedure to enable patients to have a non-legal right of redress which is flexible, fair, quick and cheap. Trusts and Health Authorities need such a system as a check on performance and as a method of identifying improvements in the delivery of patient care. The present system addresses these requirements but it is too early to say whether the reforms have been successful. Much depends on the resources and management devoted to the complaints procedures and the willingness of patients to accept second best!

Chapter 7

COMPLAINTS ABOUT GPs AND OTHER FAMILY PRACTITIONERS

Graham Girvan

This chapter explains how the NHS Complaints Procedure works in relation to complaints about GPs and other family practitioners as well as providing a brief summary of disciplinary procedures.

INTRODUCTION

If a patient has a complaint about a Family Health Service Practitioner or anyone employed by the practice it should initially be made to the practice using the practice's Local Resolution (complaints) procedure. As described in Chapter 5, the NHS Complaints Procedure is divided into two distinct stages:

- Local Resolution; and
- Independent Review.

Setting up Local Resolution complaints procedures is the responsibility of individual Family Health Service Practices, whilst Independent Reviews are the responsibility of the local Health Authority.

FAMILY HEALTH SERVICE PRACTITIONERS

Practitioners providing family health services include:

- general medical practitioners (family doctors/GPs);
- general dental practitioners (NHS dentists);

- pharmacists;
- ophthalmic medical practitioners;
- optometrists.

Terms of Service

Family Health Service Practitioners (who provide treatment or services for the NHS) are employed by their local Health Authority under a nationally agreed contract ('terms of service'). This contract includes a requirement for all Family Health Service Practitioners to be part of the NHS Complaints Procedure introduced in April 1996. Failing to operate an adequate complaints procedure would be considered a potential breach of the practitioner's terms of service and could result in disciplinary action.

WHAT SORTS OF COMPLAINTS CAN BE INVESTIGATED USING THE NEW COMPLAINTS PROCEDURES?

The NHS Complaints Procedure can be used for all types of complaint about a Family Health Service Practitioner. For example, this could include complaints about:

- clinical care e.g. complaints about treatment provided by a GP, dentist or practice nurse;
- failure to provide a home visit;
- staff attitude e.g. rudeness by a member of staff;
- financial e.g. charges made by a dentist or optometrist;
- prescription errors e.g. by a pharmacist or GP;
- administrative errors e.g. failure to arrange a referral appointment or to inform a patient of the outcome of routine screening tests;
- facilities provided by the practice e.g. appointment systems etc;
- faulty equipment/prosthesis e.g. ill-fitting dentures.

This list is not exhaustive but it demonstrates the wide range of complaints that could be investigated under the NHS Complaints Procedure.

SETTING UP LOCAL RESOLUTION PROCEDURES

Practice based complaints procedures

Each Family Health Service Practice should have a 'practice based' (i.e. set up and operated by the practice) written complaints procedure. This must comply with minimum national criteria set out by the National Health Service Executive (NHSE) along the following lines:

> **Practice Based Complaints Procedure**
>
> - the procedures will have been developed and will be managed entirely by the practice – Health Authorities will only become involved if requested and by agreement of the practitioner and the complainant
> - one person will be nominated by the practice to be responsible for overseeing the administration of the complaints procedure e.g. a 'complaints administrator'
> - practices must publicise their complaints procedure
> - practices must make sure it is clear how to lodge a complaint and to whom
> - an acknowledgement or initial response to the complaint should normally be made within two working days
> - the person nominated to investigate the complaint should make all necessary inquiries such as interviews, if appropriate, with the complainant, practitioners and practice staff
> - an explanation should normally be provided within two weeks (i.e. ten working days)
> - local schemes with additional features must be approved by the Health Authority and local representative committees

Who can complain?

Complaints can be made by existing or former patients of a Family Health Services Practitioner or by anyone who has the patient's consent to complain on his or her behalf. If the patient is unable to act, for example, as a result of mental incapacity, consent is not needed. If the complainant is considered unsuitable to act on behalf of the patient the Health Authority's Complaints Manager (or convener if the complaint is at the Independent Review stage) can refuse to deal with a particular complainant and may nominate another person to act for the patient.

Time limits for complaints

Complaints should normally be made:

- within six months from the incident that caused the problem; or
- within six months of the date of discovering the problem, provided that this is within 12 months of the incident.

If a complaint involves a serious clinical incident it may well be that the patient or his or her relative will not be in a position to make a complaint within the deadline. There is a discretion to extend this time limit and it will be the person responsible for administering the complaints procedure to take initial responsibility for considering the request for an extension.

Complaints administrator

If the complaint concerns a relatively minor matter, the complainant should be able to speak to anyone within the practice about his or her complaint – the receptionist, practice nurse, the GP. For more serious complaints, the complainant should approach the 'complaints administrator'. All practices are expected to nominate a specific individual to administer their complaints procedure. For example, this might be the senior partner or the practice manager. If a complaint is against the 'complaints administrator', the practice should arrange for someone else to handle the complaint. If the practitioner works alone, i.e. is a sole practitioner, arrangements will be made for someone outside the practice to administer the complaints procedure.

If a patient feels unable, for whatever reason, to complain directly to the practice, an approach can be made to the Complaints Manager at the Health Authority (see below).

Should a complainant change doctor?

This will very much depend upon the nature of the complaint, the strength of the relationship between the doctor and the complainant and the outcome that the complainant is seeking. Some doctors will welcome complaints and try and learn from them, others will view any criticism as a sign that the doctor/patient relationship has irretrievably broken down and have the complainant (if on the practice list) and family as well, removed.

Doctors are able to have patients removed, without giving a reason to the Health Authority. (A GP also has the option of complaining to the Health Authority about a patient.) Patients may feel that they have no further trust in their doctor and so may, in any event, vote with their feet. However, complainants or their advisers could inquire, anonymously, about the likelihood of removal before making the complaint.

Confidentiality of complaints

Complaints should be dealt with in confidence. Within the practice, only those who need to know should be told of the complaint. Personal information about the patient should not be shared with anyone outside the practice, unless the patient has given express permission for this to happen. In particular, doctors must tell patients if the investigation of any complaint will involve disclosure of information contained within their health records, to someone other than a partner of the doctor or an employee of the practice.

Locum and deputising doctors

If a complaint relates to a doctor deputising for a General Medical Practitioner, it should initially be made to the patient's registered practitioner using the practice's Local Resolution procedures. The practice should liaise with any complaints procedure operated by the deputising doctor. However, a deputising doctor cannot be required to take part in the Local Resolution procedure unless this is specifically contained within the contract between the GP and the deputy and/or their employer. If the deputy is a GP on a Health Authority medical list then it should be possible to require him or her to cooperate. If the complaint proceeds to an independent review the deputising doctor can only be required to cooperate if the above conditions apply.

Keeping records of complaints

Practices are advised to keep detailed records of complaints handling both for the purpose of using complaints to improve procedures and services and in case they are needed to enable the practice to cooperate with further stages of the complaints procedures. These records should be kept separate from the patient's health records, subject to the need to record any information which is strictly relevant to the patient's health in his or her records. Information gathered by the practitioner during the course of a complaint belongs to the practice and the Health Authority has no right of access. A Health Authority can only require the practitioner to provide information about 'action' taken under Local Resolution. For example, the practitioner would need to disclose what meetings, if any, were held to resolve the complaint but would not be required to provide details of exactly what was discussed or decided at those meetings. The Ombudsman can, however, require the practice to release any or all of the information and documentation relating to a complaint if necessary.

Investigating complaints

Each practice will have developed its own procedures for investigating complaints which will usually include a range of options from an informal verbal response to a more formal investigation by the person responsible for managing the complaints procedure. The complaints administrator may need to talk to members of staff or practitioners involved in the complaints as well as interviewing the complainant.

Disciplinary action

Disciplinary matters cannot be investigated under the NHS complaints procedure. This is a separate matter for the employing Health Authority. Unlike hospital complaints where disciplinary matters can be dealt with whilst other aspects of the complaint are still under investigation, disciplinary action involving a Family Health Service Practitioner can only take place at the conclusion of the complaints procedure. For further information on disciplinary procedures see below.

Involving the Health Authority – complaining outside the practice

Some complainants may quite reasonably be unhappy about the prospect of having their complaint dealt with by someone who is already involved in their care and who may also be the subject of the complaint, or they may simply feel too distressed to face the people involved in the incident. In this situation, the complainant should contact the Complaints Manager at the Health Authority to discuss the best way of taking his or her complaint forward. Information about the Complaints Manager at the Health Authority should be included in the practice's complaints literature.

INVOLVING THE LOCAL HEALTH AUTHORITY

How the Health Authority can assist

The Health Authority can assist complainants (and practices) to resolve complaints under local resolution in a number of ways including:

- acting as an intermediary or an 'honest broker' where the complainant does not wish to complain directly to the practice;
- advising and assisting the complainant if he or she is experiencing difficulty in getting the complaint dealt with by the practitioner;
- providing conciliation services for complainants and practitioners.

Before the Health Authority can act as an intermediary or conciliator both the practitioner and the complainant must agree to any such arrangement.

Clear lines of communication

When the Health Authority is acting as an intermediary between the patient and the practitioner, either in providing conciliation or as the 'honest broker' (i.e. neutral intermediary/'postbox') or when dealing with requests for an Independent Review, it is expected to maintain clear and constant lines of communication between the parties involved. It is recommended that this is the responsibility of a named member of staff.

'A need to know' procedure should be followed within the Health Authority, i.e. only those involved in the handling of the complaint should be aware of its existence.

Complaints about fees/charges

Some complaints, particularly about dentists and pharmacists, may involve charges or fees paid by the complainant. Health Authorities should ensure that conciliators who may become involved in the complaint fully understand the nature of such charges.

RESOLVING COMPLAINTS THROUGH CONCILIATION

Complaining directly to a practice can be very difficult for both parties but particularly for the complainant who may be very distressed and traumatised. In this sort of situation it can be helpful to have a neutral third party present in the form of a conciliator. The conciliator or mediator will try to help the practitioner and the complainant to work through the complaint and reach some form of agreement or resolution. Health Authorities are expected to make conciliation services available to practices where a conciliator is requested either by the practice or the complainant. The arrangements for employing lay conciliators and, when appropriate, professional advisers to the lay conciliators is a matter entirely for the Health Authority.

In some cases, Health Authorities may consider it more appropriate for their own staff to act as intermediaries to secure an investigation and an explanation from the practitioner, rather than providing a conciliation service.

Conciliation is considered to be most effective when used as early as possible in the Local Resolution process. Confidentiality must be strictly observed and conciliators should never be required to report details of cases to Health Authorities. They should not provide information which might be used by the Health Authority, should a complainant prove to be dissatisfied with the Local Resolution and ask for an Independent Review. This means that even if a conciliator is aware of a potential disciplinary matter, this information should not be passed on. No information should be provided which would be used by the Health Authority in any subsequent Independent Review – this applies especially to a potential disciplinary matter.

All complaints must start at local level

No matter how serious the complaint, all have to go through the Local Resolution procedure. People who go straight to the Health Authority to request an Independent Review or to the Ombudsman will be referred back for investigation under Local Resolution unless exceptional circumstances apply.

CONCLUSION OF LOCAL RESOLUTION

Written summary of the investigation

A complaint, whether verbal or in writing, should normally be concluded with a letter to the complainant giving a written summary of the investigation and its conclusion. It is recommended that such a letter should include:

- a summary of the complaint;
- an explanation of the practice's view of the events;
- an apology, where appropriate;
- the outcome of any meetings;
- details of the action taken to prevent a recurrence of the incident.

Complainants may find it helpful to refer to this list when assessing whether or not the complaint has been answered satisfactorily.

The right to request an Independent Review

The letter should also inform the complainant of his or her right to request an Independent Review which should be made within 28 calendar days from the date of the letter. This will mark the end of the Local Resolution.

It is recommended that the Local Resolution process should be completed within ten working days. If the Health Authority was involved in either providing support or conciliation this will inevitably extend the period of Local Resolution. In this event the aim would be to complete Local Resolution within 20 working days.

REQUESTING AN INDEPENDENT REVIEW

The role of the Convener

Complainants who are dissatisfied with the practice's response as a result of the Local Resolution process can request an Independent Review. A complainant could be unhappy with the outcome of Local Resolution for a number of reasons. For example, the complainant may feel that:

- the practice did not answer the specific concerns raised by the complainant;

- there was a failure to acknowledge possible errors or misjudgments;
- the investigation of the complaint was inadequate or biased;
- the practice failed to take appropriate action as a result of the complaint.

If the practice has indicated to the complainant that the Local Resolution stage has been concluded and the complainant feels that nothing further can be achieved under Local Resolution a request should be made for investigation by an Independent Review panel. This request should be made within 28 days either direct to the Convener at the local Health Authority or via the practice who should pass the request on. (See Chapter 5.)

INVESTIGATION OF DISCIPLINARY MATTERS

Disciplinary action under the old procedures

Prior to the introduction of the new NHS Complaints Procedure, complaints about Family Health Service Practitioners which involved a possible breach in the practitioners' 'terms of service' could result in a hearing before the 'service committee' of the Health Authority (FHSA). The complainant or his or her representative was expected to present the complaint before the service committee which could ultimately lead to the practitioner being subject to sanctions. In other words, the complaints procedure was also effectively a disciplinary procedure. This changed with the introduction of the NHS Complaints Procedure in April 1996.

Disciplinary matters are now kept quite separate from the complaints procedure, being dealt with independently by the Health Authority. In many cases the Health Authority will only learn of potential disciplinary matters as a result of complaints made by patients and therefore patients still have an important, albeit more limited, role in the process. Health Authorities may also learn of potential disciplinary matters as a result of routine inspections or, possibly, through reports received from professional colleagues.

The decision to take disciplinary action

Decisions about disciplinary action arising from a complaint will only be taken following the 'conclusion' of the complaints procedure. The only exception to this is if immediate action is deemed to be necessary to protect patients e.g. if patients are being put at risk or a criminal offence has been committed. Therefore, in many instances, the Health Authority will only be alerted to possible disciplinary matters and be able to take action at the conclusion of the Independent Review, following receipt of the panel's report.

If a complainant decides not to pursue his or her complaint beyond Local Resolution or, for whatever reason, abandons the complaint before the end of the Independent Review but believes the actions of the practitioner would warrant a disciplinary investigation, the Health Authority should be informed of any concerns. It is a matter for the Health Authority to decide whether or not a disciplinary investigation should be instituted. If the Health Authority decides not to take any action the complainant could consider contacting the practitioner's professional body e.g. General Medical Council, General Dental Council, etc. (See Chapter 10.)

HOW WILL THE HEALTH AUTHORITY DEAL WITH DISCIPLINARY MATTERS?

If the Health Authority identifies the need for some form of disciplinary action there are four main options available:

- informal or remedial action;
- disciplinary action;
- NHS Tribunal;
- referral to the practitioner's professional body.

INFORMAL ACTION

Health Authorities are advised to employ informal or remedial action whenever possible in preference to formal disciplinary action. It is therefore likely that a significant proportion of cases, even where a breach or breaches in the practitioner's terms of service have been identified, will be disposed of without any formal disciplinary action. The Health Authority may instead, for example, recommend further training, a change in the practice's procedures or a reduction in the number of patients on the list.

DISCIPLINARY ACTION

If the Health Authority identifies a potential breach in the practitioner's terms of service which it believes warrants formal disciplinary action, the next step is to refer the matter to the disciplinary committee of *another* Health Authority for investigation. This must be done within 28 days of receiving the report of an Independent Review Panel or, if not the subject of a complaint, within 13 weeks of the events in question.

The disciplinary committee of the independent Health Authority will hold a formal hearing to determine whether the practitioner has been in breach of the terms of service. The original Health Authority will prosecute (present) the case against the practitioner and the original complainant will be involved only as a witness. The hearing will be held in private and evidence is *not* given on oath.

The disciplinary panel will not have access to papers relating to the Local Resolution stage of the complaint which belong to the practice and will only have access to the Independent Review report if the practitioner uses it as part of his/her evidence. The Health Authority may therefore need to re-investigate the incident, taking statements from witnesses, reviewing the records, etc.

Clinical judgment is part of a doctor's terms of service although the fact that a doctor has made a clinical mistake does not necessarily mean that there has been a breach of those terms. The important test is whether or not the doctor exercised appropriate professional skill, care and attention in arriving at the decision. For example, a doctor who promptly visits a sick child and carries out a thorough examination may not be in breach for failing to diagnose the early stages of meningitis. However, a doctor who either refuses to attend or does not carry out an appropriate physical examination may well be in breach of the terms of service.

The disciplinary panel will report back to the Chief Executive of the practitioner's Health Authority with their findings and recommendations. Whilst the Health Authority must accept the findings of fact it is not bound by the committee's recommendations. If the practitioner has been found in breach of the terms of service the Health Authority may impose a financial penalty, issue a formal warning and/or place a limit on the number of patients a practitioner may treat. In serious cases, the matter may be referred to the practitioner's professional body.

Appeals

The practitioner can lodge an appeal against the disciplinary panel's decision and also against any penalty imposed by the employing Health Authority to the Family Health Services Appeal Special Health Authority. The Health Authority does not have a right of appeal because of the contractual relationship it holds with the practitioner.

THE NHS TRIBUNAL

This procedure can only be used against family practitioners, (i.e. GPs, general dental practitioners, pharmacists and opticians) by Health Authorities.

The aim of the tribunal is to promote efficiency in NHS services by preventing continued bad practice. Its remit is to decide whether the inclusion of a practitioner on a Health Authority's Medical, Dental, Pharmaceutical or Ophthalmic List would be prejudicial to the efficiency of the service in question. It can direct that the practitioner be disqualified from practising by removing or suspending the practitioner from the List. This power makes it the ultimate NHS disciplinary body for Family Health Service Practitioners. It has no other lesser sanction available to it.

Representations to the tribunal can be made by a Health Authority (usually, but not always) after a practitioner has been 'persistently' found in breach of his 'terms of service'.

Suspension order

Since December 1995, the Health Authority can also apply for a suspension order if it considers that suspension is necessary to protect patients. HSG (95) 62 states that these provisions for suspension will, for the time being, only apply to doctors and dentists, but eventually the intention is to apply supervision to all groups. Health Authorities will only be able to apply for a suspension order if there is an intention to make representations for disqualification. Suspension is an *interim measure* and not an additional sanction.

NHS tribunal

The tribunal will consist of:

- Chair appointed by the Lord Chancellor, who will have a ten year general qualification within the meaning of the Courts and Legal Services Act 1990;
- a person appointed by the Secretary of State for Health, after consultation with the Association of Health Authorities; and
- a practitioner similarly qualified to the person complained against.

If the tribunal decides to hold an inquiry, *and* the person complained against so requests, the hearing will be in public. The patient(s) and people involved in the original complaint(s) are likely to be called as witnesses by the Health Authority. Their evidence will be heard on oath and they are likely to be questioned by the person complained against's barrister or solicitor.

Referral to GMC UKCC etc

If the Health Authority, either as a result of a disciplinary panel hearing or possibly as a result of other inquiries, believes that a practitioner is not fit to practise and/or may be guilty of serious professional misconduct or whose professional performance is below an acceptable standard, it can refer the matter to the practitioner's professional body. For further details see Chapter 10.

CONCLUSION

The GP and other primary healthcare workers are the backbone of the NHS. Many people rarely see any other health professionals. The new Complaints Procedure tries to develop the idea that disputes should be settled at ground level with the practice-based Complaints Procedure being the principal method of resolution. The success of the system is unlikely to be universal because the standard of practice is so varied. It is to be hoped that the Independent Review will address this to make standards uniform and to satisfy patients.

Chapter 8

INDEPENDENT REVIEW OF NHS COMPLAINTS

Susan Polywka and Graham Girvan

If a complainant is dissatisfied with the outcome of the Local Resolution of his or her complaint, whether it is about a Family Health Service Practitioner, a Trust or a Health Authority, he or she can request an Independent Review. This is the second and final stage of the NHS Complaints Procedure.

An Independent Review offers complainants the opportunity for their complaints to be investigated by an independent panel which will conclude its inquiries with a written report of its findings. A panel investigation can be particularly beneficial where the complaint relates to clinical judgment because the panel will be advised by at least two independent assessors (and/or other appropriate practitioner) whose report(s) will be made available to the complainant at the conclusion of the investigation.

There is no automatic right to an Independent Review, only the right to request one. The guiding principle is that all opportunities for satisfying the complainant should first have been explored and fully exhausted under Local Resolution. Only where issues remain can referral to a panel be made.

This decision is the responsibility of the convener who will need to make further inquiries and seek appropriate advice. If an Independent Review is refused or the complainant is dissatisfied with the outcome of the review a complaint can be made to the Health Service Ombudsman.

REQUESTING AN INDEPENDENT REVIEW

The request for an Independent Review should be made to the convener either orally or in writing within 28 days of the conclusion of Local Resolution via the healthcare provider. The request should be acknowledged within two working days.

WHO IS THE CONVENER?

The Convener is a non-executive director of the relevant Health Authority or Trust board or an outside consultant. Save in exceptional circumstances, the Convener should not be the Chair of the board or a practising or retired clinical professional or former member of the NHS staff.

Conveners are advised that they should handle complaints impartially and that they should not defend the staff that are the subject of any complaint, but one cannot rule out the possibility that some conveners may fail to be entirely objective in their decision making. If the complainant is concerned about the independence of the convener, he or she should raise this with the Trust, and if appropriate action is not taken, refer the matter to the Health Service Ombudsman.

REQUIREMENTS TO CONVENE A PANEL

The Convener should ascertain whether all opportunities for resolving the complaint during Local Resolution have been explored and fully exhausted and what issues, if any, could be referred to an Independent Review. There is no investigation of the actual facts of the case, at this stage the objective is to establish the best way of resolving the complaint.

In order to establish whether a panel should be convened the Convener will need to:

- obtain a statement from the complainant setting out the remaining grievances (this may be set out in a letter);
- consult an independent lay chair;
- seek clinical advice (clinical complaints).

Complainant's statement

Usually the complainant is asked to make a statement, and as a guide the statement to the Convener should include:

- a summary of the events in question;
- details of the main areas of complaint/concern;
- details of what action the complainant has taken to try and resolve the complaint;

- details of the response(s) he or she has received from the healthcare provider;
- details of which aspects of the complaint remain unanswered or answered inadequately;
- why the complainant now believes that further action under Local Resolution would be unlikely to resolve the complaint;
- why the complainant believes the complaint warrants investigation by an Independent Review Panel.

As the Convener is expected to complete the inquiries within a set time (see below) the complainant may be under some pressure to prepare a statement relatively quickly. To avoid problems, complainants should seek advice about preparing a statement as early as possible, ideally before they contact the Convener (the local CHC will usually be very helpful).

The practitioner or Trust complained against will normally be informed in writing of the grievance. In the case of Family Health Service Practitioners this letter may also tell them of the name of the secretary of their local representative committee should they wish to seek advice.

Independent lay chair

The Convener must also consult with one of the independent lay chairs on the list maintained by the Regional Office of the NHS Executive. At this stage, the role of the independent lay chair is to give advice and support to the Convener and to keep a record of the complaint. If the complaint subsequently proceeds to an Independent Review the lay chair will then take over responsibility for the conduct of the panel.

Clinical complaints – clinical advice

Where the complaint relates to the exercise of clinical judgment (a clinical complaint) the Convener will need to seek appropriate clinical advice, usually from the Trust but not from anyone who is in any way associated with the complaint. The Convener may consult with an independent professional adviser drawn from a list held by the Regional Office of the NHS Executive.

In the case of complaints about FHS practitioners, the Convener will, if necessary, obtain advice from an independent practitioner, from the same profession as the practitioner complained about, whose name will come from a list of practitioners nominated by the relevant local professional committee which is held at the Regional Office. In the case of GP fundholders the advice will come from the local GP fundholding groups within the Region or, by agreement, by local medical committees working with local GP fundholding interests. If a complainant is concerned about the independence of the clinical advice he or she should raise this with the Convener and/or Ombudsman.

The Convener is not obliged to give copies to the complainant of any reports relating to any clinical advice obtained but where a panel is refused the Convener's letter to the complainant should be sufficiently comprehensive to satisfy the complainant. The Guidance encourages openness and the Convener may agree, with the clinician's consent, to allow the complainant to see the report(s).

Clinical judgment

It is not always clear when a complaint involves clinical judgment but as a guide, clinical judgment is defined as any judgment that is made by a member of the clinical professions in the NHS, by virtue of their knowledge and skill, which a layman (sic) could not make. Clinical judgment can be exercised by any of the following recognised clinical professions working within the NHS to provide patient care:

- doctors;
- nurses;
- midwives;
- health visitors;
- dentists;
- pharmacists;
- optometrists;
- ophthalmic medical practitioners;
- clinical psychologists;
- members of the professions supplementary to and allied to medicine;
- paramedics and ambulance technicians;
- laboratory and other scientific and technical staff.

THE CRITERIA FOR ESTABLISHING AN INDEPENDENT REVIEW PANEL (IRP)

In coming to the decision whether to convene an Independent Review Panel the Convener must consider:

- if any further action can be taken to satisfy the complainant, short of establishing a panel;
- if all practical action has already been taken and that establishing a panel would 'add no further value to the process';
- the advice of the appropriate clinicians if all or any of the complaint is about action taken in consequence of clinical judgment;
- the full advice of the independent lay chair.

REFUSAL OF AN INDEPENDENT REVIEW PANEL

There are only four reasons for the Convener to refuse to establish an Independent Review Panel:

- if the complainant has started legal action or there is an explicit indication by the complainant that he or she intends to make a legal claim essentially on the same set of circumstances as the original complaint;
- all practicable action has already been taken to resolve the complaint;
- further action as part of Local Resolution is still believed to be appropriate and practicable;
- the complainant has not exhausted statutory procedures which exist to deal with the type of complaint e.g. rights under the Mental Health Act.

Time period for Convener's decision

Following receipt of a request for an Independent Review the decision whether or not to convene a panel to review a complaint should be taken within:

- 20 working days in the case of a complaint about a Trust or Health Authority;
- 10 working days in the case of a complaint about a FSH practitioner.

Information about the Convener's decision

The Convener must convey the decision in writing to:

- the complainant;
- any person complained against;

- the Chief Executive of the Trust or practitioner (FHS complaints);
- the independent lay panel chair; and
- anyone else consulted.

Refusal to set up IRP

If a panel is refused the Convener must write to the complainant and the person complained against, clearly stating the full reasons for not convening a panel. Failure to do so has been the subject of criticism by the Health Service Ombudsman. The Convener must also state whether or not there is any further action which the Trust/Health Authority/FHS practitioner could take to resolve the complaint.

The complainant must also be informed of his or her right to complain to the Health Service Commissioner (Ombudsman).

Further requests for an IRP

If the Convener refers the complaint back for further investigation under Local Resolution, and the complainant remains dissatisfied after further action has been taken, the Convener can be requested to reconsider an Independent Review.

Review by the Ombudsman

The decision to refuse an Independent Review can be reviewed by the Ombudsman who will consider:

- whether the Convener's decision to refuse an independent review should be reconsidered; or
- whether it is more appropriate to investigate the substance of the complaint himself; or
- that no further action is warranted.

If the Convener is invited by the Ombudsman to reconsider a refusal to hold an Independent Review it is quite possible that the Convener may arrive at the same decision as before. The complainant would then have the option of making a further request for an investigation by the Ombudsman.

INDEPENDENT REVIEW PANEL

Terms of reference

If the Convener agrees to an Independent Review of a complaint, he or she will draw up the 'terms of reference' for the panel. This will be sent to the complainant, the person complained against and the Chief Executive of the Health Authority or Trust. The terms of reference will detail the aspects of the complaint to be included in the investigation and those matters which will be excluded, for example, disciplinary matters or points that have already been satisfactorily answered in Local Resolution. Where a complainant believes that important questions have not been included in the terms of reference representations can be made to the Convener. Nevertheless the Convener's decision is final.

IRP Members

The Trust/Health Authority will be responsible for liaising with the Regional Office of the NHSE in appointing the panel members. The Independent Review Panel will be established as a committee of the Health Authority or Trust to investigate the complaint and make a report with appropriate comments and suggestions. In the case of FHS practitioner complaints, the panel should be established within ten working days of the convener's decision (20 working days in the case of Trust/Health Authority complaints).

The panel's core membership will comprise;

- an independent lay chair
- the Convener;
- either:

  for a Trust panel, a representative of the purchaser (a non-executive member of the Health Authority or a GP fundholder);

  for a Health Authority panel, another independent lay person.

Clinical complaints – clinical assessors

When the complaint is wholly or partly about clinical matters the panel must be advised by at least two clinical assessors nominated by the Regional Office, from a list compiled with the benefit of advice from the relevant professional bodies. They will decide, in consultation with the panel, how to investigate the complaint which may include interviewing and/or examining the patient (see below).

Neither the lay chair nor the lay panel members should be current or retired NHS staff or members of any of the clinical professions. They should not be members of Trust boards or Health Authorities. They should have no previous formal links with the Trust which is involved in the complaint or the relevant Health Authority. As soon as the Convener has set out the panel's terms of reference the lay chair will then take over the conduct of the panel's business.

The complainant should be informed of who has been appointed to conduct the Independent Review.

Function of IRP

The panel will investigate the facts of the complaint taking into account the views of both sides. It will set out its conclusions, with appropriate comments and suggestions, in a written report. The panel will *not* be able to suggest that any person be subject to disciplinary action or referred to any one of the professional regulatory bodies.

Operation of the IRP

The operation of the panel in conducting its investigation and making its report is very largely at its own discretion, and ultimately that of its chair, but it should work within the following rules issued by the NHSE:

- the panel's proceedings must be confidential;
- proceedings should be held in private;
- the panel must have access to all the records held by the Trust or Health Authority relating to the handling of the complaint; Family Health Service Practitioners are only required to release information about action taken under Local Resolution, not all the information relating to the complaint;
- if the complaint is a clinical one, the panel must have access to the relevant parts of the patient's records;
- the panel must give both the complainant and the person complained against a reasonable opportunity to express their views on the complaint;
- if any of the panel members disagree about how the panel should go about its business the Chair's decision will be final;
- a tape recording of the panel's proceedings, including interviews with the parties concerned, is a matter for the panel and may only take place if both parties as well as the panel agree. The Chair is the final arbiter on whether this facility is used;
- at least one clinical assessor should be present when either party is interviewed by the panel, where matters relating to the exercise of clinical judgment are under consideration.

The panel is expected to resolve the complaint in a 'conciliatory manner' while taking a view on the facts identified. It should be flexible and choose a method or procedure that is appropriate to the circumstances of the complaint. It should not be adversarial, legalistic or confrontational. It is certainly possible that the complainant and complained against will never be brought together at the same meeting. Much of the panel's investigation might well be conducted through interview by only one of the panel members.

Role of Clinical Assessor

The role of the clinical assessor is to advise members of the panel on any matters relating to clinical judgment. Assessors should have access to all the records held by the Trust/Health Authority/ Family Health Service Practitioner together with details of the handling of the complaint. If the records are no longer in the possession of the Trust or practice being complained against, efforts should be made to ensure that they have access – photocopies where appropriate – to the relevant records to assist them in responding to the complainant. If the complainant is concerned about certain records being made available to other parties he or she should inform the Convener. Assessors should also check that the complainant has not previously been denied access to certain parts of his or her records.

Assessors may interview or examine the complainant. For example, if a complaint relates to dental treatment the patient may be examined by an independent dentist. The assessor may also interview any person complained against. The assessors should not normally discuss their findings with either party before reporting back to the panel.

Assessors' reports

The assessors will produce either combined or individual reports. These should not be given to the complainant or complained against until they have been made available to the panel. The panel may, in certain circumstances, release the reports to the parties before they publish the panel's final report if it is felt this will aid resolution of the complaint. Otherwise, the reports will be included with the panel's final report – initially in draft form.

The assessors should take care to ensure their reports contain no information which might cause serious harm to the physical or mental health of the patient or any other individual, or contain information about or provided by a third party (other than a health professional involved in the patient's care) who can be identified from the information, unless he or she has consented to its disclosure.

Rights of persons to be accompanied at IRP

When being interviewed by any members of the panel or the clinical assessors the complainant (and any other person interviewed) may be accompanied by a person of his or her choosing who may, with the agreement of the chair, speak to the members or the assessors. An individual cannot be represented by a legally qualified person acting in a legal capacity. (An officer from the CHC is usually most useful.)

The chair has discretion to allow the complainant to be accompanied by a second person, such as a relative, for emotional support, as well as an adviser, (i.e. from the CHC). Similarly, any person mentioned in the complaint may be accompanied by a trade union or professional adviser or a manager or colleague who can act as a personal adviser. Only with the approval of the chair may those accompanying the complainant or any other person interviewed contribute to the panel's proceedings.

THE REPORT OF THE INDEPENDENT REVIEW PANEL

Draft report

Upon conclusion of its investigations, the panel will issue a report with the clinical assessors' report(s) attached where present. The report cannot make any recommendations in relation to disciplinary action.

It is recommended that before issuing a final report a draft report, together with any reports obtained from clinical assessors, should be sent to the complainant and any people complained against so that they can check for factual accuracy. The draft report should be available within 30 working days of the panel being convened in the case of FHS practitioner complaints (or within 50 working days in the case of complaints about a Health Authority or Trust). The parties then have 14 days to respond and should be asked to tell the panel if they wish to show the draft report to an adviser, who has not been previously involved in the complaint, since the report is confidential. A draft report will not always be sent out before the final report is produced and complainants may wish to make a specific request that a draft report is sent.

Final report

The panel's draft report is confidential and its circulation should be restricted to:

- the complainant (and the patient, if different);
- any person named in the complaint;
- any other person interviewed by the panel;
- the clinical assessors;
- the Health Authority/Trust Chairman or Chief Executive;
- in the case of complaints about FHS practitioners/GP fundholders, the practitioners concerned;
- the regional directors of Public Health and Performance Management;
- the Health Authority chairman and Chief Executive or GP fundholder who purchased the service;
- the Chairman and Chief Executive of the independent provider, where the service was purchased by the NHS from the independent sector.

The report belongs to the chair of the panel who has the right to withhold any part of the panel's report and all or part of the assessors' reports in order to ensure confidentiality of clinical information. The NHSE guidance states that the report's overall confidentiality should be maintained to protect the confidentiality of the patient. A Trust's Chief Executive may need to show it to board members when considering what action needs to be taken in response to the report.

Where someone has only played a small part in the investigation it may not be appropriate for him or her to receive the whole report. This is a matter for the chair to decide but the patient/complainant may wish to make representations on this matter if there are concerns about personal information being made available to witnesses, etc.

The chair may feel it would be helpful to round off the Independent Review with a meeting with the complainant. If it is a clinical complaint at least one of the clinical assessors should be there to give a personal explanation of the clinical findings.

Consequences of IRP report

On receipt of the panel's report, Health Authority/Trust boards are expected to decide what action, if any, should be taken in light of the panel's findings and to ensure that such action is subsequently carried out. The panel itself will have no executive authority over any action by the Trust/Health Authority/FHS practitioner, this is a matter for the Trust or Health Authority to decide.

In the case of complaints about Trusts, the Chief Executive must within four weeks write to the complainant informing him or her of any action the Trust will be taking as a result of the report and any other matters such as a formal apology, an ex gratia payment, etc. Where the panel has suggested a review of policy which requires further consultation, the complainant should be clearly informed as to the process including the timescale and the final decisions reached. The letter must remind the complainant of the right to take any unsatisfied grievance to the Ombudsman. This letter marks the completion of the complaints process for the Trust.

Where it is a complaint about a Family Health Service Practitioner the panel will send the final report to the Chief Executive of the relevant Health Authority who will then forward copies of the report to the relevant parties with a covering letter. If the panel has made recommendations, for example, about the need for the practitioner to change certain practices, the Chief Executive of the Health Authority should inform the complainant that he or she is inviting the practitioner to respond personally to the complainant on these matters.

Disciplinary action

The Health Authority will also have to decide whether the Family Health Service Practitioner should be subject to any form of disciplinary action (see Chapter 7).

Time taken to complete IRP?

A panel reviewing a complaint against an FHS practitioner should conclude its report within 40 working days. Allowing time for the Convener's decision (10 working days), the appointment of the panel (ten working days) and for the report to be sent to the complainant and practitioner (five working days), the entire process of Independent Review should be completed within three months from the complainant's request.

A panel reviewing a complaint against a Trust or Health Authority should conclude its report within 60 working days. Allowing time for the Convener's decision (20 working days), the appointment of the panel (20 working days) and for the board's response to the report once issued (20 working days), the entire process of Independent Review should be completed within six months from the complainant's request.

FURTHER ACTION BY THE COMPLAINANT

This marks the completion of the NHS Complaints Procedure. If the complainant is dissatisfied with the outcome of the investigation there are a number of other options they could consider:

- a complaint to the Health Service Ombudsman;
- a complaint to a practitioner's professional body;
- legal action.

For further information about these options, please refer to the relevant chapters.

EXAMPLES OF COMPLAINTS

- **Case 1**

  Ms Perk's son died soon after he was born in hospital. She was aware that the midwife delayed calling a doctor for a long time, because she could not get a machine to work properly. There was then a further wait before the doctor arrived.

  She complained to the hospital and received a reply from the Chief Executive. She was not satisfied because he had not answered all her queries adequately. She spoke with a member of the local NCT group who suggested she went to the CHC. She was advised and assisted to write again explaining why she was dissatisfied with the Local Resolution and the questions to which she still wanted answers.

  The letter was passed to the Trust's Convener who discussed the complaint with the Trust's Medical Director. He then spoke to the Regional Office who gave him the name of the independent lay chair and the midwifery assessor. All agreed that an independent panel should be established.

  Ms Perks, accompanied by a woman member of the CHC, met with the clinical assessors and then with the Panel. She was sent the Panel's draft report and discussed it with the CHC member. The final report upheld her complaint and recommended the equipment in the Maternity Unit be checked more often. It is also recommended the means of communication within the Unit be reviewed. Some weeks later, she received a letter from the Chief Executive, formally apologising to her and explaining what action had been taken.

- **Case 2**

  Mr Forest was unhappy about the result of an operation on his hip. He felt that the Local Resolution had sided with the consultant since it was dealt with inside the hospital. He wrote and requested an Independent Review. The Trust's Convener discussed the complaint with an orthopaedic consultant on the Regional list. He felt that Mr Forest had been given a satisfactory answer. The independent lay chair agreed with their views and the Convener wrote to Mr Forest and to his (ex) consultant explaining that the Trust had done all that it could and that nothing would be gained from setting up an Independent Review.

  Mr Forest spoke to the CHC who advised him to appeal to the Ombudsman. The Ombudsman looked at all the correspondence and agreed with the Convener. He wrote to Mr Forest and explained why he was not going to investigate his complaint.

  Mr Forest then sought advice from a medical negligence solicitor on the AVMA panel.

- **Case 3**

  Mrs Woodford was very upset by the way she was treated at a community contraception clinic. She was unhappy with the Local Resolution because she was not able to speak with the doctor who examined her. The Convener thought that a meeting with Mrs Woodford and the doctor, chaired by herself, might resolve the complaint. The independent lay chair agreed and a full and frank discussion took place which satisfied Mrs Woodford.

CONCLUSION

The jury is still out on whether the Independent Review system is truly impartial. Only time and the quality of judgment in the individual Independent Reviews will give confidence to patients and their advisers. It is only with such confidence that the system will be used to the benefit of the patient and thereby the NHS.

Chapter 9

THE HEALTH SERVICE COMMISSIONER (OMBUDSMAN)

Richard A Oswald

Where a patient has pursued a complaint through the NHS Complaints Procedure but believes the complaint has not been satisfactorily resolved, an investigation by the Health Service Ombudsman can be requested. This chapter explains what conditions need to be satisfied for a complaint to be subject to an Ombudsman's investigation and how the complaint will be investigated.

INTRODUCTION

The role of the Health Service Ombudsman is to carry out an independent investigation of those complaints about the NHS which have not been resolved satisfactorily at local level. The Ombudsman is accountable directly to Parliament and is therefore completely independent of the NHS and the Government. Investigations are extremely thorough, and the Ombudsman has powers equivalent to those of the courts to obtain the evidence needed to reach conclusions on a complaint. The person complaining and the NHS body complained about receive a report at the end of the investigation. If the grievance is upheld the report will say what action should be taken to put matters right.

An Ombudsman typically reaches judgments on the basis not of legal argument or precedent but of equity and common sense. A key feature of a true Ombudsman is that the office is wholly independent of the service whose actions lie within its jurisdiction.

The main points to remember are that:

- the complainant must first go through the NHS internal complaints procedure by taking up the grievance with the NHS body responsible for providing the service in question;

- a complaint to the Ombudsman must be made in writing, normally by the person directly concerned;
- the complaints should normally be made within *one year* of the events in question.

THE OFFICE OF HEALTH SERVICE OMBUDSMAN – ITS ORIGINS

The first Ombudsman to appear in the United Kingdom – in 1967 – was the Parliamentary Commissioner for Administration (or Parliamentary Ombudsman). There are now also Local Government Ombudsmen for England, Scotland and Wales, an Ombudsman who deals with both central and local government services in Northern Ireland, and an increasing number of Ombudsmen (a gender neutral term) in both the public and the private sector – such as insurance, banking and legal services.

HEALTH SERVICE COMMISSIONER

The offices of Health Service Commissioner (or Ombudsman) – one each for England, Scotland and Wales – were established in 1973. All three posts have customarily been held by the same person. The Ombudsman is appointed by the Crown and is accountable to Parliament. Some staff are employed directly by the Ombudsman, but most investigation staff are seconded from the NHS or from government departments. All are based in London, except for small units in Cardiff and Edinburgh.

ROLE AND JURISDICTION OF THE HEALTH SERVICE OMBUDSMAN

Health Service Commissioners (Amendment) Act 1996

The role and jurisdiction of the Ombudsman is set out in the Health Service Commissioners Act 1993, key elements of which were amended by the 1996 Act.

Prior to the 1996 Act, clinical complaints and complaints about Family Health Services were specifically excluded from the

Ombudsman's remit. At that time the Ombudsman was restricted to investigating complaints concerning maladministration and failures in service. The 1996 Act enabled the Ombudsman to look at the whole of a complaint including clinical care. It also extended the Ombudsman's role to include Family Health Services, such as the actions of general medical and dental practitioners. These changes gave effect to the aim, proposed in the report *Being Heard* of the Wilson Review of NHS complaints procedures, that the Ombudsman should be at the apex of an integrated system for looking into complaints about the NHS.

LOCAL INVESTIGATION OF COMPLAINTS – THE NHS COMPLAINTS PROCEDURE

As a general rule, before a complaint can be considered by the Ombudsman it must first have been investigated under the Local Resolution stage of the internal NHS procedure introduced in April 1996. It should also have been considered under the Independent Review Panel stage, although a complainant may come to the Ombudsman if a request for a panel has been refused. Providers of any public service should be given a reasonable chance to resolve grievances internally before they become subject to independent scrutiny by an Ombudsman.

MATTERS WHICH LIE WITHIN THE OMBUDSMAN'S JURISDICTION

- A failure in a service provided under the NHS, whether in a NHS hospital or clinic or under a contract with a private or voluntary undertaking;
- a failure to provide a service which it was a function or duty of the NHS body in question to provide or arrange;
- a failure to release information disclosable under the '*Code of Openness in the NHS*';
- maladministration leading to injustice connected with any other action.

There is no statutory definition of what constitutes maladministration but the Ombudsman's Annual Report for 1994/95 cited, as examples, such things as avoidable delay, not following proper procedures, rudeness or discourtesy, not explaining decisions or not providing a full and prompt answer to a complaint.

Family Health Services

In the case of complaints about providers of Family Health Services (general medical or dental practitioners, local pharmacists, optometrists or ophthalmic medical practitioners) the 1996 Act refers not to failures in service or maladministration but to the 'actions' of those providers or their staff.

Establishing hardship or injustice

The Ombudsman will take up a complaint only if the matter has caused actual hardship or injustice to the aggrieved person. Therefore, speculative consequences, however real the prospect that they might occur, will not normally justify the Ombudsman's intervention.

Discretionary decisions

It is also not enough for a person simply to take exception to a discretionary decision which a NHS body has a right to take. There must be some evidence of defect in the decision-making process, such as not adhering to proper procedure or failing to take into account all relevant factors.

TIME LIMIT FOR COMPLAINTS

Why did Parliament decide to set a time limit of, normally, one year for putting a complaint to the Ombudsman? One of the reasons is that much reliance is placed in an investigation on oral evidence and memories can fade with the passage of time, reducing the prospects of reaching satisfactory conclusions. Also, natural justice demands that staff should not be under prolonged potential jeopardy of being subject to a complaint about their actions.

The following points should be borne in mind:

- the complainant should write to the Ombudsman within a year of the event or action at issue; but
- a complainant who was not aware of the matter, or its consequences, at the time should write within a year of becoming aware of it.

Complaints which are 'out of time'

Although the above defines when the time limit clock starts ticking, the one year limit can, exceptionally, be waived – e.g. because of incapacity, or if the local handling of the complaint took longer than it should have done. Always explain the circumstances if more than 12 months have passed since the cause of the complaint.

COMPLAINTS FROM NHS STAFF

The 1996 Act provided a new right for staff and practitioners in the NHS to complain to the Ombudsman if they consider that they have been unfairly treated during an investigation under the NHS Complaints Procedure. NHS staff must first pursue their concerns through the local grievance procedures. The Ombudsman can look into the way in which the original complaint was dealt with, but not into any disciplinary or other action taken by the NHS body in its capacity as employer.

MATTERS STILL EXCLUDED FROM INVESTIGATION

The Ombudsman is precluded from taking up grievances about:

- personnel issues such as appointments of staff, pay or discipline. The Ombudsman cannot bring or recommend disciplinary action but is able to inform the relevant regulatory body – such as the General Medical Council – if information obtained during an investigation, but which cannot be disclosed in the report of the investigation, suggests that a professional might constitute a threat to the health or safety of patients;
- matters for which there is a remedy in the courts or before a tribunal, unless in the Ombudsman's view it would not be reasonable in a particular case for such a course to be pursued;
- commercial or contractual matters, although complaints about NHS services to patients provided under contracts between NHS purchasers and NHS or other providers or under the GP fund-holding scheme are within jurisdiction;

- treatment in a non-NHS hospital or nursing home or other private establishment, where it is provided under arrangements made privately rather than under a NHS contract;
- generalised complaints, e.g. about staffing levels or general levels of provision;
- Government policy or the actions of government departments.

WHAT ABOUT LEGAL PROCEEDINGS?

The potential for litigation is greater for complaints about medical treatment. Accusations in a complaint letter that a health professional's actions were 'grossly negligent' can be an expression more of anger than of a real desire to litigate. Failures can often be the result not of poor treatment but of a lapse in communications or procedure. The courts, which are concerned with negligence and damages, are not a suitable vehicle for those seeking explanations or a procedural change to benefit future users of the same service. Anyone giving advice on what course of action to pursue should try to establish what sort of remedy is being sought; whether the costs and risks of legal proceedings are likely to be worthwhile; and, which course is most likely to lead to satisfactory resolution. The Ombudsman cannot secure damages or punitive action against the professional involved.

No powers of Ombudsman to investigate where legal action begun or pending

A highly defensive local response to a complaint might, quite unnecessarily, point the complainant towards litigation. Where legal action has already started the Ombudsman must decline to investigate. Occasionally it becomes clear during an investigation that inquiries are proceeding in parallel between legal representatives. That will usually result in discontinuation of the Ombudsman's inquiries. Parliament did not intend that the Ombudsman, who provides a service free to the complainant but at public expense, should help someone who sees an investigation simply as a paving exercise for litigation.

In what circumstances would it not be 'reasonable' to expect a person to pursue the legal route? So far as clinical matters are concerned, it seems likely that the Ombudsman would have regard to such matters as:

- what the complainant's general intentions are and the remedy sought;
- whether the actions at issue are likely to be appropriate for a legal remedy;
- any arguments advanced by the complainant about why it would not be reasonable to litigate.

DOES THAT LEAVE ANYTHING FOR THE OMBUDSMAN TO INVESTIGATE?

The list of excluded categories may appear forbidding, but the reality is different particularly now that clinical matters and complaints about Family Health Services are in the Ombudsman's remit. The Ombudsman's Annual Report for 1994/95 gives a good idea of the wide range of matters covered even before the extension of jurisdiction. Local complaints handling was the biggest single topic but many others were concerned with aspects of care and treatment. They included:

- age-related admission policies;
- communications about resuscitation;
- inadequate management of pressure areas and of diet;
- failure to safeguard property;
- inadequate custody and sloppy completion of patient's records;
- delay in providing treatment;
- poor staff attitudes.

REFERRING A CASE TO THE OMBUDSMAN

Who can complain?

Normally the person directly affected should put the complaint to the Ombudsman. If that is not possible, complaints may be accepted from:

- a close relative, preferably the next-of-kin;
- a personal representative, advocate or adviser acting at the clear behest of the aggrieved person;
- a member of staff, if there is no one else more suitable.

Where can complainants obtain assistance?

Help with pursuing a complaint can be obtained from Community Health Councils (or, in Scotland, Local Health Councils), Citizen's Advice Bureaux or a relevant charity providing advocacy support. It should always be made clear that the aggrieved person, if not incapable or deceased, supports the complaint. That is in order to safeguard confidentiality and because that person may need to be interviewed during the investigation.

SCREENING OF COMPLAINTS

A complaint to the Ombudsman is screened to check:

- that it is not in an excluded category;
- that it is in time;
- that it is from someone reasonably entitled to complain or to represent the aggrieved person;
- that the body complained about is within jurisdiction; and
- that the NHS Complaints Procedures can reasonably be said to have been exhausted. For example, refusal by the complaints Convener of the NHS authority, board or Trust to grant a review by an independent panel marks the end of the NHS procedure – and that refusal might itself be the subject of an investigation grievance.

COMPLAINTS WHICH ARE *NOT* ACCEPTED FOR INVESTIGATION

If a complaint to the Ombudsman cannot be investigated, a full explanatory letter is sent to the complainant. Parliament has given the Ombudsman discretion to decide whether or not to investigate any particular complaint.

COMPLAINTS WHICH ARE ACCEPTED FOR INVESTIGATION

Terms of reference

If investigation is agreed to, the Ombudsman's office sends to the complainant, and to the bodies and any individuals complained about, a summary based on the written material provided by the complainant. It is not a statement of undisputed fact, but it constitutes the terms of reference for the investigation.

THE INVESTIGATION

An investigation by the Ombudsman is extremely thorough, which is why it will usually take several months. The detailed work on a case is carried out by an investigator on the Ombudsman's staff and the information or evidence required is obtained in various ways:

- those complained about are asked to send to the Ombudsman their formal comments on and all their papers relating to the complaint;
- for clinical complaints the Ombudsman will wish to see any reports of assessors appointed to assist the NHS independent panel. The medical, nursing or other professional records will also be obtained (these are kept strictly confidential);
- the Ombudsman's investigator interviews the person who made the complaint and, after that, any other person who may be able to provide relevant evidence.

The Ombudsman has statutory powers equivalent to those of the High Court or, in Scotland, the Court of Sessions, to call for documents and to interview witnesses. Refusal to comply may be certifiable as an offence of contempt of court. Notwithstanding the statutory powers, which very rarely need to be invoked, an investigation is conducted in as informal and inquisitorial a manner as possible. Interviews are held in private, usually for complainants at their homes, and detailed notes are taken and the main points checked back before the investigator leaves. Any witness is entitled to be accompanied by a 'friend' who, for a complainant, could be another relative or someone from the Community or Local Health Council. If a solicitor is brought to the interview any associated costs will not be met by the Ombudsman unless, exceptionally, reimbursement has been agreed beforehand.

PROFESSIONAL ADVICE ON CLINICAL MATTERS

Clinical assessors

The staff of the Ombudsman has been strengthened to include advisers in hospital medicine, primary health care and nursing. Advice in other disciplines will be obtained as necessary. Those advisers will both help at the screening stage and give advice on the selection of specialist professional assessors, whose role is to examine and report upon the clinical aspects of a particular investigation. The assessors:

- will be appointed by the Ombudsman from the lists of names provided by professional and other relevant bodies to the Secretary of State for Health for the purpose of the NHS Independent Review panels;
- will serve in an individual, not a representative, capacity and care will be taken that there is nothing to cast doubt on their independence;
- will consider any professional reports made to the local panel enquiry, study the clinical records and decide whether to discuss the case with any of the professionals involved;
- will be expected to collaborate both with one another and with the staff investigator concerned;
- will draw on their own experience and expertise to

determine whether the actions of the professionals complained about were based on a reasonable and responsible exercise of clinical judgment of a standard which the patient could be entitled reasonably to expect in the particular circumstances.

ASSESSMENT OF CLINICAL ACTIONS OR DECISIONS

In reaching their conclusions, the assessors will take account of the skills and experience of the professional concerned, any standards or good practice which a professional working in the capacity in question could be expected to take into account and any other matters which in their opinion had a bearing on the decisions or action involved. They are not expected to say whether they would have decided or acted similarly, or to give advice on whether the action taken was the best possible.

Where necessary, they should say, if they can, whether the clinical consequences were the result of actions taken in the exercise of clinical judgment. The Ombudsman's investigations take account of the patient's concern about whether anyone was at fault but recognise also that clinical decisions responsibly and properly considered can, and will occasionally, lead to unintended and harmful consequences or carry an acknowledged degree of risk. That may not necessarily be the result of poor clinical judgment. The assessors' advice and reports are made to the Ombudsman, whose responsibility it is to be satisfied that their conclusions have been soundly arrived at.

THE INVESTIGATION REPORT

This is prepared once all the necessary evidence and information is available. It incorporates only that material considered necessary for the purpose of demonstrating balance, stating key facts or opinions from witnesses – however conflicting – and quoting from relevant national or local policies or procedures. Integrity and impartiality depend on the determination of conclusions (known as 'findings') which are clearly supported by the evidence.

Responsibility for deciding the content of the report rests with the Ombudsman or staff with delegated authority to exercise that function. The report is sent to:

- the complainant;
- those investigated – not only the NHS or other body concerned but also any individual whose actions lay at the centre of the complaint;
- any Member of Parliament who assisted the complaint in putting the case to the Ombudsman; and
- the relevant Secretary of State.

The report has absolute privilege, as has the assessors' advice to the Ombudsman.

FINDINGS AND REMEDY

For each of the matters investigated, including clinical aspects, the Ombudsman decides whether it should be:

- upheld;
- not upheld;
- not made out (where the evidence is not sufficient to warrant an 'upheld' finding); or
- incapable of being resolved either way (such as where conflicting evidence cannot be reconciled or is very finely balanced).

Conclusions are reached where necessary on the civil law test of the balance of probabilities. Although the Ombudsman does not have the power to cause disciplinary action to be taken or to award damages, reports can be very salutary for those involved and care is always taken to avoid arbitrariness in arriving at findings.

WHAT SORT OF REMEDY IS OBTAINED WHERE A COMPLAINT IS SUBSTANTIATED?

Such remedies may include:

- at the very least, agreement from the body concerned that their apologies should be conveyed through the report. So often the case could have been resolved much earlier if only a full and genuine apology had been given when the complaint was first dealt with;
- action such as a review of procedures, improved communications or steps to enhance skills or competence which will put things right for the benefit of future users of the service. A check is made three months later that the recommendations have been satisfactorily implemented;
- a recommendation that any expenses or financial loss, incurred directly as a result of the failure or maladministration, be reimbursed on an *ex gratia* basis. These may relate to such things as travel costs, lost property or, in rare cases, private nursing home charges;
- in some clinical cases, the provision for the first time of clear explanations or information may be a welcome remedy.

APPEAL

Parliament has provided no right of appeal against the Ombudsman's findings. The Ombudsman cannot modify the report, nor will correspondence generally be entered into, once it has been issued. Only if entirely new evidence comes to light will a fresh investigation be considered – that very seldom happens. The only remedy available to someone dissatisfied with a report is to seek a judicial review which, if successful, would render the report null and void. The Ombudsman would then have discretion to decide whether to complete a further report. To date no such proceedings have been granted against the Health Service Ombudsman.

THE OMBUDSMAN AND PARLIAMENT

It is very rare for a NHS body to dispute the findings, but if that happens the Ombudsman may lay a special report before both Houses of Parliament. The prospect of that is usually sufficient to secure compliance. A special report may also be laid, even where the findings are accepted, if the Ombudsman believes publication to be warranted because the case raises matters of public or special interest.

The Ombudsman publishes, through Parliament, a volume containing reports on a selection of the cases completed. At present two such volumes are published each year. Three main purposes are served:

- to enable the lessons from a case to be learned right across the NHS;
- to provide valuable teaching material for clinical students, professionals and others;
- together with the Ombudsman's annual report, to account to Parliament about the work of the office.

Each year the Ombudsman is examined by the Public Administration Committee of the House of Commons on the matters raised in the annual report. The Members also decide which cases in the selected case volumes merit examination. They do not have the authority to re-investigate the case, their purpose being rather to bring sharply into focus matters which warrant more public scrutiny. Relevant staff, and usually the chairman, from the body concerned are called to appear in public sessions, as may individual practitioners. Although the identity of the public bodies concerned is not protected, care is always taken both in the Ombudsman's published reports and in the Committee's work not to disclose the name of the complainant or patient.

The Committee then examines officials from the Health Departments, and occasionally Ministers, and issues its own report. That can result in action being taken on a national basis to bring about changes as a direct result of the Ombudsman's findings.

COMPLAINING TO THE OMBUDSMAN – KEY POINTS

To summarise, there are a few practical steps which, if followed, should ease the passage of a complaint submitted to the Ombudsman:

- ask the local hospital, clinic or surgery for a copy of the free leaflet about the Ombudsman's work, including what is – and is not – within jurisdiction. The leaflet is available in several languages and in versions for those with sensory or other impairments or disabilities;
- if in any uncertainty about what to do, at the earliest possible stage, consult the Community (or Local) Health Council, Citizen's Advice Bureau or relevant charity offering advocacy support;
- be clear about intentions in pursuing a complaint, and realistic in considering what outcome might be achieved;
- do not ask for an investigation of matters which are clearly outside the Ombudsman's remit. If in doubt, write anyway and a reply will be sent explaining which, if any, can be investigated;
- make the complaint in writing, either by letter or by using the form in the leaflet. State clearly what the complaint is, who is involved and when and where the events took place;
- for complaints being made outside the one year time limit explain why that is so;
- if writing on behalf of the person directly affected the reason for that should be explained and, if relevant, that person's support expressed;
- attach all the background papers, not just a selection. These should include letters to and from the bodies concerned, other related correspondence, reports and personal notes. Where originals are sent, the Ombudsman will photocopy and return them;
- provide a contact address and, if possible, a daytime telephone number.

How to contact the Ombudsman

Health Service Ombudsman for England
Millbank Tower
Millbank
London SW1P 4QP
Telephone: 0171 217 4051

Health Service Ombudsman for Scotland
28 Thistle Street
Edinburgh EH2 1EN
Telephone: 0131 225 7465

Health Service Ombudsman for Wales
5th Floor
Pearl Assurance House
Greyfriars Road
Cardiff CF1 3AG
Telephone: 01222 394621

CONCLUSION

The Ombudsman's powers, though considerable, are a last resort for those who cannot obtain satisfactory answers or action locally. The new NHS Complaints Procedures should be capable of delivering local investigations conducted with integrity, full replies expressed sensitively and in terms which can be understood, and action to put matters right. Where that fails to occur, an approach can be made direct to the Ombudsman whose investigations are thorough and wholly independent. The NHS Complaints Procedures and the Ombudsman's office are there to be used. They are an important means by which an aggrieved individual can secure improvements to benefit countless others.

Chapter 10

COMPLAINING TO A PRACTITIONER'S PROFESSIONAL BODY

Liz Thomas and Keith Miles

As with any profession, there will be individual practitioners within the healthcare professions who fall short of their profession's standards of competence and/or conduct. Patients play an essential role in reporting such cases. This chapter explains how the main health professions are regulated, the types of disciplinary procedures that are in existence and what patients can do if they believe a practitioner is guilty of misconduct.

INTRODUCTION

The gravest sanction against a healthcare professional who falls short of the standards set by his or her professional body is to be 'struck off' or 'erased' from the professional register. It is important to distinguish this from other types of action that may be taken against a practitioner. For example, a hospital may take disciplinary action against a doctor who is alleged to be seriously incompetent and as a result dismiss him or her but this will not in itself prevent the doctor seeking employment at another hospital. It is only the professional regulatory body which has the power to prevent an individual professional practising professionally.

A significant proportion of complaints received by the professional regulatory bodies will come from members of the public. In most cases, a complaint to a professional body will follow a complaint made through other channels such as the NHS Complaints Procedure. It is not a step that should be taken lightly but if a complainant believes that a practitioner has behaved unprofessionally, or is not competent to practise, then this should be brought to the attention of the relevant professional body.

PROFESSIONAL BODIES

The main health professions are each self regulated by a professional body. These professional or 'regulatory' bodies are as follows:

• General Medical Council (GMC)	Doctors
• United Kingdom Central Council for Nursing, Midwifery and Health Visiting (UKCC)	Nurses, midwives and health visitors
• General Dental Council (GDC)	Dentists
• General Optical Council (GOC)	Opticians
• Council for the Professions Supplementary to Medicine (CPSM)	Chiropodists, dietitians, medical laboratory scientists, occupational therapists, orthoptists, physiotherapists and radiographers
• Royal Pharmaceutical Society of Great Britain (RPSGB)	Pharmacists
• General Osteopathic Council	Osteopaths
• General Chiropractic Council	Chiropractors

The function of professional bodies

These have all been established by statute. Their main responsibility is the protection of the public. This is achieved by:

- setting up a register of qualified practitioners;
- fixing the standard of education and experience required for entry onto the register;

- establishing standards of professional conduct and ethics required of the registered practitioners;
- taking action against any practitioner who breaches these standards.

OTHER TYPES OF 'PROFESSIONAL BODIES'

These 'governing' or 'regulatory' bodies need to be distinguished from other types of 'professional bodies' such as the various Royal Colleges (which exist to promote high standards of professional practice and research within their specialities e.g. the Royal College of Surgeons, the Royal College of Obstetricians and Gynaecologists, Royal College of Nursing, etc.); the British Medical Association (BMA) (whose prime and legitimate purpose is to represent the interests of its members); and the Royal College of Nursing and Health Visitors Association (which performs a professional as well as a representative role). These organisations play no part in the admission, maintenance and removal from the professional register.

COMPLAINING TO A PRACTITIONER'S PROFESSIONAL BODY

All the statutory professional bodies have a responsibility to consider both complaints about the conduct of their registered practitioners and criminal convictions recorded against them. The GMC, UKCC and the GDC also have the power to investigate cases where there is evidence to suggest that the practitioner's 'fitness to practise' is seriously impaired by illness. In July 1997, the GMC introduced a new performance procedure enabling it to investigate allegations of 'seriously deficient performance'.

Standard of proof

The standard of proof required for removal of a practitioner from the Professional Register is the same as that which applies in the criminal courts, i.e. beyond reasonable doubt. In addition indirect or 'hearsay' evidence is not allowed at any hearings.

Who can complain?

Any person or organisation including a patient or a relative, a professional colleague, an employer (e.g. a Trust or Health Authority), the police (e.g. in the case of a criminal conviction), or other public authority with knowledge of the practitioner. The complaint must be within the jurisdiction of the statutory regulatory body complained to.

Types of complaints investigated

As a general rule, professional bodies will only investigate complaints which are sufficiently serious to bring into question the practitioner's registration.

The various Acts of Parliament establishing the regulatory bodies differ in the terms used to describe the breach of conduct which can result in a practitioner's removal from the register. For example, the GMC and GDC use the term 'serious professional misconduct', the UKCC uses the phrase 'misconduct' and the CPSM adds to the range with 'infamous conduct in a professional respect'.

Each organisation publishes guidelines which details what is expected of a registered practitioner and therefore the sort of conduct which could lead to removal from the register. (Copies are available from the relevant Council.)

Time limits for complaints

There are no set time limits for a complaint to a professional body. However, a complaint should be made as soon as possible to safeguard other patients and to preserve the evidence. The older the complaint the more reluctance there will be to investigate it.

Complainants can take the matter up at a local level (e.g. the NHS Complaints Procedure) first or in tandem with action in the professional arena. However, if the practitioner is likely to put other patients at immediate risk, there should be no delay in reporting concerns to the professional body.

Complaints and legal action

Unlike other complaints procedures (e.g. Ombudsman, NHS Complaints Procedure), the fact that a complainant contemplates or is already involved in litigation will not prevent a complaint to a professional body being investigated. In fact, the legal investigation often provides valuable information to help present the case to the professional body (and a solicitor experienced in conducting disciplinary cases and negligence actions may be willing to conduct both 'cases' in tandem).

GENERAL MEDICAL COUNCIL – DOCTORS

The General Medical Council (GMC) is the doctors' governing body. A person cannot practise as a doctor within the United Kingdom unless he or she is registered with the GMC (details of the system of registration can be found in Appendix 4).

Complaints about doctors

There are three separate procedures for investigating complaints about doctors:

- conduct – dealing with allegations of 'serious professional misconduct';
- performance – where the doctor's professional performance is alleged to be 'seriously deficient';
- health – where it is alleged that the doctor's ability to practise is impaired as a result of ill health.

There are some significant differences in the way in which the three procedures are investigated by the GMC, which has sole discretion as to which procedure is followed. Complainants have the greatest input in cases that are investigated under the conduct procedures resulting in a public hearing before the Professional Conduct Committee (PCC). In effect the complainant, with legal assistance, may be in a position of presenting the case against the practitioner. The new performance procedures are likely to be in private and may not result in a hearing if the doctor voluntarily complies with the procedure. Health procedures are conducted in private with little if any involvement of the original complainant.

DUTIES OF A DOCTOR

Standard and guidance

The GMC gives guidance to practitioners in a series of booklets entitled 'Duties of a Doctor'. The underlying principle is that:

> *'Patients must be able to trust doctors with their lives and well being. To justify that trust, we as a profession have a duty to*

maintain a good standard of practice and care and to show respect for human life.'[1]

and in particular doctors are charged to:

- make the care of the patient the first concern;
- treat every patient politely and considerately;
- respect patients' dignity and privacy;
- listen to patients and respect their views;
- give patients information in a way that they can understand;
- respect the rights of patients to be fully involved in decisions about their care;
- keep professional knowledge and skills up-to-date;
- recognise the limits of professional competence;
- be honest and trustworthy;
- respect and protect confidential information;
- make sure that personal beliefs do not prejudice patients' care;
- act quickly to protect patients from risk where there is good reason to believe that you or a colleague may not be fit to practise;
- avoid abusing the position as a doctor.

A breach in any of the standards of competence, care and conduct, could potentially lead to action by the GMC.

INVESTIGATION OF COMPLAINTS ABOUT DOCTORS

Screening of complaints

When a complaint is received by the GMC, it will pass through a number of different screening stages to establish whether the complaint warrants investigation and, if so, through which procedure. During the course of an investigation, a complaint may be transferred from one procedure to another as deemed appropriate. For example, a case may be transferred from conduct to health or conduct to performance but not from performance

[1] 'The Duties of a Doctor', General Medical Council, 1995.

to conduct. This latter restriction is intended to encourage doctors to voluntarily comply with performance procedures.

Pre-screening

Complaints will initially be assessed by office staff ('pre-screening'). Even at this early stage, complaints may be rejected (e.g. where the complaint is considered to fall outside the jurisdiction of the GMC, or where it is considered that the complaint is completely unfounded).

The complainant may be advised to pursue other procedures (e.g. the NHS Complaints Procedure). It is however open to the GMC to carry out its own investigation whilst other procedures are still underway. Complainants should not be deterred from submitting complaints where there are concerns about the safety of other patients.

A decision may also be taken at this early stage to refer the case for consideration under the health procedures.

The remaining cases will be referred to one of a team of medical screeners (preliminary screener) who will be appointed from medical members of the GMC.

Medical screener

The role of the medical screener is to assess the complaint and to decide which, if any, procedure it should be referred to i.e. conduct, performance, or health.

Affidavit or statutory declaration

If the screener considers a complaint relates either to serious professional misconduct or seriously deficient performance and is likely to require further action under either the conduct or performance procedures, the complainant (e.g. a member of the public or a doctor), will be required to support his or her allegations in the form of an Affidavit or Statutory Declaration (i.e. a sworn statement). This is not necessary in cases where the complainant is a public body e.g. Trust or Family Health Services Authority.

The doctor will be informed of the allegations although there is no obligation to submit a written explanation at this stage of the proceedings. The complainant will not normally receive a copy of the doctor's response.

Expert advice

The screener may seek specialist expert advice either from medical members of the GMC or for example, the Royal Colleges.

GMC lawyers

If the medical screener believes that allegations made against a practitioner may have some foundation but there is insufficient evidence on which to arrive at a decision, further inquiries may be made with the assistance of the Council's solicitor including, for example, obtaining witness statements.

Medical screener's decision

Having obtained additional evidence as appropriate (e.g. sworn statements or expert advice), the medical screener will then decide which of the following actions should be taken:

- no further action;
- refer the cases involving allegations of 'serious professional misconduct' or criminal convictions to the Preliminary Proceedings Committee (PPC);
- refer cases where there is a question of 'seriously deficient performance' for assessment under the performance procedures;
- refer the matter to the Health Committee where a complaint of misconduct or poor performance has arisen due to the doctor's ill health;
- put further GMC inquiries on hold until local disciplinary or complaints procedures have been concluded;
- send a 'letter of advice' to the doctor.

No further action

If the medical screener decides that the complaint warrants no further action, it will be referred to a non-medical screener (a lay member of the GMC) and only concluded with the lay screener's agreement.

Letter of advice

In some cases, the medical screener may decide that no further formal action is warranted but will send the doctor a 'letter of advice' (see below). This might be, for example, where the doctor has been convicted of a minor criminal offence which does not warrant formal conduct proceedings.

CONDUCT PROCEDURE

Serious professional misconduct

The conduct procedure is followed for complaints where the medical screener considers there are specific allegations which, if proven, would amount to 'serious professional misconduct', or where a doctor has been convicted of a criminal offence.

'Serious professional misconduct' is any conduct on the part of a doctor which the GMC considers sufficiently grave to warrant the sanction of striking the doctor off the professional register.

The sorts of complaints which have led to doctors being 'struck off' have included such things as gross lapses in clinical care particularly where patients have been put at risk, falsifying records, indecency, improper relations with patients or colleagues, dishonesty, fraud, falsely claiming to have certain qualifications or experience, and treatment without consent.

REFERRAL TO THE PRELIMINARY PROCEEDINGS COMMITTEE (PPC)

As indicated above, the medical screener may refer cases raising allegations of 'serious professional misconduct' to the PPC.

Criminal convictions

The PPC considers criminal convictions which are normally reported to the Council by the police. All convictions except trivial matters (e.g. speeding) are usually considered by the PPC.

The PPC will be provided with details of the conviction or copies of the complainant's statement, witness statements and other evidence as appropriate for consideration. The doctor will also have been provided with identical material and invited to make a response to the allegations. If a response is made, that too is placed before the PPC. The PPC may adjourn their proceedings if further information is considered necessary to arrive at a decision.

Powers of the PPC

The PPC includes both lay members and doctors. The proceedings are held in private and on the basis of written evidence and submissions. Where necessary the advice of the GMC lawyers is taken.

Its options are:

- no further action;
- refer to the doctor to be assessed by the Health Committee (where the problem is felt to be due to the doctor's health);
- refer the matter for investigation under the performance procedures (where there is evidence of poor performance but not serious misconduct);

- send a warning letter to the doctor and/or 'a letter of advice' (see below). A warning letter can only be used where the doctor has admitted being at fault in some way;
- refer the matter to the Professional Conduct Committee (PCC) for a disciplinary hearing on the charge of serious professional misconduct;
- make an order for the interim suspension of the doctor's registration or for interim conditional registration pending a PCC Hearing where it is deemed necessary for the protection of members of the public.

WARNING LETTERS AND LETTERS OF ADVICE

Many cases which reach the Preliminary Proceedings Committee stage are concluded with a 'warning letter' or a 'letter of advice'. (This is sometimes referred to as 'action under Chapter 15'.) A warning letter can only be used where the doctor has admitted being at fault in some way and a letter of advice is used where no admission is forthcoming. Such letters may also be sent at the screening stage where further action is not considered appropriate. The GMC is in the process of putting in place improved systems for recording complaints, including cases where no formal action is taken, so that these can be referred to in the event that further complaints are received about a practitioner.

PROFESSIONAL CONDUCT COMMITTEE (PCC)

When a decision is made to refer a case to the PCC, further evidence may need to be obtained (e.g. further witness statements, expert advice, etc.)

Who presents the case against the doctor?

The case against the doctor is brought by the complainant or by the GMC lawyers acting on behalf of the complainant. If the complainant does not wish to use the GMC's lawyers to present the case, he or she can instruct his or her own solicitors. The GMC will pay any reasonable legal fees incurred but the complainant and/or solicitor should confirm this at the outset. If the complainant is a public body, the GMC lawyers would normally present the case.

PCC hearing

Disciplinary hearings are held in public before the PCC. The lawyers acting on behalf of the complainant present the case against the doctor. Practitioners are almost always represented by lawyers appointed by their defence association. The complainant may be required to give evidence and be cross-examined by the lawyer defending the doctor.

Cases involving a criminal conviction are presented by the GMC lawyers. The hearing is to determine the gravity of the offence in the light of any mitigating circumstances and to decide what sanction, if any, should be made.

Powers of the PCC

If the doctor is found guilty of 'serious professional misconduct' or it has been established that the doctor has been convicted of a criminal offence, the PCC must decide on what action to take against the doctor including:

- concluding the case with no further action;
- placing conditions on the doctor's registration for a period not exceeding three years (e.g. not to practise single handedly as a GP);
- suspending the doctor's registration for a period not exceeding 12 months i.e. preventing a doctor from practising for a specified period;
- removing ('erasing') the doctor's name from the register, i.e. preventing a doctor practising until his name is restored to the register.

The Committee may reconsider the case before the end of the period of suspension and can extend or end the period of suspension.

To put this in context, in 1995, out of 1558 complaints received to the GMC, 50% were rejected at the screening stage. Only 93 cases were considered by the PCC (13 arising from criminal convictions), leading to 25 erasures from the Register. In 1996

66 cases went before the PCC. In 19 cases the doctor was erased from the Register. One case involved a GP who ran a nursing home where a patient died through lack of care. In nine cases the Doctor was suspended. Eleven had conditions imposed on their registration and eight were admonished.

Appeal Procedures

The doctor has 28 days to give notice of appeal to the Judicial Committee of the Privy Council against any finding or of sanction imposed by the PCC.

Restoration to the Register

The doctor can apply for restoration to the Register ten months after erasure, or if that application fails, after a further ten month interval. At that stage the PCC will consider:

- the nature and gravity of the original offence;
- the length of time since erasure; and
- the conduct of the applicant in the interval.

PERFORMANCE PROCEDURES (SERIOUSLY DEFICIENT PERFORMANCE)

Effective from 1 July 1997

In November 1995 the Medical (Professional Performance) Act 1995 received the Royal Assent. This new legislation introduced the GMC's Performance Procedures which became operative on 1 July 1997.

The legislation is not retrospective and applies to acts or omissions after 1st July 1997.

Under the performance procedures, the GMC will be able to take a broader look at a practitioner's standard of practice, perhaps arising from a number of different complaints or incidents, and where appropriate, take action to ensure that the doctor is not putting patients at risk.

The GMC's stated aim is to try and encourage poorly performing doctors to improve their practice through counselling and retraining rather than imposing sanctions as under the conduct procedures. Where a doctor agrees to comply with the performance procedures, there may be no formal hearings and the complainant may only have limited involvement in the process.

However, if a doctor fails to co-operate with the performance procedures or where he or she is judged as putting patients at 'serious' risk, the GMC does have powers to take formal action against the doctor.

Seriously deficient performance

The GMC in their guidance to the Act state:

> *'Seriously deficient performance is a departure from good professional practice – whether or not it is covered by specific GMC guidance – sufficiently serious to call into question the doctor's registration.'*[2]

This is further interpreted:

> *'A doctor's registration may be called into question by repeated or persistent failure to comply with the professional standards appropriate to the work being done by the doctor, particularly where this places patients, or members of the public, in jeopardy. This may include repeated or persistent failure to comply with the GMC's guidance in* Good Medical Practice.'[2]

The standard is not concerned with competence, which is what the doctor is capable of doing. Performance is about what a doctor does in practice.

If the medical screener decides, having received a complaint in the ordinary way and in conjunction with the lay screener, that there is sufficient evidence to justify initiating performance proceedings, the doctor will be invited to undergo 'a performance assessment' (a kind of audit). The complainant will be informed about this and any action to be taken although the assessment itself will be in private.

ASSESSMENT REFERRAL COMMITTEE (ARC)

If the doctor declines to undergo assessment voluntarily he or she will be referred to the Assessment Referral Committee.

Powers of the ARC

The ARC has the power to direct a doctor to undergo assessment within a fixed period of time if it believes the doctor's refusal is

[2]GMC, Performance Procedures, Position paper No. 2, 24th June 1996.

unjustified. If the doctor still refuses to undergo a performance assessment, he or she will then be referred to the Committee on Professional Performance.

Assessors

Where the doctor agrees to be assessed, either when initially invited by the screener or when directed by the ARC, the assessment will be conducted by a panel which will include:

- a lead assessor drawn from the same general medical speciality as the doctor being assessed;
- at least one other medically-qualified assessor from the same sub-speciality as the doctor being assessed and of equivalent status;
- a lay person.

The medical assessors on the panel will be drawn from a list of appointed specialists.

Case co-ordinator

At this stage a 'case co-ordinator' will take over the management of each case from the preliminary (medical) screener. The case co-ordinator will be medically qualified.

Assessment

The assessment may involve visiting the doctor's place of practice, examining clinical records, conducting interviews with the doctor and any third party with direct knowledge of the doctor's performance and possibly some form of formal assessment of the doctor's knowledge, skills and attitude. It is possible that complainants may be interviewed at some stage in the process.

The case co-ordinator will then decide what action, if any, should be taken. If the performance assessment revealed no significant problems, the case will be concluded at this point. Unless very serious problems have been identified, it will be up to the case co-ordinator to decide what steps need to be taken by the doctor to remedy the problem and to draw up certain requirements which the doctor will be invited to comply with. This could include such things as remedial counselling. After an initial period of remedial action, a reassessment will be undertaken and if the remedial action is deemed successful, the case will be concluded.

Assessors' Report

Following the assessment, the assessor will submit a report. This will contain a profile of the doctor's performance as well as offering advice regarding any measures which might be appropriate to remedy deficiencies in the doctor's performance and to protect the public. The complainant is not entitled to see this report.

If a doctor refuses to co-operate with the assessment team, the doctor will be referred to the CPP.

Voluntary Retirement/Removal from the Register

It will be open to a doctor invited to undergo assessment to decide, at any stage of the procedures, to retire from practice by voluntarily removing his or her name from the Register, as an alternative to continuing along the procedures. If a doctor were to adopt this course, and were subsequently to apply for restoration to the Register, he or she would then have to complete a satisfactory performance assessment.

REFERRAL TO THE COMMITTEE ON PROFESSIONAL PERFORMANCE (CPP)

The Committee on Professional Performance will be selected from the 26 Council members, including five lay members. The Committee will be assisted by one or more specialist advisers. The role of the CPP is to determine whether the doctor's professional performance has been 'seriously deficient'.

The performance screener and case co-ordinator will be able to refer cases to the CPP in the following circumstances:

- where the doctor fails to undergo assessment, having agreed to do so at the direction of the screener, or having been directed to do so by the ARC; or
- where the case co-ordinator does not accept the opinions expressed by the assessment panel in their report; or
- where, on assessment, the doctor's performance is judged to be so poor as to present a serious risk to patients; or

- where, having undergone assessment, the doctor refuses
- to agree to the requirements for further action devised by the case co-ordinator; or
- where, having agreed to those requirements, the doctor fails to comply with them; or
- where the doctor's performance fails to improve significantly after he or she has taken the recommended action; or
- where the doctor in any other way fails to cooperate with the procedures.

The doctor and any complainant in the case will have the right to be present at the Committee Hearing, to be legally represented and to address the Committee.

Powers of the Committee on Professional Performance

The CPP has statutory powers to impose sanctions on a doctor's registration including:

- suspending a doctor's registration (for an initial period of up to 12 months);
- imposing conditions on the doctor's registration (for an initial period up to three years).

Where sanctions have been imposed, the Committee will reconsider the case after an interval and may impose further sanctions. If the doctor has been suspended for two years or more, the Committee may impose an indefinite suspension. The CPP has no powers to erase from the Register.

HEALTH COMMITTEE

Fitness to Practise

Health procedures were first introduced in 1980 for 'rehabilitating sick doctors, that is, doctors whose fitness to practise is seriously impaired by a physical or mental condition'.[3]

The aim is to provide care, education and continuing monitoring to enable doctors to return to unrestricted practice.

[3]Medical Act 1983, Health Committee (Procedure) Rules 1987.

The majority of cases referred to the health procedures relate to drug or alcohol addiction or to mental illness.

> The health procedures involve four main stages:
>
> - preliminary consideration of evidence;
> - medical examination of the sick doctor;
> - medical supervision and rehabilitation of the sick doctor;
> - the Health Committee.

Information about a sick doctor may come from colleagues, employers, police, pharmacists, patients and others. The screener will invite the doctor to be examined by at least two medical examiners, usually including a psychiatrist. It is also open to the doctor to choose an additional medical examiner. The medical examiners will report on whether the doctor is fit to practise without restriction or, if not, what supervision is required and what if any limitations on his or her practice are recommended. This could include inviting the doctor to refrain from practice for a period.

If the doctor accepts the medical examiners' reports and agrees to comply with their recommendations, the medical supervisor will arrange any necessary treatment or supervision. The aim is that the doctor will be able to return to unrestricted practice without further supervision or action on the part of the GMC.

Health Committee

Cases are only referred to the Health Committee when:

- a doctor fails to co-operate with the health procedures;
- a doctor fails to comply with the recommendations of the medical examiners;
- it becomes apparent during the course of disciplinary proceedings that the complaint has arisen as a result of the doctor's ill health.

The Health Committee meets in private. The doctor may be legally represented and witnesses may be called. Complainants will not be entitled to attend (or know of the outcome).

If the Committee finds the doctor's 'fitness to practise to be seriously impaired', it has the power to:

- impose conditions on the doctor's registration for up to three years;
- suspend registration for 12 months in the first instance and in certain cases indefinitely.

The Health Committee cannot erase a doctor from the Register. The doctor can only appeal the decision of the Committee on a question of law. The Committee must reconsider the case before any period of conditional or suspended registration expires.

During 1996 50 doctors were referred under the Health Procedures. Fourteen doctors were discharged as fit to practise without further supervision. At the end of the year 167 doctors were being supervised under these procedures.

UNITED KINGDOM CENTRAL COUNCIL FOR NURSING, MIDWIFERY AND HEALTH VISITING (UKCC)

All nurses, midwives and health visitors working within the United Kingdom, must be registered with the UKCC. As part of its statutory duties, the UKCC is required to investigate complaints about the conduct of any person appearing on its list of registered practitioners.[4]

The UKCC has two separate procedures for investigating complaints about its registered practitioners:

- conduct procedures: complaints alleging misconduct which if proved would result in removal from the register;
- health procedures: complaints alleging the practitioner's fitness to practise is seriously impaired due to illness.

CONDUCT PROCEDURES

Complaints about the conduct of a nurse, midwife or health visitor are judged on the basis of 'misconduct' which is defined as 'conduct unworthy of a nurse, midwife or health visitor'. The

[4]Statutory Instrument 1993 No. 893. The Nurses, Midwifes and Health Visitors (Professional Conduct) Rules 1993 Approval Order.

UKCC, unlike the GMC, does not qualify misconduct with the word 'serious'.

Code of Professional Conduct

The UKCC has set out what is expected of its registered practitioners in its document, 'Code of Professional Conduct for the Nurse, Midwife and Health Visitor'. The Council makes it clear that:

> *'Each registered nurse, midwife and health visitor shall act, at all times, in such a manner as to safeguard and promote the interests of individual patients and clients.'*

and that he or she must:

> *'. . . ensure that no action or omission on your part, or within your sphere of responsibility, is detrimental to the interests, condition or safety of patients and clients.'*

Reasons for removal from the Register

Some frequently occurring reasons for removal from the Register:

UKCC: Examples of Misconduct

- reckless and wilfully unskilful practice;
- concealing untoward incidents;
- failure to keep essential records;
- falsifying records;
- failure to protect or promote the interest of patients/clients;
- failure to act knowing that a colleague or subordinate is improperly treating or abusing patients;
- physical or verbal abuse of patients/clients;
- abuse of patients by improperly withholding prescribed drugs, or administering unprescribed drugs or an excess of prescribed drugs;
- theft from patients or employers;
- drug related offences;
- sexual abuse of patients;
- breach of confidentiality.

There is no equivalent to the GMC Performance Procedures. However, the Council's stated expectation (see 'Code of Professional Conduct') is that, in fulfilment of his or her personal professional accountability, the practitioner

> '. . . must maintain and improve your professional knowledge and competence',

and there must be merit in considering whether to allege that the serious deficiency in performance is tantamount to misconduct.

When should a complaint be made?

The UKCC has published a booklet entitled, 'Complaints about Professional Conduct' to provide an explanation of its conduct procedures. In answer to the question, 'When should a complaint be made?', it states:

> 'Where a complaint arises from an incident associated with the practitioner's professional practice, which is not and has not been the subject of criminal proceedings, *it should be reported as soon as possible*. This helps to ensure that the incident will be fresh in the memories of potential witnesses and also that those witnesses will still be readily available. If a matter is serious enough to warrant an allegation of misconduct, it should be reported immediately rather than eventually. The formal report of a complaint alleging misconduct should not be delayed pending the completion of employment appeal procedures.'

Investigation of allegations of misconduct

Investigating Officer

Complaints about a practitioner's misconduct must be made in writing with sufficient information to enable identification of the practitioner concerned. The letter of complaint, or a summary of the allegations, may be sent to the practitioner for comment. Complaints will initially be dealt with by an 'investigating officer' who will make preliminary inquiries about the complaint, and prepare a report for the Preliminary Proceedings Committee. The practitioner will receive copies of any witness statements obtained by the UKCC.

Preliminary Proceedings Committee

The Preliminary Proceedings Committee (PPC), meeting in private, will consider all the evidence and will decide what action if any should be taken.

Powers of the UKCC Preliminary Proceedings Committee

- Order no further action;
- refer to a Professional Conduct Committee;
- refer to the Panel of Professional Screeners for investigation under the health procedures;
- order a formal caution as to future conduct; which remains on the practitioner's record for five years;
- impose interim suspension of the practitioner's registration pending further investigation where it is deemed necessary in order to protect the public or in the practitioner's own interest.

The PPC will also consider criminal convictions against a practitioner.

Professional Conduct Committee

The Professional Conduct Committee (PCC) will consider cases of alleged misconduct which have been referred to it by the PPC. It also considers applications for restoration to the Register from individuals who have previously been removed from the Register.

The PCC hearings are held in public. The Committee will concentrate on the matters raised in the formal charges against the practitioner and will not attempt to raise new matters of unsatisfactory behaviour during the hearing. The Committee will however consider any charges in the context of the practitioner's previous work record and any mitigating circumstances at the time of the incident under investigation. As discussed previously, the standard of evidence and standard of proof is 'beyond reasonable doubt'.

Powers of the UKCC Professional Conduct Committee

- Find the practitioner not guilty of the matters alleged or, where the facts are proved, not guilty of misconduct and close the case;
- find the practitioner guilty of misconduct but take no further action;
- issue a caution which will remain on the practitioner's record for five years;
- postpone judgment for a set period;
- remove the practitioner's name from the Register without a time limit or for a specified period;

- refer the case to the Panel of Professional Screeners for investigation under the health procedures;
- impose interim suspension where necessary for the public protection if the hearing is adjourned for any reason.

HEALTH PROCEDURES

Anyone who is concerned that a nurse's or midwife's fitness to practise safely appears to be seriously impaired as a result of illness, which is not of a short-term nature, is advised to report these concerns to the UKCC. The UKCC can then carry out an assessment to establish whether any action needs to be taken in relation to the practitioner's registration status.

The UKCC will draw up a statutory declaration based on the evidence brought before it which the person reporting the practitioner will be required to sign. The case will then go before a Panel of Screeners.

Other cases may be referred to the Panel of Screeners by the Preliminary Proceedings Committee and Professional Conduct Committee.

Panel of screeners

The screeners will decide whether the matter should be pursued or closed. If further action is required, the screeners will arrange for the practitioner to be examined by two medical examiners. On receipt of the examiner's reports, the screeners will decide whether the case should be:

- referred to the Health Committee;
- referred back to the Preliminary Proceedings Committee or Professional Conduct Committee (if referred by either);
- closed.

Health Committee procedures

Health Committee procedures are conducted in private.

Powers of the UKCC Health Committee

- Close the case without further action;
- refer the case back to the Preliminary Proceedings Committee or Professional Conduct Committee (if referred by either);
- suspend the practitioner's registration;
- remove the practitioner's name from the Register;
- impose interim suspension if the hearing is adjourned and this action is deemed necessary to protect the public.

GENERAL DENTAL COUNCIL (GDC)

All practising dentists, whether in NHS or private practice, must be registered with the General Dental Council. The General Dental Council is obliged by statute to investigate complaints about:

- professional conduct; and
- fitness to practise;

which are sufficiently serious to bring into question the practitioner's registration. The GDC does not operate performance procedures.

Standards and guidance

Like the GMC, complaints about the conduct of a dentist are judged on the basis of 'serious professional misconduct' but in its document, 'Maintaining standards – Guidance to Dentists on Professional and Personal Conduct' this is not defined.

The GDC's approach is to give guidance as to how a dentist is expected to behave, both professionally and personally and to indicate what matters may lead to a charge of serious professional misconduct.

Conduct procedures

The GDC conduct procedures operate in a similar way to those of the General Medical Council, with the same range of committees, although the preliminary screening procedure is done by the President of the Council.

Preliminary Proceedings Committee

The President may refer reports of convictions, complaints and/or information relating to conduct to the Preliminary Proceedings Committee (PPC) which normally meets twice a year in private.

Complaints from members of the public must be supported by a statutory declaration/affidavit which the dentist will be invited to comment upon/submit an explanation.

Powers of the GDC Preliminary Proceedings Committee

- To take no further action because a prima facie case has not been made against the dentist;
- to take no further action but to warn the dentist that it may reconsider this decision if further information comes to its notice;
- to refer the matter to the Professional Conduct Committee for a public inquiry;
- to suspend the practitioner's registration in the interests of public safety but only after the dentist has been allowed to make representations.

Professional Conduct Committee

The Professional Conduct Committee normally meets twice a year. If it finds a dentist has been convicted or has been guilty of serious professional misconduct, there are a number of options open to the Committee:

- the Committee may conclude the case with an admonition;
- judgment may be postponed until a future meeting when the Committee will consider the dentist's conduct during the intervening period. Postponement is generally for one year;
- the Committee may direct that the dentist's registration be suspended for a specified period not exceeding 12 months;
- the Committee may direct that the dentist's name be erased from the Dentists Register.

Appeals

There are similar appeals procedures to that of the GMC.

Fitness to Practise

The Committee also has the option of directing that the matter be referred to a Health Committee. The Dentists Act 1984 gives the General Dental Council powers to act in cases where the fitness to practise of a dentist is seriously impaired by reason of a physical or mental condition. The details of the health procedures are set out in the General Dental Council Health Committee (Procedure) Rules 1984. The procedures are similar to those of the GMC except that cases are initially considered by the President of the Council.

Complaints about private dental treatment

Most complaints about dentists will not come within the jurisdiction of the GDC because they fall outside the GDC's specific statutory powers to investigate (i.e. serious misconduct and fitness to practise). In addition, an increasing proportion of dental treatment is now provided on a private basis and therefore falls outside the scope of the NHS Complaints Procedure. This means that a complainant may not have recourse to any of the statutory complaints procedure. The GDC is working towards setting up a complaints procedure for private dental treatment but this is in the early stages and requires a change in the legislation. However, the GDC in its ethical guidance to dentists recommends that dentists carrying out private work should have a practice based procedure in line with the NHS Local Resolution procedure.[5] Where a dentist refuses to respond to a complaint about private treatment, then the complainant should bring this to the attention of the GDC.

GENERAL OPTICAL COUNCIL (GOC)

The General Optical Council regulates optometrists (often called ophthalmic opticians) and dispensing opticians.

Standards and guidance

The GOC accepts the guidance on professional ethics and conduct provided by the respective professional membership organisations: the College of Optometrists and the Association of British Dispensing Opticians.

Serious professional misconduct

The GOC will consider complaints of 'serious professional misconduct' in a two stage committee process. However, unlike the GMC and GDC, it does not have the power or the machinery to consider any allegations that fitness to practise is seriously impaired by illness, or that of interim suspension at the preliminary committee stage.

Complaints about the service or product supplied by the optician

The GOC can only investigate complaints about misconduct. It *cannot* deal with other types of complaint, e.g. complaints about the standard or cost of the service, spectacles or lenses. There are other avenues of complaint available to deal with these:

[5]Professional Conduct and Fitness to Practise, General Dental Council 1993

- the Optical Consumer Complaints Service (OCCS): an independent service which will help to resolve complaints between patients and their opticians. The address of the OCCS can be found at the end of this chapter;
- NHS Complaints Procedure: for services provided under the NHS;
- local Trading Standards office: complaints about the product or standard of service received.

COUNCIL FOR THE PROFESSIONS SUPPLEMENTARY TO MEDICINE (CPSM)

The CPSM is responsible for regulating chiropodists, dietitians, medical laboratory scientists, occupational therapists, orthoptists, physiotherapists, radiographers, prosthetists, and arts therapists. These professional titles are not protected in the same way as other professional groups (e.g. doctors, nurses etc.), because practitioners are *not* required to be registered with the CPSM except where they work in the NHS or for local Authorities. Those that are registered can use the term 'state registered' to identify that they are fully qualified. New legislation is planned within the next two years so that only registered, and therefore qualified, practitioners can use these professional titles.

The CPSM will consider matters that are 'infamous conduct in a professional respect', and like the GOC operates a two stage committee process. Again it has neither the power or the machinery to consider any allegations that fitness to practise is seriously impaired by illness, or to impose interim suspension.

Standard and guidance

Each of the professional groups has its own statutory regulatory board, the CPSM acting in a co-ordinating role (under the proposed legislation, a single statutory body is likely to be created). The individual boards have prepared a 'Statement of Conduct'[6] to provide guidance about the kind of conduct that it considers to be 'infamous conduct in a professional respect'. Copies of these documents can be obtained from the bodies concerned.

[6]'Statements of Conduct': Board of the Council for the Professions Supplementary to Medicine, various dates 1993–1995

ROYAL PHARMACEUTICAL SOCIETY OF GREAT BRITAIN (RPSGB)

The Royal Pharmaceutical Society of Great Britain is the regulatory body for pharmacists. Unlike other statutory bodies, the RPSGB does not place a restriction on the types of complaints it will investigate. This enables it to deal with complaints which fall outside the conduct procedures.

Standard and guidance

The guidance setting out the standard expected of a registered practitioner can be found in the RPSGB's 'Medicine Ethics and Practice', a Guide for Pharmacists, published by the Pharmaceutical Society twice a year.

The RPSGB states in the preface to the 'Code of Ethics' that it '. . . is intended to set the standard of professional conduct for all pharmacists.' The first principle which the Code then declares is that, 'a pharmacist's prime concern must be for the welfare of both patient and other members of the public.'[7]

Conduct procedures

In relation to conduct procedures, the position of the RPSGB is, in summary, that a complaint can be made by any individual about a breach of professional standards on the part of a pharmacist. The matter is investigated by the Society's Professional Standards Department and, if it is considered necessary, is referred to the Disciplinary Committee for consideration.

GENERAL OSTEOPATHIC COUNCIL

The General Osteopathic Council (GOsC) has been established by the Osteopaths Act 1993 to develop, promote and regulate the profession of osteopathy. It is also responsible for professional education, standards and conduct. The statutory Register for Osteopaths is targeted to open during May 1998. Thereafter, the GOsC may regulate registered osteopaths and will consider allegations of professional misconduct, and incompetence. Fair and open investigative procedures will be put in place, and ultimately cases will be heard by the Statutory Fitness to Practise Committees of the

[7]See Medicine Ethics & Practice', Royal Pharmaceutical Society of Great Britain, 1995

Council.[8] Sanctions will include suspension or removal of an osteopath from the Register, but there is no power to fine an osteopath, or order that compensation be paid to a complainant.

Under the Act, two years after the Register is open (the transitional period), it will be an offence for persons to describe themselves as osteopaths unless they are registered with the GOsC. To attain registration, applicants will initially have to satisfy the Registrar that they have been practising osteopathy lawfully, safely and competently. Following the transitional period, entry to the Register will be through recognition of qualifications. The General Council itself consists of osteopathic and lay members.

GENERAL CHIROPRACTIC COUNCIL

The General Chiropractic Council[9] is another new statutory regulatory body which will also be opening a register to practitioners in late 1998. There will be a transitional period of two years following the introduction of the statutory register before all practising chiropractors must be registered. Details of the conduct procedures are still to be announced.

Other complementary therapies

Osteopathy and chiropractice are currently the only complementary or alternative therapies where practitioners will be required by law to be registered with a professional body in order to practise. There is no statutory regulation of other branches of complementary medicine although most do have membership organisations for their practitioners which operate varying degrees of voluntary regulation, including complaints procedures. However, because there is no legal requirement for a practitioner to become a member of one of these professional associations, a practitioner whose membership has been revoked will still be able to practise.

The British Acupuncture Council is currently working towards statutory regulation and already has in place voluntary regulatory systems similar to the existing professional bodies. The Society of Homeopaths regulates over 1500 homeopaths and

[8]See Osteopaths Act 1995
[9]See Chiropractors Act 1994

operates regulatory procedures. However, until such time as statutory regulation is introduced, there is no requirement for a practitioner to be a member of these particular organisations.

CONCLUSION

There is no doubt that sanction of being 'struck off' is a deterrent to all healthcare professionals. It is also undoubtedly true that the serious miscreants in the healthcare professions are dealt appropriately by the professional bodies. The worry is self regulation itself and whether these organisations are really capable of protecting the public, educating and maintaining and reinforcing standards. The public has a right to expect standards to be set high and to be effectively enforced.

Addresses of Professional Bodies

The General Medical Council
178 Great Portland Street
London W1N 6JE
Tel: 0171 580 7642

The United Kingdom Central Council
23 Portland Place
London W1N 4JT
Tel: 0171 637 7181

The General Dental Council
37 Wimpole Street
London W1M 8DQ
Tel: 0171 887 3800

The General Optical Council
41 Harley Street
London W1N 2DJ
Tel: 0171 580 3898

The Council for Professions Supplementary to Medicine
Park House
184 Kennington Park Road
London SE11 4BU
Tel: 0171 582 0866

The Royal Pharmaceutical Society of Great Britain
1 Lambeth High Street
London SE1 7JN
Tel: 0171 735 9141

General Osteopathic Council
Premier House
10 Greycoat Place
London SW1P 1SB
Tel: 0171 799 2442

General Chiropractic Council
Register opens late 1998. A permanent address is not currently available.

Professional associations – Complementary Medicine (non-statutory bodies)

British Acupuncture Council
Park House
206 Latimer Road
London W10 6RE
Tel: 0181 964 0222

Society of Homeopaths
2 Artizan Road
Northampton
NN1 4HU
Tel: 01604 621400

Optical Consumers Complaints Service
PO Box 4685
London SE1 8YH
Tel: 0171 261 1017

Chapter 11

MEDICAL TREATMENT AND THE CRIMINAL LAW

Robin Stewart QC

This chapter deals with the medical profession and the criminal law. It explains the differences between criminal law and the civil law and gives examples of how doctors can be prosecuted under the criminal law.

INTRODUCTION

In the treatment of, and in dealing with, their patients, doctors can intentionally or recklessly fall foul of the criminal law. The consequences are usually serious. A conviction of any of the offences listed below may well lead to a term of imprisonment. Further, the fact of the conviction will be reported to the General Medical Council, and the doctor can expect then to appear before the GMC's Professional Conduct Committee on a charge of serious professional misconduct. To put matters into perspective, GMC statistics show that there were only 12 doctors convicted of criminal offences in relation to their professional work in 1994, 13 in 1995 and 15 in 1996.

WHAT IS THE DIFFERENCE BETWEEN CRIMINAL AND CIVIL PROCEEDINGS?

There are four main differences between criminal prosecutions and civil proceedings:

The standard of proof

In civil proceedings, a claim that a doctor was negligent must be proved on the balance of probabilities. In criminal proceedings, the standard of proof is much higher – the magistrates or jury must be sure of guilt before they can convict: the legal phrase is proof beyond reasonable doubt.

Investigation and control of criminal proceedings

In a civil case, the claimant usually has solicitors. They investigate the facts and launch the proceedings. In criminal cases, the victim (or in the case of a child, the parent) makes a complaint to the police, who then take statements and investigate it. The Crown Prosecution Service decide what, if any, charges to bring, and the CPS prosecute the proceedings.

How the case is tried

Civil claims for damages for negligence against doctors are tried by a judge sitting alone. In criminal cases, trial is by magistrates on less serious charges, or by judge and jury in more serious cases. In civil cases, the evidence of the injured plaintiff is often not contentious. In criminal cases, however, the victim is likely to have to give evidence in court, and to be cross examined on it. Special procedures exist for taking the evidence of children.

The verdict

In a civil claim, the downside for the doctor (apart from professional repute) is limited to compensation which is usually paid by the Health Authority, insurers or the relevant defence society. In a criminal case, no question of damages arises. A convicted doctor is liable to a criminal penalty, usually a fine or a term of imprisonment.

OFFENCES WHICH MAY BE COMMITTED BY DOCTORS TOWARDS PATIENTS

Manslaughter

When a doctor is treating a patient, he or she owes to that patient a duty of care. If he or she is then in breach of that duty of care, and if that breach causes the death of the patient, then the doctor is liable to be convicted of manslaughter if he or she was guilty of gross negligence so as, in the view of the jury, to justify a criminal conviction.

Gross negligence may be found if any of the following states of mind are proved:

- indifference to an obvious risk of injury to health;
- actual foresight of the risk, coupled with the determination nevertheless to run it;
- an appreciation of the risk coupled with an intention to avoid it, but also coupled with a high degree of negligence in the attempted avoidance;
- inattention or failure to advert to a serious risk which goes beyond mere inadvertence in respect of an obvious and important matter which the defendant's duty demanded that he or she should address.

An illustration is provided by the case of 'A'. He was the anaesthetist during an eye operation. The anaesthetist had to sit by the patient, ensuring the safety of the patient by observing him throughout the operation and by giving careful attention to the different monitoring devices. The patient was connected to a ventilation machine to breathe for him. The machine had a gauge which recorded the inhalation and exhalation of breath. 'A' failed to notice that the air ventilation machine had become disconnected, though it was his essential, and in effect sole, duty to see that the patient was breathing satisfactorily. When the machine became disconnected, the patient stopped breathing. As a result, he suffered a cardiac arrest and hypoxia (deprivation of oxygen). In consequence, he died. 'A' was charged with and convicted of manslaughter. [*R v Prentice & Others* [1994] 98 Cr App R 262].

Not surprisingly any manslaughter case involving a doctor becomes headline news. In 1993, there were no criminal convictions for manslaughter before the GMC; whereas in 1994 there was one and in 1996 there were two – one case of grossly over prescribing drugs and the other a case of recklessness in which the circumstances are not known.

Assault

Consent to medical treatment is widely regarded as the key to the doctor/patient relationship. As a general principle, medical treatment given without consent constitutes both the tort of trespass to the person and the criminal offence of assault. Consent must be freely given, and it must relate to the procedure that the doctor performs. If, for example, a patient with an injured hand gives consent for it to be repaired under anaesthetic, but not to its amputation, the doctor may not amputate, even though on examination that appears to be necessary.

There are two main situations where consent to medical treatment is not necessary. Firstly, in certain circumstances medical treatment may be given to patients suffering from mental illness without their consent (sections 56–64 of the Mental Health Act 1983). Secondly, medical treatment may, in an emergency, lawfully be given to anyone without his or her consent.

There appear to have been no doctors convicted of assault on a patient in 1994–1996 but one doctor was erased from the Register for treatment without consent.

Indecent assault

An indecent assault always amounts to a breach of the criminal law. Of course a proper medical examination by a doctor may of necessity require the patient to strip, and involve examination of the genitalia. But, for example, the paediatrician who 'touches up' his child patient, commits a criminal offence, and is liable to prosecution and conviction. The difficulty is often one of proof, with victims being shy and embarrassed about complaining. 'Dr S', a paediatrician convicted recently, had become besotted over a period of years with various girls whom he was treating. His downfall came when letters he had written to some of the girls came to light. They revealed an improper and indecent relationship. Once it became known that some girls had complained, others came forward.

In 1994, there were four doctors convicted of indecency by the courts, and a further seven doctors found guilty by the Professional Conduct Committee. There were two suspensions from practice, and nine erasures from the Register. In 1995, there were four doctors convicted by the courts with a total of nine doctors found guilty by the Professional Conduct Committee leading to five erasures.

In 1996 there were four doctors convicted by the criminal courts with a total of nine found guilty by the PCC leading to six erasures.

Abortion

It is lawful under the Abortion Act 1967 (as amended) for a doctor to terminate a pregnancy, provided that two registered practitioners are of the opinion formed in good faith that:

- the pregnancy has not exceeded its 24th week; and that its continuance would involve risk, greater than if the pregnancy were terminated, of injury to the physical or mental health of the pregnant woman or any existing children of her family; or
- the termination is necessary to prevent grave permanent

injury to the physical or mental health of the pregnant woman; or
- the continuance of the pregnancy would involve risk to the life of the pregnant woman greater than if the pregnancy were terminated; or
- there is a substantial risk that if the child were born it would suffer from such physical or mental abnormalities as to be seriously handicapped.

Subject to that, it is an offence to supply or to use poisons or instruments to secure a miscarriage.

There were no doctors convicted in 1993; but in 1994 there was one doctor convicted before the GMC and he was erased. There were no doctors convicted of performing unlawful abortions in 1996.

Female circumcision

It is an offence to excise, infibulate, or otherwise mutilate the whole or any part of the labia majora or labia minora or clitoris of another person; or to aid, abet, counsel or procure the performance any of those acts by another person on that other person's own body [Female Circumcision Act 1985].

These acts are not unlawful:

- in a surgical operation, performed by a registered medical practitioner, which is necessary for the physical or mental health of the person on whom it is performed. However, in determining whether an operation is necessary for the mental health of a person, no account is to be taken of the effect on that person of any belief that the operation is required as a matter of custom or ritual. Thus the circumstances when any of these acts may be 'necessary' in a surgical operation, must be rare; or
- if they are performed on a person who is in any stage of labour or who has just given birth, and they are so performed for purposes connected with that labour or birth, by a registered medical practitioner or a registered midwife, or by a person undergoing a course of training to become a registered medical practitioner or a registered midwife.

In 1993, 1994, 1995 and 1996 there were no criminal convictions, but in 1993 one doctor appeared before the GMC for arranging to perform a female circumcision, and his name was erased from the Register.

Attempt to pervert the course of justice

It is not often that a doctor will put himself into the position of committing this offence.

If a course of public justice has been embarked upon in the sense that proceedings of some kind are in being or imminent, or investigations which could or might bring proceedings about are in progress, then it is an offence to do any act which tends and is intended to pervert or interfere with that course of public justice.

In a recent case, 'Dr S' prescribed a drug for a patient. The patient had an adverse reaction and died. The Coroner's officer was informed and started to make his usual enquiries into the death. Thus a 'course of public justice' was embarked upon, which could or might bring about any proceedings – viz the Coroner's inquest, or a civil claim for damages, or a police investigation and criminal case relating to the death. The doctor, realising that he might be thought to be worthy of blame, altered some of the practice's computer records as to the treatment of the patient. When this was discovered, he was prosecuted, and convicted of this offence.

There were no such convictions before the GMC in 1993, 1994, 1995 and 1996.

However in 1996 a doctor was found guilty of serious professional misconduct when he provided confidential information to a court without a patient's consent.

Fraud, dishonesty, obtaining by deception

If a doctor submits false claims for payment to the relevant NHS authority – for example in relation to prescriptions, or to night visits, or to some other treatment of a patient – he commits an offence under the Theft Act 1968.

In 1993, one doctor had a criminal conviction, and another faced a charge of financial dishonesty before the GMC. One was erased, and one was suspended. In 1994, six doctors were convicted of offences of financial dishonesty; a further three appeared before the GMC on similar charges. Of these four were admonished, the registration of two was made conditional and three were erased. In 1995, five doctors were convicted for financial dishonesty, and were found guilty of serious professional misconduct resulting in erasures from the Register.

In 1996 there were six cases of financial dishonesty or fraud, including obtaining by deception, false accounting and obtaining drugs by deception. Five were found guilty of serious professional misconduct of whom two were erased from the Register and one doctor was referred to the Health Committee.

CONCLUSION

It is not only doctors who can be prosecuted under the criminal law – the recent case of Beverley Aylett illustrates this. However, the high regard which society has of the medical profession means that a criminal conviction will almost always result in removal from the professional register even if it is not strictly connected with the practice of medicine. Drink driving is a good example – the GMC is currently inviting all doctors convicted of drink driving to be medically examined. This is intended to establish at an early stage doctors who may have alcohol problems.

Chapter 12

COMPLAINING ABOUT PRIVATE HEALTH CARE

Richard Ennals

This chapter is dedicated to the memory of my father, Owen Ennals. It sets out the avenues of complaint available to those dissatisfied with their treatment in the private healthcare section.

There are currently 6.4 million people with private medical insurance, the private acute healthcare sector having experienced a major expansion in the 1980s. The deficiencies in the regulation of the private sector are becoming more apparent and in particular, the continuing absence of any statutory complaints procedures for patients. Private hospitals are not covered by the NHS Complaints Procedure nor do private patients have any recourse to an independent investigation by the Health Service Ombudsman. In the wake of an untoward incident in a private hospital complainants seeking an explanation or an acknowledgement of mistakes are often advised (if these are not forthcoming) that their only option is to sue. This is likely to be arduous and potentially extremely costly and may not be particularly helpful if the patient's primary concern is to prevent the same thing happening to someone else. In fact, a number of other options do exist which cost the patient nothing and which can lead to a satisfactory resolution of a complaint, and may even be of assistance if compensation is subsequently sought.

Avenues of complaint

These options include the following avenues of complaint:

- the hospital's complaints procedure;
- an investigation by the local Health Authority;
- complaining to the individual practitioner;
- a complaint to a practitioner's professional body e.g. GMC, UKCC.

Other options which it may be useful to explore include:

- withholding payment;
- complaining to the health insurance company;
- complaining to the Trading Standards Office;
- advising the individual Charity Commission (most hospitals are registered as charities).

Prior to making any complaint it is important to first obtain copies of all the relevant medical and nursing records (under the Access to Health Records Act 1990) including both hospital notes and those held by the consultant (see Chapter 18 and Appendix 6).

COMPLAINTS PROCEDURES WITHIN PRIVATE HOSPITALS

All private hospitals are expected as part of the registration requirements to have in place as good practice a clear written procedure for complaints, and details of this should be set out in their patient information booklet. If this information cannot be found, it should be requested either from the hospital management or from the nursing homes' unit of the Health Authority responsible for registering the premises, who should hold a copy.

Independent Healthcare Association – guidance on complaints

Most private hospitals will be members of the Independent Healthcare Association (the IHA)[1] and if that is the case, it may be helpful to ask the IHA for a copy of its 'Code of Practice for Patient Complaints'. This publication, drawn up as guidance for its members, sets out quite comprehensive procedures for hospitals to investigate complaints. It recommends that there should be a full investigation by a designated hospital official to determine whether or not the complaint is justified. It must also be established as to what degree any complaint may be about perceived failure on the part of the patient's consultant, who is not a staff member.

[1]The Independent Healthcare Association, 22 Little Russell Street, London WC1A 2HT Tel: 0171 430 0537

Minor complaints

Minor complaints, according to the IHA, should be the subject of a report to management, and all reports should be reviewed to ensure that prompt, courteous and appropriate action has been taken. If necessary, the IHA states, senior management should write to the patient to ensure that matters have been resolved to his or her satisfaction.

Complaints about charges

Most patients will be insured for their treatment and where complaints relate to charges the IHA recommends that patients should contact their insurance company for advice before complaining to the hospital. Patients should ideally be informed in advance of admission of the hospital's and consultant's fees, and on discharge should be given an itemised account in sufficient detail to enable the patient to identify services received.

Clinical complaints

For the most serious complaints relating to treatment and the quality of clinical care, the IHA states that the hospital management and senior nurse should undertake an efficient fact gathering exercise, and this should involve interviewing all the staff involved. After due contact with the patient's consultant and, if necessary, the involvement of the hospital's Medical Advisory Committee, the senior management must give the customer as full an explanation as possible.

The IHA advocates that if on completion of the investigation it transpires that the hospital and/or consultant was at fault, acknowledgement of this to the patient is important, together with the appropriate compensation or rectification proposal. Notably, the IHA recommends to its members at this point that apologies for errors with explanations, if relevant, should be tendered. If, however, it seems that the patient still remains dissatisfied, it recommends that the hospital should advise the patient to consult a solicitor.

In practice, complainants may find that the IHA's guidance is not always adhered to. Commercial insurance and legal considerations may also influence the handling and outcome of a complaint. For example, if a complaint indicates serious failures on the part of the hospital it is not unreasonable to consider that concerns for its reputation or fear of admitting liability may mean that the full explanation, acknowledgement of mistakes and apology advocated by the IHA may not always be forthcoming.

Patients and their relatives may therefore still remain dissatisfied and aggrieved even after the hospital's own investigation. If that is the case, they should then consider taking their complaint outside the hospital.

COMPLAINING TO THE REGISTERING HEALTH AUTHORITY

Registered Homes Act 1984

All private hospitals must be registered with the local Health Authority in accordance with the Registered Homes Act 1984. Under the Act, private hospitals (referred to in the legislation as nursing homes) are required to ensure that there is adequacy in the provision of facilities and services to patients and that there is adequate record keeping. It is the responsibility of the local Health Authority to ensure compliance with the Act including that the person in charge of the hospital who is legally required to manage the premises is a 'fit' person (see below). The name of the registering Health Authority can be found on the Certificate of Registration that should be displayed in the hospital's entrance.

Private hospitals must advise patients of their right to complain to the Health Authority in the event that they are dissatisfied with the internal investigation. Patients should contact the Health Authority's Registration and Inspection of Nursing Homes Officer with details of their concerns. It may also be advisable to copy any correspondence, particularly if problems are encountered, to the Health Authority's Chief Executive and Director of Public Health.

If the authority undertakes to conduct an investigation, it is important to secure in writing an indication of its duration. An unnecessarily lengthy or unsatisfactory investigation by an NHS authority can be referred to the Health Service Ombudsman for review. A letter from the complainant's MP to the authority's Chief Executive may also help to speed up an investigation.

A useful publication to obtain is 'Independent Acute Hospitals and Services – Supplement to the Handbook on the Registration and Inspection of Nursing Homes' produced by the National Association of Health Authorities and Trusts (NAHAT)[2].

This publication provides detailed guidelines to assist Health Authorities to investigate complaints about poor care and untoward incidents in private hospitals.

[2]The NAHAT has now merged with the NHS Trust Federation to form the NHS Confederation. Its guidelines are available from: The Publications Department, the NHS Confederation, Birmingham Research Park, Vincent Drive, Birmingham B15 2SQ Tel: 0121 471 4444

WHAT SORTS OF MATTERS WILL A HEALTH AUTHORITY INVESTIGATE?

For Health Authorities to investigate complaints they must first be satisfied that the complaint indicates a breach or breaches of the registration requirements. Regulations 7 and 12 of the Rules and Regulations (SI 1578) set out some of these requirements. Whilst these deal largely with secondary, non-clinical matters, such as that there should be adequacy in the provision of food, crockery and laundering facilities, there are nonetheless a number of areas covering clinical treatment and care. For example, hospitals must:

- provide adequate professional, technical, ancillary and other staff;
- provide and maintain adequate medical, surgical and nursing equipment and adequate treatment facilities;
- make adequate arrangements for patients to receive medical services;
- make adequate arrangements for the recording, safe keeping, handling and disposal of drugs;
- provide adequate arrangements for the prevention of infection, toxic conditions or spread of infection;
- take adequate precautions against the risk of accident;
- make adequate arrangements either with the Health Authority or otherwise for the care of patients in medical emergencies;
- keep proper records including an adequate daily statement of the patient's health and condition and details of any investigations made, surgical operations carried out and treatment given.

The NAHAT publication comments and enlarges on this legislation, citing examples of good practice.

Even within the limited remit of the Registered Homes Act, the Health Authority can carry out a comprehensive investigation of a complaint. For example, in addition to interviewing management, it can also interview all hospital staff involved in any untoward incident (something not generally possible for a solicitor conducting a pre-action investigation). It should also be able to interview consultants concerned where any perceived act of omission or commission involve issues relevant to the authority's statutory duties under the Act.

The Health Authority has the right to inspect the patient's notes. Failure to furnish such documents when they are requested is an offence.

Complaints about clinical treatment can often indicate serious failures in the registration requirements. Even when an incident does not strictly breach the regulations, the Health Authority should, as a matter of good practice, undertake some investigation, especially when the incident has resulted in harm to the patient.

Fitness of the person in charge

The Health Authority must have regard to questions relating to the continuing fitness of the person in charge. Establishing that the director or matron of a private hospital is fit to remain employed is one of the most important aspects of an Authority's registration duties. Serious failure in a hospital's standards resulting in harm to a patient may raise questions as to this fitness. According to the findings of Registered Homes Tribunals (which cover all private hospitals) fitness implies more than competence. It also denotes integrity, truthfulness, honesty, probity and morality. According to NAHAT, fitness also includes the ability to promote good practice.

Report of the Health Authority investigation

The Health Authority should produce a full report at the conclusion of its investigation which should set out the reasons for its investigation, the nature of the clinical problem investigated, the method of the investigation, and its findings. To ensure that the report is factually correct, contributors – which should include the complainant – should be shown a draft copy before a final report is produced. Complainants should then be supplied with a copy of the Authority's final report.

Where appropriate, the Health Authority should make recommendations for improvements, and after the inspection team has ensured that its recommendations have been implemented, a follow-up report should be made. Where failure in the hospital's clinical practices or procedures have been identified, the Health Authority must also check that similar failures are not being repeated in other independent hospitals registered with it.

In rare cases the Authority may consider a prosecution under the Registered Homes Act (Part IV), but the heavy burden of proof required and economics will mean that this happens rarely.

In theory, a properly conducted Health Authority investigation can represent a very effective way of investigating serious complaints about private hospitals and for ensuring that action is taken to protect future patients. Regrettably, few Health Authorities appear to promote this important avenue of complaint. Indeed, it seems that the NAHAT guidelines as a whole are not sufficiently consulted. In Health Service Guidelines sent out to Health Authorities in September 1995 (HSG[95]41), the NHS Executive states: "Insufficient weight is being given by some registration officers to the series of guidelines published by the National Association of Health Authorities and Trusts."

Finally, patients who have had an unsatisfactory response to a complaint about private health care could consider bringing their concerns to the attention of the Operational Policy Unit 1, Human and Corporate Resources Directorate of the NHSE at the Department of Health. This unit deals specifically with private healthcare regulation and the Registered Homes Act.

Referral of practitioners to their professional bodies

If the Health Authority's investigation reveals misconduct on the part of any of the doctors or nurses involved in the case, the guidelines emphasise that the Health Authority must refer these practitioners to their professional bodies. There is an implicit duty to do so and this should not be left to patients or relatives. If the GMC or UKCC proceed with their own investigation, the guidelines state that members of the Authority's inspection team should also be prepared to give evidence.

COMPLAINING ABOUT A PRIVATE CONSULTANT

Complaints about treatment provided by a private consultant present particular difficulties because the consultant who treats the patient at the hospital is rarely a member of the hospital's staff but is a private contractor who has been granted 'admission rights' to the hospital. It is with the consultant (and not the hospital) that the patient is contracting for treatment. The consultant bears the primary responsibility for the patient's treatment even when the treatment takes place on the hospital's premises. The hospital itself may be reluctant to respond to or to become involved in specific questions relating to the consultant's treatment, leaving it up to patient to raise their complaints directly with the doctor.

Guidance for doctors for responding to complaints

Doctors carrying out private work must subscribe to one of the medical defence organisations: the Medical Defence Union (MDU)[3] or the Medical Protection Society (MPS)[4]. These organisations provide insurance cover for any claims made against a doctor. Both organisations have published comprehensive guidance on how doctors insured with them should respond to complaints. These include 'Pitfalls of Practice' by the MPS and 'Talking to Patients' by the MDU. These publications stress the importance of giving a full factual account of what has happened and where appropriate, making a full apology.

Unfortunately, complainants may find that not all doctors are disposed to put this guidance into practice which means that they may have to look at other options for resolving their complaint.

Medical Advisory Committee

If a complaint concerns serious failures in a consultant's clinical judgment or practices, or indeed in those of resident staff, it may be helpful to bring this to the attention of the hospital's Medical Advisory Committee. Serious clinical failings should be a matter of concern for any responsible MAC.

If still dissatisfied, and if they consider that there has been serious professional misconduct on the part of a doctor, private patients can also complain to the General Medical Council as well as considering pursuing a claim for medical negligence.

Complaining to GMC/UKCC etc.

A serious complaint about an individual practitioner which brings into question the practitioner's fitness to practise should be referred to the relevant professional body e.g. the General Medical Council (GMC) in the case of doctors and the United Kingdom Central Council (UKCC) in the case of nurses. Details of the various procedures can be found in Chapter 10.

It is interesting to note that the UKCC, specifically enjoins its registered practitioners not to conceal untoward incidents, (see Chapter 6 'Complaining to a Practitioner's Professional Body')

[3]The Medical Defence Union, 3 Devonshire Place, London W1N 6DE Tel: 0171 486 6181
[4]The Medical Protection Society, 50 Hallam Street, London W1N 6DE Tel: 0171 637 0541

as this is a frequently occurring reason for removal from the Register. Other reasons include: failure to keep essential records/falsifying records; failure to protect or promote the interests of patients; and reckless and wilfully unskilful practice.

In line with the UKCC, the GMC issued new guidance in 1998 imposing a duty on doctors to provide a full explanation in the event that something goes wrong.[5]

OTHER OPTIONS FOR INVESTIGATING COMPLAINTS

Withholding payment

If a patient believes that he has not received a proper service then one option would be to withhold payment from the hospital and/or consultant.

When withholding payment, the patient should inform the hospital and/or consultant in writing giving full reasons. If the treatment is being funded by health insurers, then the patient should contact them as soon as possible both to advise them of the situation and to seek their advice.

The complainant needs to be very cautious when withholding payment, for the hospital/consultant may sue for recovery of the debt. If the private hospital and/or doctor do take legal action for non-payment, then the patient will have to establish that the treatment provided was negligent and/or that there was a breach of contract. It would be advisable to seek an initial legal opinion from a solicitor experienced in medical negligence claims.

Complaining to the insurers

The majority of patients who use private hospitals have private medical insurance. Whilst it could be seen as in the insurance company's commercial interest to investigate complaints about serious clinical incidents, no health insurer currently appears to have a proper written policy for investigating such matters and will not normally intervene. Instead, patients or relatives who contact their insurers will usually be told that its remit extends no further than to reimbursing its subscribers for the costs of their treatment, up to the limits in their policy, and that only if the complaint is about costs or facilities will it consider becoming directly involved.

However, if a complaint does raise serious questions about the standard of treatment offered by a particular hospital and/or

[5] Good Medical Practice 15.7.98 GMC

consultant, then it may still be worth reporting these concerns to the insurers. Insurers have considerable control over which consultants and hospitals can be used by their subscribers and incidents reported by complainants may ultimately influence which hospitals and consultants are recognised within their scheme. If the allegations are independently supported by, for example, the report of a Health Authority investigation, this will obviously help to substantiate any complaint made.

Complaining to the Trading Standards Office

Private hospitals, nursing homes and specialist clinics are all service providers, and if patients or relatives are dissatisfied with the quality or the costs of the service they have received, they might consider contacting the local Trading Standards Office for advice. Complaints may indicate breaches of the Supply of Goods and Services Act 1982, the Trade Descriptions Act 1968 or the Consumer Protection Act 1987.

Complaining to the Charity Commission

Of the approximately 220 private hospitals in England and Wales over a third are registered as charities or form part of a registered charity. If a patient has received substandard treatment with adverse consequences in a charity hospital, and if complaints by the patient or family have not been responded to satisfactorily by the hospital's management, they could consider taking their complaint to the trustees of the charity.

If the patient complains to the trustees and is not satisfied with the investigation, consideration could be given to taking a complaint to the Charity Commission.[6] The Commission seeks to ensure that trustees are aware of and are acting within the purposes of the charity as set out in its governing document, and it is possible that the Commission's involvement in the matter, with its powers to advise trustees and to ensure that they comply with the law, may assist in the satisfactory resolution of the complaint.

INVESTIGATION FOLLOWING A DEATH

Coroners

In certain circumstances following a death a Coroner can decide whether a post-mortem examination and an inquest are required.

---

[6]The Charity Commission, St Alban's House, 57–60 Haymarket, London SW1Y 4QX Tel: 0171 210 447

This can be a useful route of investigation. For further details see Chapter 13.

Medical certificates for cremation

If a death was not subject to a Coroner's investigation, another possible source of information and inquiry could be the medical certificate for cremation (if the body is to be cremated).

Detailed forms must be completed and signed by a total of three doctors, so as to eliminate the possibility that there may be anything untoward about the death before the body is disposed of irretrievably. It is a criminal offence to make a false declaration on these forms. If a subsequent investigation reveals a medical/nursing error contributed to the death the Home Office can review the forms and request the Crown Prosecution Service to consider criminal action under the Cremation Act 1902.

Defamation

Private hospitals are commercial concerns which are sensitive to adverse publicity. Private patients, on the other hand, may reasonably feel that 'going public' is the only option remaining if the other avenues have been exhausted. However, a word of caution: a private hospital may construe any allegations made against it as defamation (libel or slander) and could take the step of threatening proceedings. The complainant should take legal advice before embarking on such a course of action.

OTHER PRIVATE CARE PROVIDERS

Private nursing homes

Patients or relatives dissatisfied with a nursing home's investigation of a serious complaint should raise their concerns with officers of the Health Authority's nursing homes unit. NHS patients receiving care in a private nursing home can complain using the NHS Complaints Procedure. It may also be helpful to contact one of the specialist voluntary organisations for advice, e.g. Counsel and Care, Age Concern, etc.

Private residential homes

Complaints about services provided by an independent residential home funded by the local authority should initially be dealt with by the home. Complainants who are dissatisfied or prefer to complain directly to the Social Services Department (SSD) may do so. Social Services Departments operate a three stage complaints procedure which concludes with an investigation by a review panel. Private residents in an independent home have the option of complaining to the home and/or raising their concerns with the SSD responsible for registering the home. Residential homes will generally be registered with the local authority under Part I of the Registered Homes Act 1984, unless they are deemed to provide 'nursing care'.

Private psychiatric hospitals and homes

Depending on the type of care offered, a residential home offering psychiatric care may be registered either with the local authority or the Health Authority or in some cases come under the jurisdiction of both authorities. If it is NHS treatment being provided within an independent facility then a complaint can be made using the NHS Complaints Procedure.

Fertility clinics

Private fertility clinics are subject to regulation under the Registered Homes Act 1984 and the Human Fertilisation and Embryology Act 1990. Complaints should initially be made to the clinic, all clinics being required to have a formal complaints procedure and a designated complaints officer. If it has not been possible to resolve the complaint with the clinic, the complainant should contact the Human Fertilisation and Embryology Authority (HFEA)[7] who may wish to investigate the matter, particularly if it relates to possible breaches in the licensing requirements. The HFEA is responsible for setting up a code of practice for IVF treatment, for ensuring that clinics meet these guidelines and for licensing and inspecting all relevant premises including NHS premises and research units. The HFEA also provides detailed information on IVF clinics and guidance for prospective patients.

Abortion clinics

Premises which perform terminations of pregnancy must be approved by the Department of Health (DoH) in accordance with the Abortion Act 1967 as well as being registered with the local Health Authority under the Registered Homes Act 1984. Further guidance was issued by the DoH in 1994 detailing the requirements for approval under the 1967 Act. Approval by the DoH is reviewed every two years. If a complaint cannot be resolved with the clinic, complaints which indicate breaches in the Registered Homes Act 1984 can be referred to the local Health Authority.

---

[7]Human Fertilisation and Embryology Authority, Paxton House, 30 Artillery Lane, London E17 7LS Tel: 0171 377 1871

Where the complaint is very serious or relates to possible breaches in the requirements of the Abortion Act 1967, the complainant should contact the DoH's inspection staff.[8]

Cosmetic clinics

If a cosmetic clinic is performing invasive procedures, it should be registered under Part II of the Registered Homes Act 1984 and will be subject to the normal regulatory and inspection requirements. Alternatively, complainants could approach the local Trading Standards Office. If injury or loss have been incurred the complainant should seek advice from a solicitor.

PRIVATE PRACTITIONERS

Complaints about individual private practitioners (e.g. dentists, opticians, physiotherapists etc.) should be referred to the relevant statutory professional body (see Chapter 10).

COMPLEMENTARY THERAPIES

If treatment has not been carried out on premises subject to regulation under the Registered Homes Act 1984, and the practitioner is not qualified as a doctor or nurse, then the complainant should consider complaining to the practitioner's professional association (see Chapter 10), if he or she belongs to one, or approaching the local Trading Standards Office. If injury or loss has been incurred then the complainant should seek the advice of a solicitor.

CONCLUSION

Patients should not be deterred from pursuing their rights against doctors and hospitals who operate in the private sector; much can be achieved. Nevertheless it has to be said that the system cries out for reform and regulation. Until then only grit and courage will make the present arrangements work for the patient.

[8]Department of Health, Wellington House, 133–155 Waterloo Road, London SE1 8UG Tel: 0171 972 2000

Chapter 13

THE CORONER'S INQUEST

Tom Osborne

If a patient dies and the family believes that this was as a consequence of medical treatment (or lack of treatment), asking the Coroner to hold an inquest into the death can be a very effective way of ensuring that the circumstances surrounding the death are properly investigated.

INTRODUCTION

Where a death occurs in circumstances where the family feel aggrieved at the way that the deceased has been treated either by their medical practitioner or whilst in hospital, then it is open to them to bring the circumstances of the death to the attention of the Coroner and invite her to investigate the matter and hold a formal inquest. Very often the inquest and therefore an independent inquiry into exactly what happened is far more beneficial to the family than an action for compensation in the civil courts. This is particularly the case where the claim involves the death of a child, or adult with no dependants, where the amount of compensation would be minimal.

The inquest gives the family an opportunity to ask those involved in the treatment and care of the deceased searching questions as to their conduct and the procedures that were followed. Many families, if they are adequately represented at the inquest, very often do not wish to take the matter further once the inquest has been concluded. In other circumstances it may provide vital information to those advising the family to enable an application for legal aid to be submitted or indeed to support the civil action.

THE CORONER

The office of the Coroner is one of the oldest in the English legal system dating back at least to the twelfth century. The Coroner is responsible for investigating deaths reported to her which lie within her appointed district. Since 1888 Coroners have been appointed by the local authority which is also responsible for payment of the Coroners' expenses and remuneration. A Coroner can be a solicitor, barrister or doctor of five years' standing. She is an independent judicial officer and can only be removed from post by the Lord Chancellor.

The Coroner's rules

Coroner's inquests today are regulated by the Coroners Act 1988. The rules regulating the practice and procedures of inquests are those that applied under the previous legislation and are known as the Coroner's Rules 1984. A brief summary of the rules as they apply to inquests is included at the end of this chapter.

The Coroner is obliged by statute to investigate certain categories of death but is not necessarily required to hold an inquest in every case if, after preliminary enquiries, she is satisfied that death was due to natural causes. These are specific circumstances where the Coroner must proceed to an inquest hearing. Details are provided below. The procedure for investigating deaths can be summarised as follows:

- death reported to the Coroner;
- post-mortem examination and preliminary inquiries;
- inquest opened for formal identification of the deceased and adjourned;
- investigation by Coroner's office e.g. interviewing witnesses, and obtaining evidence;
- inquest resumed for a full hearing and Coroner's verdict.

Coroner's officer

The Coroner is usually assisted in his function by the Coroner's Officer. This post is usually held by a serving police officer. He or she is the Coroner's representative and will make the arrangements for the removal of a body; he or she will search for evidence and interview witnesses and liaise with any of the lawyers representing the deceased. He or she will also make all the arrangements for the inquest including the summoning of witnesses and the jury. He or she also acts as the clerk and usher at the inquest.

NOTIFYING THE CORONER OF A DEATH

Most deaths are *not* brought to the attention of the Coroner. Where the cause of death is clear and there are no untoward or suspicious circumstances, the attending doctor will prepare a medical certificate showing the cause of death. The death will then be registered and the body will be released for burial or cremation.

Deaths which must be reported to the Coroner

The Registrar of Births, Deaths and Marriages has a duty to report any death to the Coroner where any of the following circumstances apply:

- the deceased did not receive medical treatment in her last illness;
- the Registrar has been unable to obtain a completed death certificate giving the cause of death;
- the death certificate indicates that the deceased was not attended by a medical practitioner for a period of 14 days prior to death or immediately after death;
- the cause of death appears to be unknown;
- the Registrar has reason to believe that a death was unnatural, or to have been caused by violence, or neglect, or by abortion or occurred in suspicious circumstances;
- death occurred during, or immediately after an operation or before the deceased recovered from the anaesthetic (even if death occurred some weeks or months later);
- death was due to industrial disease or industrial poisoning;
- deaths which occurred in legal custody;
- deaths where there are allegations of negligence including medical negligence.

Stillbirths

Stillbirths do not come within the Coroner's jurisdiction unless there is any doubt that the infant was alive at the time of birth (and subsequently died) in which case it may be possible for the Coroner to become involved.

Who can report a death to the Coroner?

Any person who has concerns or suspicions about the cause of another person's death (or believes that it comes within one of the categories listed above), should report those concerns to the Coroner. This could include:

- doctors;
- the police;
- the Registrar of Deaths, Births and Marriages;
- any other person e.g. family, friends, carers, members of the general public.

Where the circumstances of a death require it to be reported to the Coroner, the Registrar should either ensure that the appropriate person has reported the death or failing that, report the death herself. If the appropriate person e.g. doctor, does not report a death, he or she may be subject to censure by the Coroner.

Medical negligence

In the case of deaths occurring during the course of medical treatment, it is quite possible that a death would not routinely be reported to the Coroner even though the family might have identified concerns over the treatment or lack of treatment afforded to the deceased. The medical practitioner(s) attending the deceased may be satisfied as to the cause of death and may therefore not feel it appropriate to report the death to the Coroner. It is therefore very important that the family or their legal representatives make their concerns known to the Coroner (or the Registrar of Deaths) before accepting release of the body so that the Coroner can carry out appropriate investigations including a post-mortem in order to investigate the family's concerns.

The family may wish to obtain assistance at this stage, either from a legal representative or other advice agency e.g. AVMA or the local CHC, to ensure that the pathologist and/or Coroner is fully appraised of all the circumstances surrounding the death.

THE POST-MORTEM EXAMINATION AND PRELIMINARY INQUIRIES

Pathologist

If a death is reported to the Coroner, it would be fairly exceptional for the Coroner not to arrange a post-mortem examination. The Coroner's Rules now strongly recommend that only a pathologist with suitable qualifications and experience and with access to laboratory facilities should be employed to carry out the post-mortem. A pathologist is a qualified doctor who specialises in the examination of diseased tissues and post-mortems.

Medical negligence

Where there are allegations of medical negligence, by Rule 6 of the Coroner's Rules, if the deceased died in hospital, the post-mortem should *not* normally be made by a pathologist connected with the hospital. The family may, if appropriate, wish to bring this to the attention of the Coroner. This rule does not apply if the obtaining of another qualified pathologist would unduly delay the examination but this should not normally present a problem.

It is possible for the relatives of the deceased to arrange for their own independent pathologist to attend the post-mortem. The relatives will need to act quickly because the post-mortem would normally be carried out within a few days of the death being reported to the Coroner.

Copies of the post-mortem must be supplied by the Coroner to properly interested parties including the family and the legal representatives of the deceased.

THE DECISION TO HOLD AN INQUEST

Post-mortem without any inquest

If a death is reported to the Coroner, she will normally carry out preliminary investigations including a post-mortem examination. If the death is then determined as being due to natural causes and there are no untoward circumstances surrounding the death, the Coroner will issue a death certificate and a disposal certificate allowing the burial or cremation to take place, and the Coroner's inquiry will be brought to a close.

Deaths requiring an inquest

An inquest must be held if there is reasonable cause to suspect that the deceased died:

- a violent or unnatural death;
- a sudden death where the cause is unknown;
- in custody;
- or in circumstances where other statutes require an inquest to be held e.g. criminal cases (murder, manslaughter, infanticide);

- suicides;
- accidents e.g. road, aviation, rail, domestic;
- industrial accidents and diseases;
- deaths in prison or police custody;
- deaths where negligent medical treatment is alleged;
- deaths where the cause is still unknown following a post-mortem.

Criminal cases

In cases where criminal charges are likely to be brought, the inquest is immediately adjourned and the matter referred to the Director of Public Prosecution (DPP). At the conclusion of any criminal proceedings, the coroner may then hold a hearing to conclude the inquest. If no criminal proceedings are brought following referral to the DPP the inquest will be re-opened and a verdict reached.

THE INQUEST

An inquest is a public hearing, conducted by the Coroner, held to determine who the deceased was, when and where he or she came by his or her death. The inquest hearing may be held in a purpose built Coroner's Court if such a facility is available, or at some other appropriate location e.g. the local hospital.

Opening and adjourning the inquest

If the Coroner is satisfied that the circumstances of the death require her to hold an inquest, a preliminary hearing is usually held for the purposes of formal identification of the deceased. It is not normally necessary for the family to be represented at this preliminary hearing. Once this hearing has taken place, the Coroner will then be able to release the body for burial or cremation. The full inquest hearing will then take place some weeks – or often several months – later depending on how long the investigation takes to complete. The reason for 'opening and adjourning' the inquest in this way is to enable the family to arrange the funeral rather than having to wait until after the full inquest.

Inquest jury

Most inquests are conducted by the Coroner without a jury. A jury is still necessary under certain circumstances including:

- where a death occurred whilst the deceased was in police custody; or
- where the death occurred in circumstances, the continuance or possible recurrence of which is prejudicial to the health or safety of the public or any section of the public.

It may be useful in medical accident circumstances for the family or legal representative to write to the Coroner inviting her to hold an inquest on the basis that it is in the public interest to do so. Thereafter the Coroner can be advised that he must summon a jury.

Legal and other costs

An inquest is a public inquiry and relatives will only incur costs if they decide to carry out their own independent investigations. Such costs could include:

- representation by a lawyer at the inquest;
- any independent medical reports;
- copies of notes and records from the hospital.

Legal Aid

Unfortunately legal aid is not available for representation at an inquest although there has been suggestion in recent years that the Lord Chancellor may be prepared to extend legal aid to inquest proceedings.

Legal advice and assistance may be available to a deceased's family under the 'Green Form' scheme. This will not include representation.

Legal expenses insurance

If the deceased was covered by an insurance policy which included legal expenses insurance, it may be possible, in certain circumstances, to use such a policy to finance legal representation at an inquest. The deceased's family should discuss this possibility with an experienced medical negligence solicitor.

Privately funding representation

The costs for privately funding legal representation at an inquest could on average range from anything between £500 to £3000, depending on the sorts of investigations that are carried out prior to the inquest e.g. expert medical opinions. Some solicitors (and barristers) may, in certain circumstances, be willing to come to an arrangement whereby no fee ('pro bono') or only a nominal sum is charged for representation at the inquest perhaps, for example, if the family or dependants intend to pursue a claim for medical negligence.

Obtaining financial assistance from the Health Authority

In recent years, more and more Health Authorities and Trusts are prepared to meet the legal costs of a family to be represented at an inquest where the conduct of the hospital or its staff may be fairly criticised. An approach to the Trust should be made at an early stage as the family may then be in a position to arrange legal representation.

THE INQUEST HEARING

The hearing will be conducted by the Coroner with or without a jury. She will summon and examine the witnesses who have evidence to give concerning the death of the deceased. Thereafter such witnesses may be cross examined by representatives of the family or other interested parties such as the Health Authority/hospital or representatives of the medical staff. If the circumstances surrounding the death are of a technical nature, the Coroner may sit with an adviser.

Witnesses

The Coroner will decide which witnesses to call but it is open to the family to make representations to the Coroner if they feel that additional witnesses should be called. It is also open to individuals to put themselves forward as potential witnesses. Witnesses are obliged to attend an inquest if called and may be subpoenaed. Certain witnesses will be required to attend the inquest in person, whilst other witnesses may be asked to submit written evidence which may be read out at the inquest.

An inquest hearing may take only an hour or so to complete. In more complex cases, the hearing could continue for several days or in exceptional cases, several weeks or months e.g. major disasters involving multiple deaths. Inquests where medical treatment is being brought into question will usually take at least half a day, and in anything but relatively straightforward cases, possibly one or two days.

THE INQUEST VERDICT

If the Coroner is conducting an inquest without a jury, once the evidence has been concluded, it is for the Coroner to reach her verdict after she has given the representatives the opportunity to address her on points of law. There is no right for any party to address him on the facts of the case as presented.

If a jury has been summoned, the Coroner must sum up the proceedings and direct the jury on the law to assist them in arriving at their verdict.

The verdict must determine:

- WHO the deceased was;
- HOW or by what means the deceased came by his or her death;
- WHEN and WHERE he or she died.

The verdict must **not** be framed in such a way as to determine:

- criminal liability on the part of any named person;
- civil liability of any person or organisation.

Whilst there are a number of common verdicts there is no statutory requirement for the verdict to be in any particular form. In the case of *R v Southwark Coroners Court ex parte Kendall (1988) 1 WLR 1186*, it was stated that the verdict should be expressed in concise and ordinary language so as to indicate how the deceased came by her death.

The common verdicts are as follows:

- natural causes;
- want of attention at birth;
- suicide;
- accident/misadventure;
- open verdict;
- stillbirth;
- lawful killing;
- unlawful killing;
- self-neglect or lack of care.

Lack of care

The Court of Appeal in the case of *R v North Humberside Coroner ex parte Jamieson (1995)* defined neglect or lack of care as follows:

> 'Neglect i.e. lack of care in this context means a gross failure to provide adequate nourishment or liquid, or provide or procure basic medical attention or shelter or warmth to someone in a dependent position because of youth, age, illness or incarceration who cannot provide it himself or herself. Failure to provide medical

> attention to a dependent person whose physical condition is such as to show that he or she obviously needs it may amount to neglect. So it may be that if it is the dependent person's mental condition which obviously calls for medical attention . . . in both cases the crucial consideration will be what the dependent person's condition, whether physical or mental, appeared to be.'

To justify such a verdict there must be a clear cause or connection between the neglect and the death.

It has been the writer's experience that the Coroner can be persuaded to reach a verdict and to add that 'neglect/lack of care was a contributing factor'.

APPEALING THE CORONER'S DECISION

There is no right of appeal against the decision or verdict reached by the Coroner, although the decision may be subject to statutory review or can be challenged by the means of Judicial Review procedure if the Coroner acted wrongly.

Statutory Review

An application to quash an inquest verdict or to overturn a Coroner's decision can be made by any interested party. Such an application should be made to the Attorney General who will then decide whether the matter warrants referral to the High Court. The High Court can quash an inquisition provided that:

- authority is given by the Attorney General;
- the inquest has already been held;
- there must have been fraud, rejection of evidence, irregularity of proceedings, insufficient inquiries or other reason;
- since the inquest new facts or evidence have been discovered.

If the above criteria are met the court will order another inquest to be held and the original decision will be quashed.

Judicial review

In addition to the statutory powers mentioned above, it is open to any party to make an application to the High Court for leave to proceed by way of Judicial Review if an error has been made in the decision making process. An application for Judicial Review can be made *ex parte* (only requiring evidence from one party i.e. the applicant) although it must be remembered that this is a discretionary remedy and it is unlikely that the court will grant an order if the outcome, despite the error made, would be the same.

Legal Aid

Although not available for inquests, legal aid is available for an application to the High Court whether by Judicial Review or under the statutory powers, if the applicant qualifies on financial grounds and the Legal Aid Board is persuaded that the applicant has reasonable grounds for bringing the proceedings and being successful.

PRACTICAL SUMMARY

Legal representation

Where a death occurs in circumstances where the medical treatment is called into question, the family should whenever possible contact a solicitor immediately. Ideally, the solicitor should be someone who specialises in medical negligence, particularly if the family is considering a claim for damages arising out of the death.

Post-mortem

The solicitor (or a family member) should contact the Coroner without delay, make their concerns known and if appropriate, should object to the pathologist at the hospital where the deceased died carrying out the post-mortem. They may also wish to suggest that the Coroner employs a specialist pathologist e.g. a neonatal pathologist in the case of a neonatal death.

If it is possible and the family have the means to do so, then the family's own nominated medical practitioner (e.g. pathologist) could attend the post-mortem examination. If this could not be arranged in time, the family can arrange a subsequent private post-mortem if it is felt this would be beneficial e.g. if the cause of death is still uncertain or conflicts with other evidence.

Notifying the Coroner

The Coroner to be notified is the Coroner where the body of the deceased is lying, whether the cause of death arose within his or her jurisdiction or not. This applies even if the person died abroad; if his or her body is returned to England, the Coroner covering the district where the body is returned to would then have jurisdiction to investigate the death.

Medical records

The notes and records from the GP and the hospital should be requested. If possible, these should be looked at by a medical practitioner who will be able to advise on the care afforded to the deceased. This will assist in identifying the issues that need to be addressed at the inquest.

The Coroner should be requested to hold an inquest on the basis that it is in the public's interest to do so. When she agrees to hold an inquest, he should then be informed that he has no alternative other than to summon a jury.

Before the actual inquest an informal approach should be made to the Coroner for the disclosure of the pathologist's report and witness statements that the Coroner is going to read out. It is not usually possible to obtain copies of witness statements obtained during the course of the pre-inquest investigation unless they are going to be submitted in evidence at the inquest.

Representation and questioning of witnesses

At the inquest itself, the family can act alone or be represented by a solicitor or barrister. Each witness is first sworn in and then examined (questioned) by the Coroner. Any questions should be aimed at discovering the facts rather than to make accusations. Witnesses can then be examined by any other interested party with the consent of the Coroner. If during the course of the inquest it appears that someone is not present or represented whose conduct may be criticised, then the Coroner should be asked to adjourn the inquest to require his or her attendance.

Incrimination

During the course of the inquest the Coroner may warn any witness that he or she is not obliged to answer any questions which may incriminate him or her.

Addressing the Coroner on matters of law

Once the evidence has been called each party may address the Coroner on matters of law but not on matters of fact.

The Coroner should be addressed on the question of neglect where it can be clearly shown that there is a cause or link between the lack of care and the death of the deceased.

Verdict

The Coroner or the jury (if one has been summoned) will then retire to consider the evidence and arrive at a verdict.

Transcripts

In addition to the Coroner's notes of the inquest, the proceedings are usually taped. It is possible to obtain transcripts of inquest proceedings but a fee is usually charged. The family may want to check what arrangements are available prior to the inquest.

WHAT IF A FAMILY CANNOT AFFORD LEGAL REPRESENTATION?

If a family is not in a position to have a legal representative present at the inquest, assistance may be obtained in preparing for the inquest from the following organisations:

- Action for Victims of Medical Accidents;
- Inquest;
- Community Health Council;
- Mind (deaths related to mental health);
- Victim Support.

Details of these organisations can be found in Appendix 6.

If the family has specific concerns which they feel need to be addressed at the inquest, then they should make these concerns known to the Coroner at an early stage, preferably in writing as well as verbally. This will help to ensure that the Coroner's inquiry deals with the family's specific concerns and perhaps which witnesses the Coroner should call.

If possible, the family should try and obtain copies of any relevant medical records and if necessary seek advice on the medical issues, for example, from AVMA or the local CHC.

Prior to the inquest, the family should prepare lists of questions or issues that they would like particular witnesses to respond to. If the family is concerned about their ability to raise questions at the inquest hearing and is unable to find anyone else to do this on their behalf, then they could consider writing to the Coroner with questions which they would like the Coroner to address at the inquest. The Coroner should be willing to comply with such a request.

An inquest is an invaluable opportunity for investigating the circumstances surrounding a death and, if properly conducted, can help families to come to terms with their loss. It is therefore important that whenever possible families do seek advice so that full use can be made of the unique opportunity that it represents.

THE CORONER'S RULES

Coroners Act 1988

Coroners and inquests are regulated by the Coroners Act 1988.

Section 8(1) of the Coroners Act 1988 provides:

(a) Where a Coroner is informed that the body of a person ('the deceased') is lying within his district and there is reasonable cause to suspect that the deceased:
(b) has died a violent or an unnatural death;
(c) has died a sudden death of which the cause is unknown;
(d) has died in prison or such a place or in such circumstances as to require an inquest under any other act;

then whether the cause of death arose within his district or not, the Coroner shall as soon as practicable hold an inquest into the death of the deceased either with or subject to Section 3 below without a jury.

CORONER'S RULES 1984

The rules regulating the practice and procedures of inquests are known as the Coroner's Rules 1984. The following is a brief summary of the rules as they apply to inquests, with particular reference to medical accidents.

Rule 6

Pathologist independent

When deciding which medical practitioner should perform a post-mortem, the coroner must have regard to the following:

> (c) if the deceased died in a hospital the Coroner should not use a pathologist connected with the hospital to carry out the post-mortem if the conduct of any member of staff at the hospital is likely to be called into question or if a relative of the deceased asks the Coroner that some other pathologist should conduct the post-mortem. The Coroner can over-rule such a request if it would unnecessarily delay the examination.

Rule 7

This deals with whom the Coroner should notify of the carrying out of a post-mortem. These will include relatives, the hospital, the family GP and other statutory authorities including the police. Any person who has an interest is entitled to be represented by a legally qualified medical practitioner. This does not mean a doctor with a legal qualification but simply a recognised doctor although the Coroner does have discretion to allow others to attend.

Rule 10

Pathologist's report

The pathologist must deliver his report to the Coroner and must not supply copies to any other person.

Rule 17

Public hearing

Provides that an inquest must be held in public unless it would be against the interests of national security.

Rule 19

Notification of an inquest

Outlines who should be notified of the date of the inquest which will include any relative or spouse or any other person who has notified the Coroner of wishing to be notified.

Rule 20

Representation at an inquest

Any parent, child, spouse or personal representative or any beneficiary under a policy of insurance or the insurer or any other person who in the opinion of the Coroner has a proper interest is entitled to attend (the inquest) and to ask questions either in person or by Counsel or a solicitor.

Rule 21

Witnesses

Witnesses at the inquest will first be examined by the Coroner and lastly by his or her representative.

Rule 22

No witness should be obliged to answer a question which incriminates himself or herself.

Rule 24

Any person whose conduct is likely in the opinion of the Coroner to be called into question shall be given notice of the intended inquest. If necessary it can be adjourned for him to attend.

Rule 36

The proceedings and evidence at an inquest shall solely be directed towards determining:

(a) who the deceased was;
(b) how, when and where the deceased came by his death;
(c) the particulars for the time being required by the Registration Acts.

Neither the Coroner nor the jury shall express any opinion on any other matters.

Rule 37

Documentary evidence

The Coroner may admit at an inquest documentary evidence relevant to the purpose of the inquest which may include medical reports and notes unless a person objects. Before admitting the document into evidence the Coroner shall at the beginning of the inquest announce his or her intention publicly.

Rule 39

The Coroner shall take notes of the evidence at every inquest. (These will normally be held for at least 15 years.)

Rule 40

No person shall be allowed to address the Coroner or the jury as to facts.

Rule 41

Where the Coroner sits with a jury he or she shall summon up the evidence to the jury and direct them as to the law before they consider their verdict.

Rule 42

Criminal liability

No verdict shall be framed in such a way as to appear to determine any question of criminal or civil liability on the part of the named person.

Rule 43

A Coroner who believes that action should be taken to prevent the recurrence of fatalities similar to that in respect of which the inquest is being held may announce at the inquest that he or she is reporting the matter in writing to the personal authority who may have power to take such action and he or she may report the matter accordingly.

Section III

MEDICAL NEGLIGENCE AND LEGAL ACTION

Chapter 14

INTRODUCTION – SUING FOR COMPENSATION

Arnold Simanowitz

The following section of the book deals with how people who have been injured can recover compensation for that injury – the law which applies, the courts involved and the procedure which must be followed. This chapter introduces the subject and puts it in context, dealing with the history of medical negligence litigation, the issues involved and the way the main players have influenced and continue to influence how patients are able to obtain their rightful compensation under the law.

> *'Early in the inquiry it became increasingly obvious that it was in the area of medical negligence that the civil justice system was failing most conspicuously to meet the needs of litigants in a number of respects.'*
>
> *Lord Woolf, Master of the Rolls*[1]

History of medical negligence litigation

Anyone who today approaches the subject of suing for compensation for a medical accident will find that medical negligence litigation is a branch of the law recognised by the courts, with its own literature, special rules of procedure and specialist solicitors. It would be hard for them to believe that as recently as 1982, when AVMA was founded, those few cases involving medical negligence which were litigated[2] were dealt with as a minor branch of the law which deals with personal injury generally.

Personal injury covers cases where injury, physical or mental, is caused to the person of the individual. Clearly medical negligence can cause such injury and indeed, as we shall see later in this chapter, unless it does so no claim can be made. But there are so many special circumstances and considerations which apply when a person is injured while under medical care, that many of

---

[1]Access to Justice, the Final Report to the Lord Chancellor on the Civil Justice system in England and Wales 1996.

[2]In 1981 only 800 Legal Aid Certificates were issued in Medical Negligence Cases.

the procedures which apply to personal injury are not appropriate and it is necessary to have special procedures which apply to medical negligence cases.

In 1982 that was not the case. There were no specialist solicitors, the first text book on medical negligence was not published until 1988[3] and until Lord Woolf's Inquiry in 1996 (see Chapter 23 Medical Negligence After Woolf) the Lord Chancellor in promulgating new rules for the conduct of personal injury cases steadfastly refused to recognise that medical negligence was in any way different from ordinary personal injury actions.

Medical negligence litigation did not finally come of age until Lord Woolf's inquiry when he was persuaded to set up a special working group to look separately into medical negligence which led to his decision that such litigation required special treatment.

Number of cases

It was not, however, the number of cases which led to such a conclusion. Although by 1996 the number of cases started had increased greatly since 1981. The annual expenditure on legal aid for medical negligence was only £50.2 million out of a total spent on personal injury litigation of £284.7 million.

What makes it different?

So what is it that makes this litigation different from all other so that it requires a different approach by all involved in it? There are numerous reasons and in this introduction I can only touch on the most fundamental one because to deal with that issue fully as well as consider all the others would require a much more detailed consideration. The fundamental difference is the relationship between patients and doctors and the status of doctors in society. A medical negligence action is not simply about money, indeed it is often hardly about money at all. That of course makes it difficult for such actions to fit into the general scheme of the courts because historically the role of the courts is simply to deal with money and property.

The doctor/patient relationship

From the patient's point of view a medical negligence claim involves breach of trust on the part of the most caring of professions; from the doctor's point of view it is seen as a personal attack on his or her competence and integrity. That is not to say that

[3]Medical Negligence: A Practical Guide by Charles Lewis published by Frank Cass & Co Ltd [now in its 3rd edition].

every medical negligence action has at its core the behaviour of one particular doctor. Indeed, it is becoming more and more recognised that a large number of accidents result from a breakdown in the team procedures and it is often difficult if not impossible, as well as unnecessary, to pin the blame on one particular individual. Nevertheless both sides perceive the doctor as being at the heart of the problem and this has dictated, if not bedevilled, the approach to these cases.

The moral dimension

Because the doctor/patient relationship lies at the heart of medical negligence claims, they cannot be treated in the same way as, for example, a traffic accident. Doctors are, by the Hippocratic oath, under a duty to care for their patients and specifically to do them no harm. When an accident takes place that duty does not simply disappear entitling the doctor to walk away from the problem.

There is an argument that says that a doctor owes a patient even more care when he or she, or another member of the profession, damages that patient. They therefore have a duty to ensure that an injured patient gets all the care that is needed, which may include compensation to enable them to restore the quality of life, or some of it, which they may have lost as a result of the accident.

The defence organisations

Until 1991 doctors, whether or not they were working in a NHS hospital, were held personally liable if they were found to be negligent. This meant that all claims involving a doctor were dealt with by that doctor's defence organisation. If the doctor was a hospital doctor then the Health Authority would be involved as well (this was before the days of the Trusts – see Chapter 2) but effectively the defence would be run by the solicitors for the particular defence organisation to which the clinician belonged. (The Medical Defence Union (MDU) and the Medical Protection Society (MPS) in England and Wales, and the Medical and Dental Defence Union (MDDUS) in Scotland.)

Although the defence organisations indemnify clinicians who have to compensate patients, that is pay any compensation which is required to be paid, they are not regarded as insurers in law. That is because there is no binding obligation on them to meet any claim and they do have the right to refuse to do so. This, and the fact that clinicians were always seen as being in the front line of any claim, had serious consequences for patients and medical negligence litigation generally.

Firstly, although the defence organisations had the right to refuse indemnity, in the main the doctors could depend on them to meet any claim. Patients, however, cannot be certain that the defence organisations will pay up in the end. Although such situations are rare, it is possible for the defence organisations to refuse to indemnify a doctor and then if the doctor did not have the money to pay the patient would not receive the compensation to which he or she was entitled.

Defensive medicine

More importantly, however, with the doctors in the front line, was the attitude engendered by the fear of litigation. Faced with the threat of a steeply rising number of claims against them, leading to steeply rising payments to their defence organisations, doctors began to claim that this was leading to their carrying out unnecessary treatment, including operations, simply to protect themselves against being sued. This was especially so in the case of caesarean sections where it was said that there was a significant increase in the number being carried out because of the fear of litigation.

Little did doctors realise that if they were really practising this 'defensive medicine' they were in breach of their ethical code. A doctor is obliged to practise in the best interests of the patient, not of the doctor. If the doctor carried out treatment for legal rather than medical reasons he or she could be in serious trouble with the General Medical Council (see Chapter 10).

Furthermore, far from protecting from litigation, defensive medicine could itself lead to litigation. If, for example, something unavoidable went wrong during a caesarean or a patient had an adverse reaction to a drug, and it could be shown that the doctor had carried out the operation or dispensed the drug for legal rather than medical considerations, a claim could well lie where it otherwise would not have done because, save for operating or prescribing a drug when the clinical indications did not require such action, the doctor had not in fact been negligent.[4]

In fact the issue of defensive medicine has turned out to be a myth rather than a reality; a concept, like so many other concepts in this area of the law, imported from the USA in which country it may or may not be more of a reality. The truth is that not only

[4]For an article illustrating this see: Defensive Medicine: Myths and Facts: Jones and Morris, Journal of the MDU, Vol 5, Summer 1989.

has research shown that doctors are not affected to a great extent by the fear of litigation in taking clinical decisions, but even the claim that they do is virtually no longer being made. That may have something to do with the fact that insofar as NHS hospital doctors (who represent the vast majority of doctors subject to medical negligence claims) are concerned, they are no longer in the immediate firing line nor liable to the massive increases in payments to the defence organisations.

NHS (Crown) indemnity

This results from the circular HC[89]34 which provided that as from 1st April 1990 the Trusts would be liable to indemnify any doctor employed by them who was required to pay compensation to a patient as a result of negligence in the course of the treatment of the patient. Accordingly the responsibility for handling and funding existing and future claims, arising from the acts or omissions of hospital or community medical or dental staff in the course of their NHS employment, passed from the medical defence organisations to Health Authorities and Trusts. This was (and sometimes still is) wrongly called Crown Indemnity but is in fact NHS indemnity. The result is that NHS hospital doctors are no longer personally liable to pay the compensation but it is payable by the Trust or Health Authority which employs them.

They therefore do not have to look to their defence organisations for indemnity although they are still entitled, and are well advised, to seek advice from those organisations. The defence organisations still cover general practitioners as well as other doctors in respect of their private work. Accordingly the defence organisations do not have anywhere near the same call on their resources and as a result there has not been the same pressure on doctors' contributions to those organisations. Interestingly, following the reduction in that pressure there has been far less talk from the doctors or their leaders about defensive medicine.

The Clinical Negligence Scheme for Trusts

Once the Trusts became liable to meet all claims arising out of the negligence of doctors employed by them it was clear that they would become subject to the same financial pressures as those previously suffered by the doctors and their defence organisations. A number of substantial pay-outs in close proximity could wreak havoc with a Trust budget.

Indeed, it was not uncommon to see Trust managers complaining that because patients were securing large awards against a Trust they were responsible for the closure of wards.

This attitude was even worse than the defensive medicine claims prevalent under the previous system and did sometimes have the effect, which appeared to be sought by the managers, of discouraging injured patients with bona fide claims and substantial needs from taking legal proceedings.

In order to assist the Trusts the Clinical Negligence Scheme for Trusts (CNST) was established in 1990[1]. Under this scheme Trusts who join make regular payments, based on their record of claims, into a central fund and claims against them relating to incidents which occurred on or after the 1st April 1995 are then met from that fund. It is not an insurance scheme but simply a method by which payments are spread over a regular period so that Trusts can better plan their budgets.

There are other important facets of the scheme not the least of which is that the scheme insists on the Trusts instituting risk management systems which hopefully will reduce the level of avoidable accidents.

The National Health Service Litigation Authority

The CNST is administered by a special Health Authority which was set up by the Act, the National Health Service Litigation Authority (NHSLA). In addition to administering the CNST the NHSLA also administers the scheme which has been set up to meet claims arising before 1st April 1995. That scheme, known as the Existing Liabilities Scheme (ELS) (8 See FDL[95]56 and EL[96]11) is funded by a central levy on Health Authorities. Under the scheme the Trust or other body meets the first £10,000 and 20% between £10,000 and £500,000 and the remainder is met entirely by the fund.

The NHSLA has overall control over how claims against both these funds are handled. It lays down strict requirements. It will only make payment if three conditions are met:

- it is informed about the claim when it is made;
- its views on handling the claim must be taken into account;
- any offer to settle is approved by it.

It will be seen, therefore, that for the first time there is one body which has an overall view and can control how claims against NHS hospitals are handled. This could have a major effect on the way such claims are dealt with.

Lord Woolf's inquiry

The other major influence on the conduct of medical negligence litigation in recent times has of course been Lord Woolf's report.

It has already been mentioned that Lord Woolf in his report finally identified medical negligence as a discrete speciality. Sarah Leigh in her chapter deals with the inquiry and the report in detail. As at the time of writing the detail of the rules to cover medical negligence are by no means clear. Nevertheless, even the proposals that were made are having an effect.

Case management

The objective of the report is to make the litigation more open, quicker and cheaper. Because lawyers are notoriously conservative there is a danger that whatever rules are made in order to try and achieve these objectives, they will try to find ways around them so as to maintain the procedures to which they are used. For this reason a major plank in the Woolf reforms is case management by the court itself. This means that the court will oversee how the case progresses and will be in a position to regulate such progress in such a way as to ensure that delay and cost are reduced.

The changes discussed above have transformed the scene in medical negligence litigation. To date all have improved the situation for those seeking compensation for a medical accident. Insofar as Lord Woolf's reforms are concerned they have the potential to make even more dramatic improvements. That is dependent, however, largely on whether adequate resources are invested, in order to make them work. Otherwise the short cuts which could result will simply lead to time and costs being saved at the expense of a thorough investigation. Accordingly, whilst the courts and the legal system may be made more accessible, justice may not.

Whilst strict rules governing the conduct of litigation can help the litigants to some extent they will always suffer from two defects in this particular litigation. In the first place the spirit of the implementation of the rules is often far more important than the letter. So, for example, whilst a strict rule can require particular evidence to be disclosed by a certain date, total inflexibility could mean that obviously vital evidence is excluded simply because of bureaucratic requirements. This could lead to great injustice and hardship. There will therefore always be scope for manipulation of the rules by the parties. The second defeat is that the rules can deal only with the position once litigation has begun. Insofar as medical accidents are concerned many disputes should never find their way to litigation and it is in the interests of all parties that litigation is avoided. That can only be achieved by cooperation between the parties and their representatives.

The Clinical Disputes Forum

One of the more important aspects of the Woolf inquiry was the way in which all parties interested in the issue of compensation for medical accidents were persuaded to get together to consider the issues. For those who were brought up in the old tradition where defendants and plaintiffs, and their representatives, were as adversarial and difficult towards one another as possible, this cooperation was both startling and gratifying. In order to continue that cooperation following the publication of the Woolf report, the Clinical Disputes Forum (CDF) was established.

Comprising the same people who were involved in the medical negligence side of the Woolf inquiry, its object is both to work out procedures for resolving disputes without recourse to litigation and to ensure that when litigation does take place it is conducted in a cooperative manner and in the interests of both sides.

It has, for example, produced a protocol which, by requiring the mutual disclosure of information at the earliest possible time, could lead to unmeritorious claims not being brought or unmeritorious defences not being maintained; it will look at the extent to which compensation could be incorporated in the NHS complaints procedure; and it is looking at the relevance of mediation to medical negligence disputes.

Mediation

Mediation has been defined as a facilitative process in which disputing parties engage the assistance of a neutral third party who acts as a mediator in their dispute. The neutral has no authority to make any decisions which are binding on them, but uses certain procedures, techniques and skills to help them to negotiate a resolution of their dispute by agreement without adjudication. The idea is extremely attractive in principle and mediation has been shown to work in many kinds of dispute, particularly family and commercial. For medical negligence the idea has special attraction in its ability to reduce confrontation, deal with other issues between the parties such as the doctor patient relationship and result in a "win-win" situation which must be to the advantage of all parties.

Whether mediation can be applied fairly to medical disputes is another matter. One of the major objections is the discrepancy in the position of the defendant, who has all the information and medical skills, and that of the plaintiff who is entirely dependent on his or her experts whether legal or medical.

In order to evaluate the suitability of medical negligence for mediation the DoH set up a pilot scheme in two Health Regions. That pilot will be academically evaluated during 1998 and will be crucial in enabling Trusts and other healthcare providers as well as patients to decide whether mediation is to play a major role in resolving clinical disputes.

At the end of the day, whatever cooperation is developed, however user-friendly litigation does or does not become, and whatever alternative schemes are developed, the courts are going to remain a major recourse for those seeking compensation. The following chapters are intended to give a greater understanding of how the law and the courts operate.

Chapter 15

THE LAW AND MEDICAL NEGLIGENCE

Simeon Maskrey QC and Paula Sparks

This chapter explains the legal requirements necessary to prove medical negligence and explains some of the terms used by lawyers.

INTRODUCTION

A medical negligence action is a claim for compensation. It is brought when a person has suffered injury as a result of doctors, nurses or other medical staff doing something they should not have done or failing to do something that they should have done.

It is important for potential claimants to understand what a medical negligence action is not. It is not a mechanism designed to punish or discipline the doctor or nurse who did something wrong. It is not a means to bring a change in hospital practices – although it may incidentally have that result. It is not a way of bringing about an apology or a public acceptance that something went wrong. Except in very limited circumstances it cannot be used to compensate for worry, distress, grief, humiliation or injured feelings.

A medical negligence action is concerned about *compensation* for *injury*, brought about by someone else's *negligence*. Let us look at each of those emphasised words before we consider the legal principles that go to make up a medical negligence action.

Compensation

This means money; it is also called by lawyers 'damages'. Thus, if one is looking for compensation one is looking for 'damages'.

Injury

This means physical or psychiatric injury and any financial loss that is brought about by the physical or psychiatric injury. Hurt feelings do not amount to an injury. Distress does not amount to an injury. There has to be an identifiable bodily injury or a recognisable psychiatric injury before compensation can be obtained. Note that the financial loss has to be caused by the injury before it will result in compensation. If a hospital mixes up some admission dates so that a patient's operation is cancelled at the last minute and it costs that patient £100 in lost wages, he or she cannot claim compensation in a medical negligence action. That is because the financial loss was not brought about by any injury that the patient suffered. On the other hand, if the patient was left unable to work because the hospital staff wrongly amputated his or her leg, he or she would be able to claim compensation for his or her lost wages.

Negligence

This is the most difficult concept of all; put very broadly it means that the doctor, nurse or hospital concerned must be shown to have acted in a way that a reputable, reasonable doctor or nurse would regard as incompetent. There is no need to show that the doctor deliberately injured a patient. Equally it is not enough to show that the doctor simply made a mistake. What must be proven is that it was a mistake that no responsible doctor or nurse would have made.

The basis of a medical negligence action

In summary, in a medical negligence action a plaintiff is seeking damages (compensation) for personal injury loss and damage (injury) arising from the negligence of a doctor, a nurse or a hospital authority.

PARTIES TO THE ACTION

Adversarial system

In England and Wales, there is what is termed an 'adversarial system'. All that means is that there are two sides pitched against each other, the plaintiff and the defendant.

The plaintiff

The person who has been injured and who is bringing the action (otherwise known as the claim) is called the plaintiff. There may be more than one plaintiff in an action. For example, if both mother and baby were injured during delivery, there would be two plaintiffs.

The defendant

The defendant is the person who it is alleged caused the injury by acting wrongfully or the NHS Trust or other legal entity responsible for that person.

It is usual to bring the action against the legal entity responsible for the doctors and nurses, e.g. the Trust, rather than the doctors and nurses themselves.

More than one defendant

There can be more than one defendant just as there can be more than one plaintiff. Thus, if it is said that a GP and two hospital doctors made mistakes and that the combined effect of those mistakes was to cause the plaintiff injury, the claim for compensation would be against the GP (the first defendant) and the NHS Trust responsible for the hospital doctors (the second defendant).

THE ELEMENTS OF NEGLIGENCE

There are a number of essential elements in any negligence action. The plaintiff must prove:

- the defendant owed him a duty of care;
- that the defendant was in breach of that duty of care;
- that this breach caused the plaintiff injury; and
- the consequences and effect of the injury on the plaintiff.

Let us take each of those elements in turn.

DUTY OF CARE

Not everyone has a responsibility in law towards everyone else. A driver has a legal responsibility to other road users, but a bystander has no legal responsibility to a distressed swimmer in a lake. As the driver has a legal responsibility, he or she must exercise reasonable care for the other road users. It is this responsibility in law that is known as the duty of care.

Limits on the duty of care

It may seem obvious that a doctor owes a duty to those under his care. But there are limits to that duty. The doctor does not owe a duty to the employers of the patient or to the patient's friends or (except in limited circumstances) to the patient's relatives. Therefore although the doctor may negligently injure a valued employee, and although as a consequence of that injury the employer is unable to fulfil a contract and loses money, the employer cannot sue the doctor for compensation. This is because the doctor did not owe the employer a duty of care, only the patient. In an ordinary medical negligence action where a plaintiff has come under the care of a GP or hospital doctor there will be no difficulty in establishing that that GP or hospital doctor owed a duty of care.

BREACH OF DUTY

Breach of duty or 'negligence'

A breach of duty is also known by lawyers as 'negligence'. There is no precise definition of breach of duty of care; each case will be decided on its facts.

The 'Bolam test'

The most often quoted description of the breach of duty was given in 1957 in a case called *Bolam v Friern Management Committee* where the judge set out what was required to prove a breach of duty. It is worth reciting here a little of what he said:

> 'In the ordinary case which does not involve any special skill, negligence in law means this: some failure to do some act which a reasonable man in the circumstances would do, or doing some act which a reasonable man in the circumstances would not do: and if that failure or doing of that act results in injury, then there is a cause of action . . . [W]here you get a situation which involves the use of some special skill or competence, then . . . the test is the standard of the ordinary skilled man exercising and professing to have that special skill. A man need not possess the highest expert skill at the risk of being found negligent . . . It is sufficient if he exercises the ordinary skill of an ordinary competent man exercising that particular art.'

The judge then went on to consider what should happen where a doctor carried out a procedure that some members of his profession considered to be appropriate and others considered to be inappropriate. He said this:

> 'A doctor is not guilty of negligence if he has acted in accordance with a practice accepted as proper by a *responsible body of medical*

men skilled in that particular art . . . Putting it the other way round, a doctor is not negligent, if he is acting in accordance with such a practice, merely because there is a body of opinion that takes a contrary view.'

Responsible body of medical opinion

From these remarks, it is possible to distil what is meant by a breach of duty (otherwise known as negligence).

- The doctor has to exercise the skill of the competent man exercising that particular art. Therefore we do not judge the GP by the standards of the consultant neurologist. We do not say that the GP was negligent or in breach of duty in failing to diagnose meningitis simply because a consultant neurologist in the same circumstances would have found no difficulty in doing so. We judge the GP by the standards of an ordinary competent GP exercising the skills to be expected of a GP. The GP is not expected to have and will not have the specialist knowledge of the consultant neurologist.
- The doctor must exercise the ordinary skill of the ordinary competent man. That means that he is not expected to act in accordance with the standards of those pre-eminent in that field. The standard to be expected of a consultant neurologist is that of the ordinary competent neurologist, not the standard of the leading neurologists in the best teaching hospitals.
- When assessing whether the doctor has exercised the ordinary skill of the ordinary competent man exercising that particular art account must be taken of his or her level of training or expertise. We expect the junior doctor to exercise the ordinary skill of the ordinary junior doctor in the particular speciality under consideration.
- There will be times when a doctor has performed an operation or procedure in a way that is regarded as wrong by many others who have his or her knowledge, expertise and seniority. That is not enough to establish a breach of duty and thus negligence if there also exists a responsible body of professional opinion that would regard what the doctor did as correct even if that body of opinion amounts to a minority of the profession.

It is not enough for a doctor to come to court with one or two others and to say 'they would have done what I did' and expect to be acquitted of negligence. If a small group of doctors favoured a particular procedure in the face of contrary literature and research, guidelines from the Royal Colleges and the opinion of the overwhelming majority of their fellow doctors, it is unlikely that a court would regard that group as a "responsible body" of opinion.

BREACH OF DUTY WHICH LEADS TO THE PHYSICAL OR PSYCHOLOGICAL INJURIES (CAUSATION)

There are many cases where a doctor may have been in breach of duty but the breach did not cause any injury. The GP who negligently fails to examine a patient who dies 24 hours later will not be held liable to pay compensation if the patient would have died in any event. The hospital doctor who fails to diagnose meningitis will not be held liable to pay compensation if the correct diagnosis was made later by somebody else and no adverse consequences followed from the breach of duty. The plaintiff must always prove that it is more likely than not that the injury was caused by the breach of duty.

Potential plaintiffs often find it hard to come to terms with the fact that a doctor may have been in serious dereliction of his or her duty and yet it may have made no difference to the eventual outcome.

It is not enough for the plaintiff to prove that the breach of duty increased the chance of some adverse result occurring. In *Hotson v Fitzgerald* [1985], the Judicial Committee of the House of Lords decided that where a plaintiff had a 75% chance of the bone in his hip dying because of an accident, but the negligence of the doctors turned that 75% chance into a certainty, the plaintiff was not entitled to compensation. The reason was because it was more likely than not that the bone would have died in any event. Therefore it was more likely than not that the negligence of the doctors did not make any difference to the eventual outcome of the case. Therefore on a balance of probabilities the negligence of the doctors did not cause the plaintiff any injury. The trial judge, who had wanted to give the plaintiff 25% of the compensation he would have received had the negligence of the doctors been the sole cause of the bone dying, was found to have been wrong.

The plaintiff must show that the acts or omissions resulting in the breach of duty caused or materially contributed to the outcome.

INJURY

So the breach of duty must cause injury.

It must be reasonably foreseeable that the breach of duty could cause some sort of injury, although it is unnecessary for the precise form of the injury to be foreseeable.

Injury may mean a worsening of a condition or a failure to recover from a condition that previously existed. There is no need to prove that the negligence of the doctor made a patient worse, if the whole idea of the treatment was to make him or her better and he or she would have been made better had it been properly carried out.

Injury includes death. If patients die as a result of medical negligence their estate and their dependants can bring an action for compensation. Whilst their dependants have not themselves suffered an injury they may have suffered financial loss as a result of the death. They can be compensated for that financial loss. In addition, Parliament has decided that certain relatives (a wife or husband or the parents of a child under the age of 18) can receive £7,500 compensation for bereavement. That is an exception to the general rule that a plaintiff cannot have compensation for grief or injured feelings.

Effect of the injury

Once it has been proved that the patient has suffered an injury as a result of the breach of duty by the doctor or nurse the plaintiff is said to have proved liability. That means that he or she is entitled to compensation. How this is calculated is fully explained in Chapters 19 and 20.

Contributory negligence

There may be occasions where a defendant will argue that the plaintiff contributed in some way through his or her own negligence towards the injury he or she has sustained, in other words there was contributory negligence. In these circumstances, the defendant has the burden of proving the plaintiff's negligence. In medical cases this may arise where, for example, a patient fails to follow the doctor's instructions or to re-visit a GP following a worsening of symptoms. The effect of a finding of contributory negligence may be to reduce compensation. Thus, if the injury is due to the negligence of the doctor and the negligence of the patient in equal proportions, compensation will be reduced by half.

THE BURDEN AND STANDARD OF PROOF

It has to be emphasised that it is for the plaintiff to prove what happened, how it happened and what effect it had upon him or her. That may seem unfair, especially as in many medical negligence actions the plaintiff will not have the first idea of what occurred because e.g. she was under a general anaesthetic at the time.

Balance of probabilities

When a fact is in dispute or when a plaintiff is trying to establish what would or would not have occurred but for the negligence of the doctor, nurse or hospital it is necessary to prove the fact or the event upon 'a balance of probabilities' i.e. it is more likely to have occurred than not. The plaintiff does not have to prove that the doctor did inject the wrong drug; only that it is more likely than not that he or she injected the wrong drug. And the plaintiff does not have to prove that the injection of the wrong drug did cause the injury alleged, only that it is more likely than not that it caused or materially contributed to the injury alleged.

THE DECISION TO PURSUE A MEDICAL NEGLIGENCE ACTION

The decision to bring a medical negligence action is not one that should be taken lightly. It is expensive, time consuming and imposes a terrible strain upon all of the participants. If the case is contested, it may take years before it comes on for trial. At court the plaintiff will have to give evidence in public, and the case may be reported in the press. To lose may have devastating personal and financial consequences on the plaintiff. It follows that action should only be brought if the plaintiff is committed to the case, understands what it entails and is prepared to suffer the consequences of losing. It should only be brought when there is clear evidence of a breach of duty causing injury. And it should only be brought if the size of the award that may be made justifies the risk of losing and the time and emotional commitment that will be required.

CONCLUSION

Important points to be remembered

- The plaintiff must prove the case on (the balance of probabilities) in that it is more likely than not that each important fact, event or consequence occurred.
- Poor note keeping by a doctor may make the plaintiff's job of proving the case difficult or even impossible. Proof that the note keeping was of a poor standard does not amount to proof that the doctor caused the injury.
- The plaintiff must prove that there was a breach of duty. Not every mistake amounts to a breach of duty. The plaintiff must prove that the doctor acted in a way that could not be supported by any responsible body of medical opinion.
- The plaintiff must prove that the breach of duty caused him or her to suffer a physical or psychiatric injury.
- The plaintiff must prove the consequences of the injury and that the *type* of injury was foreseeable.
- The plaintiff must prove that any financial loss as a result of the injury was foreseeable.
- The plaintiff must be committed to overcoming the risks and stresses imposed by legal action.

Chapter 16

UNDERSTANDING THE ENGLISH LEGAL SYSTEM

Paula Sparks and Liz Thomas

In this chapter we shall look at the legal system – how the courts operate and the role of the people, such as judges and lawyers, who are usually closely involved in the process. We shall also look at the way in which law is made and the legal principles upon which the claims are founded.

INTRODUCTION TO ENGLISH LAW

Civil and criminal law

There are two main branches of law in this country: civil and criminal. Criminal law is essentially concerned with wrongs committed by individuals which may result in punishment by the State whereas civil law concerns wrongs between individuals that may result in compensation. It is possible that an incident will give rise both to a criminal prosecution by the State and a claim in medical negligence by the injured individual.

Medical negligence cases in civil law are usually based in the law of negligence dealing with the duty of care between the doctor and the patient, or contract where there is a private agreement between the doctor and the patient. Other civil wrongs such as assault and battery are sometimes relevant to medical cases. These 'wrongs' are called torts by the lawyers.

There are also other civil laws dealing with relationships between companies, transfer of property, taxation and so forth which it is not necessary to cover in this chapter.

CIVIL LAW

Tort

A 'tort' is a civil wrong (as opposed to criminal) committed by one party against another and for which the injured party may claim compensation.

Negligence

Negligence is the tort most commonly applied in medical cases where it is alleged there has been poor medical care. To establish a claim under the tort of negligence, it is necessary to show that there has been a breach of a duty owed to an individual which has resulted in an injury or loss. (See Chapter 15)

Contract law and NHS patients

A contract is an agreement between two or more parties which is enforceable under the law and which creates binding responsibilities. With respect to medical negligence actions, as there is no direct financial relationship between the *patient and the NHS*, there is not considered to be a contractual relationship. It is therefore not possible to bring a claim for 'breach of contract' in respect of the provision of medical services or lack of care where the patient was being treated under the NHS.

Contract law and private patients

However, there is a contractual relationship between private patients and their medical carers. Private patients may be able to sue concurrently in both tort and contract. For practical purposes however the duty owed by doctors to use reasonable care and skill by virtue of the contract with their client will usually be identical to the duty of care owed in tort.

THE DEVELOPMENT OF ENGLISH LAW

Both civil and criminal law have developed over many centuries from two main sources:

- common law;
- statute law.

There are two other sources of law, equity and European law, but these are outside the scope of the current discussion.

COMMON LAW

Common law[1] is the body of law which has developed as a result of decisions made by judges (judicial decisions) in numerous cases over many centuries. These decisions, referred to as case law or precedents, have provided a legal framework for deciding other cases. Common law is continually being developed and refined as new cases come under consideration by the courts.

Judicial precedent

Common law (or case law) is based on precedent. A precedent is a previous decision made by a judge which sets out a principle binding on another court deciding on a similar case. The court system is a hierarchical structure – County Court, High Court, Court of Appeal and House of Lords. Judicial precedent works on the basis that lower courts are bound by (i.e. must be in accordance with) the decisions of higher courts. Thus High Court and County Court judges are bound by decisions made in the Court of Appeal and Court of Appeal judges are bound by the decisions made by the House of Lords.

Legal principle – *'ratio decidendi'*

Judges only have to follow the legal principle (*ratio decidendi*) established in a case. All other matters referred to in the judge's decision (perhaps relating to the individual facts of the case) are non-binding and so cases which are factually very similar may result in quite different decisions in law. This could mean, for example, that a legal precedent established in a case where the injured party was unsuccessful in his or her claim could be subsequently employed in a case resulting in a successful action on the part of the injured party and vice versa.

Decisions made by foreign courts

English courts can also refer to decisions made by judges in other countries which have a comparable 'common law' system (e.g. Hong Kong, Canada, Australia, New Zealand, some States in USA). Although these decisions are of a general persuasive value only and do not bind the English courts.

Some areas of law are made up almost entirely of common law (case law) as opposed to statute law. Medical negligence is one of

[1]The origins of the term 'common law' date back to the twelfth century when the process began of bringing together all the locally held customary laws and rules and creating a unified body of law – the common law – which would apply throughout the land.

these areas. Thus, one of the main principles of medical negligence law – the standard of care to be adopted by the courts – is primarily based on the judge's ruling in the case of *Bolam v Friern Barnet Management Committee*. (See page 216)

Recording the judicial decisions

A legal system based on precedent (case law) obviously relies on cases being reported. A formal system for reporting cases was first instituted in 1870 with the creation of the Incorporated Council of Law Reporting for England and Wales which led to the publication of the Law Reports. Whilst cases are reported in other publications, the Law Reports are still considered the most authoritative. The development of computer databases now makes it much easier for lawyers to access relevant precedents (authorities).

STATUTE LAW

Statute law is law that has been created as a result of legislation passed by Parliament. This legislation is contained within formal documents, known as statutes or Acts of Parliament. A statute (Act) represents the ultimate source of law in that if it conflicts with common law, the law contained within the statute prevails. Even if a judge thinks that a particular statute is unfair he or she is powerless to change it. The only way of changing the law made by Parliament is for Parliament to enact new legislation. Parliament makes lots of new laws each year. It can also repeal (abolish) laws and can overturn common law, even though it may have been established for centuries.

Delegated legislation – statutory instruments

When new statutes are created, they often require a considerable amount of fine-tuning in the form of detailed regulations in order to implement them. The details of an Act are often left to other bodies to complete, such as government departments. The regulations that accompany an Act, known as 'statutory instruments', have the same legal standing as the original statute and are referred to as delegated (or subordinate) legislation.

Judicial interpretation

Judges also have an important role in interpreting how statute law should be applied by the decisions they reach in individual cases. Such decisions may create new legal precedents which will then dictate how an Act will be applied in future cases.

JUDICIAL REVIEW

Judicial review is a process by which the courts can exercise a supervisory role over inferior courts, tribunals or other bodies or individuals who are responsible by statute for performing public duties or acts. Judicial review can be used by individuals to challenge decisions of bodies such as Health Authorities, Coroner's Courts, education authorities, the General Medical Council, tribunals, etc., as well as challenging delegated legislation (regulations).

The grounds for Judicially reviewing a decision (or act) broadly fall within the following categories:

- procedural irregularity in the way in which a decision was arrived at;
- the public authority acted in a way that went beyond the power of that which was authorised ('ultra vires');
- it conflicts with UK or EC legislation;
- was so unreasonable that no reasonable body would have made it.

Judicial review has been used to challenge decisions relating to allocation of resources by patients trying to secure health care for themselves or their relatives. In one case, for example, the parents of a child with a life threatening condition argued unsuccessfully that the Secretary of State was in breach of her duty to provide health care by not providing resources for a life saving operation. The decision not to allow the parents in that case to proceed reflects the general reluctance of the courts to interfere with allocation of resources in the Health Service.

Before an application can be made for Judicial review, leave must be obtained from a judge within three months of the event that is to be challenged under Judicial review. A person making an application for Judicial review must be seen to have appropriate interest in the action ('locus standi'). If a Judicial review is granted the court has a number of remedies available to it:

- quash the decision under review ('*certiorari*') and require the public body or inferior court to reconsider the decision in a lawful manner (even though this may result in the same decision being arrived at);
- prevent a public body from making an unlawful decision ('prohibition');
- force a public body to act in accordance with its statutory duties ('mandamus');
- grant an injunction either preventing a public body from taking certain action or requiring certain action to be taken ('injunction');
- make a declaration which formally states the rights of an individual under the law;
- award damages in certain circumstances.

THE LAW IN PRACTICE

It can be seen that the law governing a particular situation or dispute may arise from both statute and common law and depending on whether a crime has been committed, will be dealt with in either the criminal or civil courts. Medical negligence is normally dealt with in the civil courts under the tort of negligence (and in certain circumstances, trespass) but there will be exceptional cases, where the actions of an individual or individuals breach criminal law and may therefore also give rise to criminal proceedings in the criminal courts.

Court structure

Which court hears a dispute depends upon the type of law under which the dispute is to be determined, the seriousness of the case and the geographical location of the parties.

Civil Proceedings

Civil actions (claims) are commenced either in the County Court or High Court.

County Courts

County Courts are local courts designed to be easily accessible to the public and with less technical rules of procedure. In fact their rules have become very complicated over time and so efforts are currently being made to simplify the procedure and to give more help to litigants (the parties to an action). There will be a County Court in every large town and city in the country.

Medical negligence actions

County courts will try all medical negligence actions where the compensation claimed is below £25,000 except where the issues involved are particularly complicated. They are allowed to deal with actions where the compensation claimed exceeds £25,000 although the larger the claim or the more complicated the issues involved the less likely it is that the County Court will be appropriate. Actions valued at £50,000 or less must be started in the County Court although they may be transferred to the High Court if at a later stage it is felt that they involve complicated issues and that this would be more appropriate.

The High Court

The High Court deals with the most serious and complicated claims. Its work is divided into three divisions: Queen's Bench, Chancery and Family. Medical negligence claims are heard in the Queen's Bench division. There is a High Court in the major cities in England and Wales. However, a High Court judge is not always available to try claims for compensation in these major cities and accordingly many litigants opt to have their cases tried in London.

CRIMINAL PROCEEDINGS

Criminal cases, which are concerned primarily with punishment rather than compensation, are heard in criminal courts. The criminal courts are the Magistrates' Courts and Crown Courts.

Magistrates' Courts

The Magistrates' Courts hear cases which involve less serious allegations although all criminal cases must start in the magistrates' court even if they are to be heard in the Crown Court. It would be very unusual for a case involving allegations of a crime committed in the course of medical treatment to be brought in a Magistrates' Court as these types of allegations are regarded as very serious. Certain civil actions are also heard in the Magistrates' Court including matrimonial and family matters.

Crown Courts

These more serious criminal cases will be brought in the Crown Courts. Chapter 11 looks in more detail at the sort of behaviour which may result in a criminal prosecution being brought against medical professionals.

HOW COURTS DECIDE ON CASES

Adversarial system

In England and Wales, we have what is termed an 'adversarial system'. That essentially means that there are two sides set up against each other. In civil cases the two opposing sides will be the plaintiff (the injured party) and the defendant (the offending party) and in criminal cases, the prosecutor (acting for the Crown) and the accused. Each party is responsible for preparing its side of the case – finding witnesses and gathering evidence to support its case.

Court Procedures – White Book & Green Book

The rules governing High Court procedures are set out in the publication, 'The Supreme Court Practice', otherwise known as the 'White Book', and for County Court procedures in 'The County Court Practice', otherwise known as the 'Green Book'.

Trial

If the two sides cannot reach agreement between themselves to settle the dispute, then the case will be heard before a judge (and where appropriate jury) at trial. Most civil cases, and all medical negligence cases, will be heard by a judge alone whereas all defendants to an allegation of criminal misconduct have the right to a jury trial. A jury will only be called (empanelled) for a small pre-defined category of civil actions.

The judge (and jury) will hear both sides and then pass judgment or arrive at a verdict (jury).

All trials are conducted in public. Except in the rarest of cases the press will have free access to the proceedings and will be able to publish what goes on.

JUDGES

Law Lords

The most senior judges are those who sit in the Appeal Courts. They are either Law Lords or are Knights (or Dames).

High Court judges

The High Court judges who try the most complicated and serious cases are also Knights. They are referred to in Court as 'my Lord'/'my Lady' and in the newspapers as 'Mr Justice X'.

Circuit judges

In the County Court judges are known as Circuit judges and are referred to as 'your honour'. They are not usually Knights.

District judges/ Masters

Procedural and pre-trial management of cases are dealt with by District Judges who are referred to as 'Sir' or 'Madam'. In the Royal Courts of Justice London pre-trial judges are known as Masters. Both District Judges and Masters are solicitors or barristers of at least seven years' standing.

Criminal cases

Judges who sit in the Crown Court will either be High Court judges for the very serious cases (such as murder) or Circuit judges. Some part time judges deal with less serious cases. They are known as Assistant Recorders.

APPEALS

There is a right of appeal from both the civil and criminal courts to the Court of Appeal: the Criminal Division for criminal cases and the Civil Division for civil cases.

Court of Appeal

Appeals from the High Court or the County Court will be made to the Civil Division of the Court of Appeal which is headed by the Master of the Rolls.

Where the law is uncertain or leaves a gap, appeals may be allowed to the appeal judges. At the Court of Appeal the judges rely upon the court transcript, any documents and legal argument from barristers. They will only hear live witnesses in certain exceptional circumstances.

House of Lords

Exceptionally, an appeal may be made from the Court of Appeal to the House of Lords. The formal title for judges who sit in the House of Lords is Lord of Appeal in Ordinary. More commonly however they are known as Law Lords. The Lords sit in a panel (usually) of five in the common rooms of the House of Lords to hear appeals which are based upon the arguments of the barristers. The Lords do not deliver a judgment as in the other courts, their opinion is set out in speeches which they make in the House of Lords which has special sittings for this purpose. A vote is taken on whether or not the appeal should be allowed.

EUROPEAN COURT OF HUMAN RIGHTS

If an appellant is unsuccessful in the House of Lords there is only one other avenue of appeal. It is very rarely invoked because of the very narrow grounds on which an appeal may be based. This is an appeal to The European Court of Human Rights based in Strasbourg. It deals solely with issues of human rights and few cases fall within its remit to consider alleged breaches of the European Convention of Human Rights. Furthermore, before an appeal can be made to the Court all domestic remedies should have been exhausted. In practice this means that all rights of appeal must be exercised before an application can be made.

Civil Court Structure in England and Wales

↑

European Court of Justice

↑

House of Lords

↑

Court of Appeal
(Civil Division)

↗ ↖

County Court
(Cases worth under £25,000)

High Court
(Cases worth more than £50,000)

OTHER TYPES OF COURTS

Coroner's Courts

The job of the Coroner's Court is to investigate sudden or unexpected deaths where the cause of death is unknown or occurred in suspicious or violent circumstances. Coroner's Courts are presided over by a Coroner and are inquisitorial as opposed to adversarial. Details of how Coroner's Courts operate can be found in Chapter 13.

Tribunals

These are described as 'administrative courts'. Tribunals function in a similar way to a court but specialise in certain types of disputes e.g. industrial tribunals, rent tribunals, social security tribunals, etc. Tribunals deal with disputes between individuals and the State, as well as certain types of disputes between individuals.

Alternative Dispute Resolution (ADR)

This refers to alternative methods of resolving disputes on a non-adversarial basis and thereby avoiding the excessive costs involved, both personal and financial, of taking a matter to court. ADR schemes involve a third party acting as a neutral mediator or conciliator between the two parties with the aim of facilitating dispute resolution between the parties. If the parties are unable to reach agreement, then it is open to them to seek resolution through the courts. Pilot mediation schemes for dealing with medical negligence disputes have already been in operation.

Arbitration

Arbitration is another alternative to court proceedings and is generally used in commercial disputes. Proceedings are held in private and the person conducting the proceedings, the arbitrator, usually has a specialist knowledge of the subject matter under dispute. Only if both parties agree will a dispute be resolved through arbitration. The arbitrator will listen to both parties and then arrive at a decision, whereas in mediation it is up to the parties to reach their own decision. In addition, the decision or award of the arbitrator is enforceable through the courts.

LAWYERS

Bringing a medical negligence action makes contact with lawyers inevitable. That will either be because the plaintiff has a lawyer to act for him or her, or because the defendant does. Defendants will almost invariably have a lawyer and only in very exceptional cases would a plaintiff proceed with a medical negligence action without legal assistance.

The legal profession in England has two main branches: solicitors and barristers.

Solicitors

The solicitor is usually the first lawyer that a client will have contact with. The solicitor's function is to investigate the case and prepare it for trial. In some cases, the solicitor may conduct the trial, especially if it is in the County Court. In medical negligence cases it would be more usual for a barrister to be instructed. The solicitor will be in overall control of the conduct of the case (e.g. he or she will instruct the experts and the barrister etc.).

In England and Wales there are in the region 70,000 solicitors in practice. Solicitors are governed by the Law Society which imposes certain rules and standards of conduct. Before a solicitor can practise, he or she must obtain a valid practising certificate from the Law Society.

Most solicitors have very general practices. Like family doctors, they tend to deal with the whole range of problems that people bring to them, from conveyancing to crime. There are only a relatively small number of solicitors who have specialist practices where they deal almost exclusively with one area of the law. There is however increasing pressure for solicitors (and barristers) to become more specialist in response to the increasing complexities of the law.

Medical negligence is a notable example of an area of the law where specialist expertise is essential. Anyone considering pursuing a medical negligence action would be well advised to seek out an experienced medical negligence solicitor rather than risk going to a non-specialist solicitor. Details of medical negligence specialists can be obtained from AVMA who can also advise on other aspects of the case, or a list of the members of the Law Society's Medical Negligence Panel Solicitors can be obtained from the Law Society.

Legal executives

Many firms employ legal executives as well as solicitors. Legal executives are less qualified than solicitors and in theory carry out some of the more mundane day to day work on cases under the supervision of a solicitor. However, legal executives tend to specialise in particular areas of the law and as a result, some legal executives can develop a special expertise. In effect they may in fact be far more competent than some of their solicitor colleagues in a particular area. There are some legal executives who specialise in medical negligence. One of the main restrictions on the work carried out by a legal executive is in relation to his or her right of audience in court which prevents a legal executive from conducting a trial.

Barristers

The role of the barrister is to conduct cases in court, provide opinions on difficult legal problems, advise on the conduct of a case and to prepare the formal documents ('draft the pleadings') necessary to bring a case to trial. Barristers are referred to as

'Counsel' when appearing in court or providing advice to clients. They practise from 'chambers' (sets of chambers) – the term used both to describe the offices occupied by a barrister or group of barristers and to describe a group of barristers practising from a set of chambers. Barristers work independently of one another, meaning that barristers from the same set of chambers may act on opposite sides in the same case. The barristers working within a set of chambers will between them employ clerical staff and a clerk. The clerk is responsible for managing the chambers and dealing with solicitors.

The barristers' governing body is the Bar Council (General Council of the Bar) which is responsible for setting professional standards. Barristers should not take on work which they are not competent to handle. They are however expected to abide by the 'cab rank' rule which means that they should accept instructions on a case even if it goes against their own beliefs or involves a client or a matter which they would prefer not to deal with. However, there are sufficient exceptions to the rule to allow barristers to legitimately turn down cases.

The barrister is not employed by anyone and is wholly independent of the solicitor. Any approach to a barrister for advice must be made through a solicitor – the barrister usually cannot deal directly with the client. There are exceptions e.g. 'direct professional access' whereby certain approved professions e.g. chartered accountants, may have direct access to a barrister. Ombudsmen may also instruct barristers without using a solicitor.

There will almost always be a barrister on both sides in the High Court. If the solicitor has decided to use a barrister (and most do) the client will usually meet him or her on no more than two or three occasions – meetings with the barrister are referred to as 'conferences' – before the trial itself. All other dealings with the barrister will be through the solicitor.

In the same way that it is important to employ a specialist solicitor for a medical negligence action, it is also important that the barrister instructed to advise on the case is experienced in medical negligence.

Queen's Counsel (QC)

A Queen's Counsel (QC) is a senior barrister whose work has been recognised as of a high standard. QCs are sometimes brought in on very complex cases where an important point of law is involved or a very large sum of money is at stake. QCs are referred to as 'leaders' whereas other barristers are referred to as 'juniors'.

CONCLUSION

The English legal system is complicated especially to non-lawyers. Many of its traditions are sound and largely enhance the perception of 'justice being seen to be done'. It is hoped that this chapter has made it easier for the patient involved in litigation to understand the system in which the claim proceeds.

Chapter 17

CLAIMING ON TIME: THE LAW OF LIMITATION AND MEDICAL NEGLIGENCE

Frank Burton QC

The general rule in personal injury law is that a plaintiff has three years to sue from the date when he or she suffers an injury or knew that he or she was suffering such an injury. If an injured person is out of time to sue then the court may, in certain circumstances, allow the claim to proceed. This chapter details how the law governing these various situations works and explains how claimants can bring themselves within the law.

INTRODUCTION

The meaning of limitation

Most people would agree that if a person has a right to compensation and wishes to make a claim he or she should make the claim within a reasonable time. In most circumstances it would be wrong to allow him or her to start proceedings many years after the event. Parliament has therefore made laws imposing time limits for bringing legal action, hence the term limitation.

Limitation Act 1980

The law which governs these time limits is the Limitation Act 1980. Under the 1980 Act, the general rule for personal injury actions, which includes medical negligence, is that plaintiffs have three years to sue from the date when they suffer an injury or alternatively, three years from the date when they knew that they had suffered such an injury. This latter date is referred to in shorthand as 'the date of knowledge'.

The Limitation Act 1980 deals with other classes of action as well as personal injury but only the sections relevant to personal injury actions are dealt with here.

THE LIMITATION PERIOD

Primary limitation period

The three year time limit from the injury or the date of knowledge is referred to as the 'primary' limitation period.

Children

In the case of minors, that is people under the age of 18 years, the three year limitation period does not start to run until they reach the age of 18 (Section 28). This means that they have until their 21st birthday in which to bring a claim for personal injury. The action can, however, be brought while they are still under age by their parents or any other appropriate person who agrees to act as their next friend.

People under a disability

Persons suffering from a mental disability within the meaning of the Mental Health Act 1983, namely those who are incapable of managing and administering their own property and affairs, have three years to bring a claim after the cessation of the disability.

It will therefore be noted that there is no limitation period in respect of a permanently brain damaged claimant – minor or adult. Such persons may have claims brought in their name at any time up to three years after their death. So, for example, in a case reported in 1995[1], the Appeal Court reinstated a case brought 28 years after a medical accident that occurred to a plaintiff at the age of nine months, which had been struck out by the lower court.

Once started, however, a case brought even on behalf of a permanent patient may be struck out if not progressed reasonably quickly[2].

Fatal cases

In fatal cases, the people authorised to deal with the estate (known as the 'personal representatives') or the dependants of the deceased have three years from the date of death to bring a claim or, if it is later, three years from their own date of knowledge.

Personal injury claims which have become 'statute barred'

If court proceedings are not begun within the relevant limitation period, the action becomes 'statute barred'. This does not in itself prevent a personal injury plaintiff from issuing proceedings after the expiration of the limitation period but the defendant will almost invariably plead limitation in his or her defence and unless the courts are willing to exercise discretion

[1]Headford v Bristol and District Health Authority (1995) Med L.R. 61
[2]Hogg v Hamilton (1992) P.I.Q.R. 387

to display the limitation period under Section 33 of the Limitation Act 1980, the case will not be allowed to proceed.

Professional negligence claims against lawyers

If a lawyer fails to prosecute a medical negligence action so that it either becomes statute barred (out of time) or struck out for want of prosecution, the client may have a claim against the lawyer for professional negligence. Such an action would be subject to the basic six year time limit for non-personal injury actions.

NEGLIGENCE, NUISANCE AND BREACH OF STATUTORY DUTY

Section 11 of the Limitation Act 1980, defines the types of cases where the three year limitation period would apply:

> 'any action for damages for negligence, nuisance or breach of duty (whether the duty exists by virtue of a contract or of provision made by or under statute or independently of any contract or any such provision) where the damages claimed by the plaintiff for the negligence, nuisance or breach of duty consist of or include damages in respect of personal injury to the plaintiff or any other person'.

Most medical accidents will be dealt with under the law of negligence or, if the injured person was a private patient, also under the law of contract, but in either case are subject to the three year limitation period for personal injury claims.

Trespass or deliberate assault

An exception may arise in personal injury actions which involve a trespass or deliberate assault. The House of Lords found in the case of *Stubbings v Webb* (1993)[3] that breach of duty as it applies in Section 11, does not include deliberate assaults such as indecent assaults or rape. Accordingly, a claim for personal injury caused by such an act will fall outside the definition of personal injury set out in Section 11 and will therefore be subject to the six year

[3]Stubbings v Webb (1993) A.C. 498

limitation period for actions in tort and contract without qualification (extension) rather than the three years plus possible extension which applies to other actions for personal injury.

THE 'DATE OF KNOWLEDGE'

Working out when a person 'knew' he was suffering from an injury can be difficult, particularly with medical injuries. For example, if someone undergoes medical treatment to repair a fractured bone in his or her leg, and is left with a permanent disability, that person may have no reason to suspect that the treatment was at fault or that the cause of his or her disability was other than an unavoidable consequence of the original injury – unless and until someone advises them otherwise. This is different from other types of personal injury actions, e.g. a road traffic accident where the person is generally immediately aware that he or she has been involved in an accident and therefore that his or her injuries are likely to be attributable to that event.

Section 14 of the Limitation Act defines 'date of knowledge':

'In Sections 11 and 12 of this Act references to a person's date of knowledge are references to the date on which he or she first had knowledge of the following facts:

(a) that the injury in question was *significant*; and
(b) that the injury was attributable in whole or part to the *act or omission* which is alleged to constitute negligence, nuisance or breach of that duty; and
(c) the *identity of the defendant*; and
(d) if it is alleged that the act or omission was that of a person other than the defendant, the identity of that person and the additional facts supporting the bringing of an action against the defendant;

and knowledge that any acts or omission did or did not as a matter of law, involve negligence, nuisance or breach of duty is irrelevant.'

Time does not run against a plaintiff therefore until he has knowledge of four types of facts namely that the injury was significant, attributable to acts or omissions of the defendant, the identity of the defendant, or in some circumstances, the identity of the person who would be vicariously liable for the defendant.

Knowledge

The courts have had great difficulty in deciding what exactly constitutes knowledge. The most recent authoritative statement on knowledge is to be found in the product liability case of Nash v Eli Lilly and Co[4] which concerned actions arising out of the effects of the drug Opren which included skin sensitivity, abnormal hair growth and liver and kidney failure. The Court of Appeal in *Nash* laid down the following definition:

> '. . . knowledge is a condition of mind which imports a degree of certainty and that the degree of certainty which is appropriate for this purpose is that which, for the particular plaintiff, may reasonably be regarded as sufficient to justify embarking upon the preliminaries to the making of the claim for compensation such as the taking of legal and other advice.'

In other words, if a person is sufficiently certain that someone has caused him or her a medical injury to start arranging to consult a lawyer or someone else who can give legal advice he or she will be considered to have the knowledge at that time and the three years will then begin to run. When deciding whether a person acted reasonably in not making some such arrangements, account must be taken of the intellectual capacity of that person to understand information and also how that person in fact understood the information.

The effect of an expert's opinion of knowledge

Frequently in medical negligence cases there is a negative expert opinion before a second opinion is positive. In those circumstances time is not suspended until the second positive opinion but runs from the date of the plaintiff's firmly held belief (see *Nash*). However, if the plaintiff has a belief that an act or omission caused his or her injury but feels that confirmation of the belief is required by an expert then time does not run. These fine distinctions make it increasingly difficult to give unambiguous advice as to when the plaintiff did have knowledge within the meaning of the Act. In the case of *Whitfield v North Durham Health Authority*[5], the Court of Appeal emphasised that all the plaintiff had to know was the essence of the complaint against the medical practitioner and all the Court had to enquire into was how far the plaintiff

[4]Nash v Eli Lilly and Co (1993) 4 All E.R. 383
[5]Whitfield v North Durham Health Authority (1995) 6 Med L.R. 32

had knowledge in broad terms of the facts on which the complaint was based (see also *Gregory v Ferro (GB) Limited)*[6].

SIGNIFICANCE, ATTRIBUTION, IDENTITY AND CONSTRUCTIVE KNOWLEDGE

Significance

The plaintiff must know that the injury was significant. Significance is defined by Section 14(2) as:

> '... an injury is significant if the person whose knowledge is in question would reasonably have considered it *sufficiently serious to justify his or her instituting proceedings for damages* against a defendant who did not dispute liability and was able to satisfy judgment.'

This is a very low threshold of injury because even relatively trivial matters might be worth suing over if the defendant is able to pay damages and accepts liability. The only likely area of dispute is over whether the particular plaintiff concerned would *reasonably* have considered the injury worth prosecuting. In the case of *Nash*, the court indicated that the test was partly subjective, namely would this particular plaintiff have considered the injury sufficiently serious, and partly objective, namely would he have been reasonable if he did not regard it as sufficiently serious. Such an analysis must take into account the plaintiff's particular intelligence and circumstances. In the case of *Stephen v Riverside Health Authority*[7], the court found it reasonable that the plaintiff did not sue in respect of skin discoloration and anxiety arising out of excessive radiation. The injury only became sufficiently serious and significant when she learned that the overdose of radiation could cause cancer. Accordingly the proceedings had been started within three years from the date of knowledge and she was able to proceed with the case.

The courts have emphasised that significance is to be determined by looking at the first injury and not at any subsequent deterioration.

---

[6]Gregory v Ferro (GB) Limited (1995) 6 Med L.R. 321 C.A.
[7]Stephen v Riverside Health Authority (1990) 1 Med L.R. 261

Attribution

The second type of fact that the plaintiff must have knowledge of is 'attribution':

> 'that the injury was attributable in whole or part to the act or omission which is alleged to constitute negligence, nuisance or breach of that duty.'

This is one of the most difficult concepts to explain and it cannot be done simply. That is because there have been numerous cases on this question alone and the courts themselves, whilst repeatedly saying that it is a simple matter, have not been able to agree exactly what it means.

The most recent authoritative statement on what constitutes attribution appears in the case of Mrs Dobbie in 1994[8]. Mrs Dobbie was admitted for a biopsy on a lump in her breast on the 27th April 1973, and the surgeon considered that the lump was pre-cancerous and carried out a left mastectomy without microscopic examination and allegedly without her consent.

Shortly after, on 14th May 1973, it was found that the lump was in fact benign and Mrs Dobbie was told of this on 11th June 1973. She developed a significant psychiatric reaction to the loss of her breast but took no steps to claim until she heard about a similar case reported in a newspaper and on the local radio. She issued proceedings in 1989. The trial judge found that time began to run against Mrs Dobbie when she was informed about the laboratory analysis of the lump in June 1973, because at that time her injury was capable of being attributed to the defendant's fault. Accordingly Mrs Dobbie was out of time but she then appealed this decision.

The Court of Appeal dismissed Mrs Dobbie's appeal and in doing so reviewed the leading authorities on attribution. First, the court confirmed that 'attributable to' meant 'capable of being attributed to' and not 'caused by'. Secondly, the court emphasised that the plaintiff did not need to know that the defendant's act or omission was capable of being attributed to some fault. Knowledge of fault, i.e. knowledge that the act or omission amounted to a case in law, was to be specifically excluded on the clear words of the Limitation Act (S14(1)). Thirdly the court confirmed that all that was need for knowledge was a broad understanding of the essence of the act or omission. It concluded

[8]Dobbie v Medway Health Authority (1990) 3 Med L.R. 217

that Mrs Dobbie knew within hours, days or months of the operation that she had suffered a significant injury which was capable of being attributed to, or alternatively, it was a clear and direct result of an act or omission of, the Health Authority. What she did not appreciate until later was that the Health Authority's act or omission was arguably negligent or blameworthy. That fact of fault (i.e. that she did not know what had happened was negligent), however, did not stop time beginning to run.

In other words, although Mrs Dobbie might have thought that the doctor knew best in removing her breast notwithstanding that the biopsy had shown that the growth was not cancer, and therefore did not know, or even believe, that the doctor had done something wrong, she should still have sought legal advice. Because she had not done so, and because she knew that the injury, that is, the removal of her breast, was capable of being attributed to the doctor, she had not started her legal action in time. (See also *Whitfield v North Durham Health Authority*)[5]

In contrast with this decision is the case of Mr Forbes in 1996.[9] Mr Forbes was operated on in 1982 for a by-pass and the operation failed and a second operation was carried out the next day. That operation failed also and he was told that he needed to have his leg amputated to prevent gangrene and this was done on the 5th November 1982. Mr Forbes obtained a report in 1992 indicating that the practitioners had been negligent not to perform the second operation sooner. The defendant contended that all that was needed was knowledge that there was a period of time between the first and the second operations, that the second operation was not successful and as a result the plaintiff had his leg amputated. The court dismissed this approach and indicated that the plaintiff did not know that the loss of his leg was capable of being attributed to the act or omission of the defendant until the receipt of the opinion by the vascular surgeon.

The court therefore held that Mr Forbes did not have actual knowledge. Unfortunately, Mr Forbes still did not win the case because he was held to have 'constructive' knowledge, explained below.

The reader may find it difficult to reconcile the position regarding Mrs Dobbie's breast and Mr Forbes' leg, and these

---

[9]Forbes v Wandsworth Health Authority (1996) *The Times* 21 March

distinctions may one day be the subject of further deliberation in the House of Lords where perhaps it is not too much to hope that the position will be clarified.

Identity of the defendant

In medical negligence and breach of contract actions, the identity of the practitioners concerned is unlikely to give rise to difficulties. The situation can be more difficult in, for example, pharmaceutical cases where a drug might be produced by a number of different manufacturers. In those circumstances, time may not run until the identity of the particular manufacturer is ascertained.

Constructive knowledge

The Limitation Act imposes a duty on a claimant to act reasonably to obtain information about her claim; she cannot simply say that she did not think about making inquiries.

Section 14(3) provides:-

'For the purposes of this section a person's knowledge includes knowledge which he might reasonably have been expected to acquire:

(a) from facts observable or ascertainable by him: or
(b) from facts ascertainable by him with the help of medical or other appropriate expert advice which it is reasonable for him to seek;

but a person shall not be fixed under this sub-section with knowledge of a fact ascertainable only with the help of expert advice so long as he has taken all reasonable steps to obtain (and, where appropriate, to act on) that advice.'

This important sub-section imposes a duty on a plaintiff to act reasonably to obtain information about her claim. If a plaintiff does not act reasonably, the court will fix her with 'constructive' knowledge on the assumption that had she acted reasonably she would have obtained relevant knowledge and information. In other words, the court will identify when it would have been reasonable for the plaintiff to have acquired relevant knowledge and treat this as the plaintiff's date of knowledge.

But does the reasonableness depend on the character and circumstances of the person concerned, or is it what people generally would consider reasonable? The courts have held that in the main it would depend on the particular plaintiff, but the court should also take into account what people generally would do. Once again the courts try to face both ways at the same time which makes life very difficult for patients and their advisers.

The general drift of recent authorities is towards fixing plaintiffs with an earlier date of *actual* knowledge and an earlier date of *constructive* knowledge. A prudent patient would therefore be well advised to establish at an early stage precisely what did go wrong and what were the causes. Legal advisers should increasingly attempt to work within the three year primary limitation period if at all possible and in any event to obtain expert evidence quickly and issue proceedings as soon as possible. In the short term there is likely, as previously indicated, to be an increased reliance on applications to court for discretion under Section 33 of the Limitation Act which is dealt with below. In Mr Forbes' case the court held that it would have been reasonable to seek advice after the loss of his leg and accordingly his case was out of time.

DISCRETION UNDER SECTION 33 FOR PERSONAL INJURY CLAIMS WHICH ARE OUTSIDE THE LIMITATION PERIOD

When a personal injury plaintiff has failed to start an action before the expiration of the three year limitation period, then the only prospect of continuing with the claim would be to ask the court to exercise its discretion to disapply the limitation period so that the action can proceed even though it is out of time. The court has a free discretion within Section 33 of the Limitation Act 1980 to disapply the limitation period in personal injury actions. In most personal injury actions, there is no 'long-stop' (maximum) time limit beyond which a case would be considered statutorily too stale to proceed and even in cases where the plaintiff has an unanswerable claim against his or her legal advisers for failing to issue a writ within time, the court is entitled and has allowed the case to proceed under Section 33.

Claims where Section 33 discretion cannot be exercised

The only major class of action excluded from Section 33 discretion are those cases where a second writ has been issued because the first writ was never served or lawfully renewed or where the first action was struck out for want of prosecution or discontinued for some other reason. In such cases, which frequently occur in medical negligence actions, the only possible way forward is where a date of knowledge within the meaning of Section 14 of the Limitation Act 1980 can be found to have occurred within three years prior to the issue of a second writ.

Guidelines on discretion

Even though the court is entirely free to exercise its discretion, it must still have regard to the guidelines in the Limitation Act which specify the matters which must be taken into account by the court in deciding whether or not a case should be allowed to proceed. These are as follows:

- the balance of prejudice to each party;
- the six specific factors contained in Section 33 (see below);
- all the circumstances of the case.

The plethora of cases involving the application of Section 33 cannot be treated as precedents because of the disparate factual circumstances they give rise to and because judicial conceptions of discretion and equity vary. Medical negligence actions feature frequently in reported limitation cases and often involve analysis of the plaintiff's date of knowledge coupled with an application for section 33 dispensation.

The balance of prejudice to each party

The court is required to consider the prejudice that each party would suffer in the event that the decision to allow a statute barred claim to proceed went against them. In other words, would it be more unfair to the plaintiff if the claim *were not* allowed to proceed or more unfair to the defendant if the claim *were* allowed to proceed.

Prejudice or unfairness to the plaintiff will in almost all cases be the loss he or she will suffer if his or her claim is not allowed to proceed. The more substantial the plaintiff's claim, the more prejudice he or she would suffer if not allowed to proceed. For example, a person who has been paralysed would suffer greater economic prejudice than someone who had suffered a relatively minor injury. Similarly, a plaintiff with a strong claim on liability would potentially be more prejudiced than someone who has a weak claim with little prospect of success. The court will also take into account whether or not the plaintiff has an alternative legal remedy in the form of an action against his/her solicitor for failing to bring the case in time.

The prejudice that a defendant might suffer could include the economic prejudice arising out of having to resist a weak claim or as a result of changes in insurance arrangements; evidential prejudice in that the defendant's ability to defend an action may have been weakened by the delay; and personal prejudice in that the defendant may have a claim hanging over him or her for many years potentially causing undue stress and affecting his or her reputation or business.

The court will weigh up all these factors and any others the parties may put forward in deciding where the balance of prejudice lies.

DISCRETION

Section 33 (3) lays down six factors which the court should have regard to when considering exercising discretion to disapply the limitation period:

The length of, and reasons for, the delay on the part of the plaintiff

Obviously if a plaintiff is fully aware of the right to claim compensation but does nothing about it for many years and then suddenly decides to sue, it is highly unlikely that the court will allow the case to proceed. Generally speaking, however, if the plaintiff has a good reason for the delay, the shorter the delay the more likely the court is to allow the action to proceed.

An example of an extensive delay where the judge allowed the action to proceed occurred in the case of *Doughty v North Staffordshire Health Authority*[10]. The action concerned the negligent removal of a port wine stain going back some 20 years and which was started some 13 years after the plaintiff's date of knowledge. The reason for condoning the delay was that it was caused by discouraging advice from the lawyers and consequently problems with legal aid. The case was allowed to proceed even though the surgeon who was alleged to have been responsible had in the meantime had a stroke and was unable to give evidence.

[10]Doughty v North Staffordshire Health Authority (1992) 3 Med L.R. 81

The effect of the delay on cogency of the evidence

The delay referred to here is delay since the expiry of the limitation period and is considered to be the most significant factor in the exercise of the court's discretion. Very few cases, like *Doughty* (*ibid*), are allowed to proceed where the defendants establish that they would suffer significant evidential prejudice if the limitation period were disapplied.

If a case depends on the recollection of incidents which took place more than 20 years previously, the defendants are clearly going to be prejudiced in terms of the availability of evidence to defend the action after such a long time lapse. Medical negligence actions primarily based on the interpretation of expert evidence which have the benefit of written clinical and nursing notes are accordingly more likely to be allowed to proceed than those which raise issues concerning consent and warning as to risks which largely hinge on oral recollections. In *Baig v City and Hackney Health Authority*,[11] the trial judge refused to allow a statute barred action to proceed, *inter alia* because the part of the plaintiff's action based upon a failure to warn or to discuss the merits and potential dangers of a stapedectomy performed 17 years prior to the issue of proceedings meant that the practitioners concerned could have no valuable recollection of what had been said at the time (see also *Wilding v Lambeth Southwark and Lewisham Area Health Authority*)[12].

Alternatively, when all the notes are available and where there is little reliance on oral recollection, a court is more frequently sympathetic to a Section 33 dispensation. See *Bentley* (*ibid*), *Doughty* (ibid), *Waghorn v Lewisham and North Southwark Area Health Authority.*[13] For recent cases going the other way on this point, see *Gregory v Ferro (GB) Limited Al* (1995)[6] and *Whitfield v North Durham Health Authority* (1995).[5]

The conduct of the defendant after the injury including the response to requests for information

If the defendant doctor or Trust has been misleading or failed to answer the patient's questions, then the court is more likely to allow the plaintiff to proceed. It is quite surprising that there have not been more successful applications for discretion based on this ground bearing in mind how little doctors have told patients in the past and how difficult it has been to obtain information.

[11]Baig v City and Hackney Health Authority (1994) 5 Med L.R. 221
[12]Wilding v Lambeth, Southwark and Lewisham Area Health Authority Lexis May 1982
[13]Waghorn v Lewisham and North Southwark Area Health Authority 23 June 1987 (unreported)

The duration of the disability arising after the cause of action

This subsection deals with plaintiffs who develop a 'disability' after the commencement of the limitation period and is a factor which the court will consider in the exercise of Section 33 discretion. Disability here refers to a mental rather than a physical disability (although some judges have interpreted it as including physical).

How quickly the plaintiff acted once he knew all facts

Plaintiffs and their lawyers must act reasonably quickly otherwise they will fail in an application for discretion. Once a plaintiff has personal knowledge in respect of the cause of action upon which he or she sues, the court will enquire into how expeditiously the action was progressed before issue of the proceedings both in respect of the plaintiff's behaviour and that of his or her lawyers. Sometimes the court will excuse the plaintiff when it is the lawyer who is slow. In the case of *Doughty* (*ibid*), the court was willing to excuse the dilatoriness of the lawyers and exonerated the plaintiff from any personal blame in respect of failing to chivvy her lawyers because she was busy looking after her handicapped son. That is not likely to happen often, however, and the courts are more likely to say 'sue your lawyer!'

Obtaining legal advice

Obviously if the patient thinks that all is not well he or she should at least seek medical advice. If the medical advice incorrectly reassures her that everything reasonable was done then she may well be excused.

Negative legal advice is frequently a problem for plaintiffs in medical negligence actions where there is often difficulty in obtaining a favourable medical opinion on negligence and causation. This may lead to the discharge of a legal aid certificate. In *Bentley v Bristol and Western Health Authority*[14], the plaintiff received two negative legal advices from two counsel based upon negative medical opinion but a third set of solicitors obtained a report from a well-known orthopaedic surgeon indicating that there had been undue traction during a process which damaged the sciatic nerve. The judge held that if he had been required to exercise section 33, he would have done so in the plaintiff's favour because at all times the plaintiff was striving to carry her claim forward. In addition there was little evidential prejudice.

[14]Bentley v Bristol and Western Health Authority (1991) 2 Med L.R. 329

Other circumstances

The six factors listed above which the court must have regard to are not exclusive because section 33 requires the court to 'look at all the circumstances of the case'. Having considered all the specific matters laid down by the Act, the court must then look at the circumstances of the case as a whole.

Circumstances will be individual to any particular case but reported decisions indicate that the court is likely to have particular regard to the strength of the plaintiff's or defendant's case, to the amount of damages involved, whether the plaintiff is legally aided or not, whether a defendant is insured and whether there is a good claim against the plaintiff's solicitors if the claim is not allowed to proceed.

It will be seen that the court has many factors which it must carefully weigh up in deciding where the balance of prejudice lies. At the end of the day, however, the judges must exercise their discretion and that discretion cannot be challenged unless it can be shown that the judges failed to consider any of the specific factors laid down by the Act or did take into account matters which they should not have done.

CONCLUSION

It was said at the beginning of this chapter that the general rule was that proceedings ought to be commenced within three years of the act of negligence. The principle underlying this is that the courts want to hear cases where the evidence is still fresh so that justice can be done. Patients who are victims of medical negligence are advised to seek advice as early as possible so that the considerable problems of overcoming the three year rule are avoided.

Chapter 18

LEGAL PROCEDURES: PRELIMINARY INVESTIGATION TO TRIAL

Paul McNeil

This chapter will provide a route map describing all the milestones and pitfalls on the road from seeing a solicitor at the beginning to hearing the pronouncement by a judge at the end of the case. In particular, it will cover:–

- how to involve a solicitor in your claim;
- what steps the solicitor will need to take to investigate the claim and gather the evidence;
- how the legal costs can be funded;
- an explanation of the legal procedures;
- what to expect from the lawyers, medical experts and the court;
- the tactics that are used by both sides.

INTRODUCTION

Choose the right lawyer

Medical negligence cases are complicated, often involving complex factual, medical and legal issues. For this reason, any victim of medical malpractice should seek the advice of a solicitor who has experience in such claims. Clients who have suffered badly at the hands of the medical profession do not deserve to also suffer at the hands of the legal profession. Choose the lawyer carefully. AVMA and the Law Society have lists of suitable, experienced and sympathetic lawyers who are widely recognised as being reliable. Most lawyers will agree to provide an initial consultation free or at a modest charge. Use this to establish the lawyer's credentials and whether you are likely to be able to develop an ongoing professional relationship.

What the legal process can achieve

A word or two about the legal process. It is geared simply to enable an aggrieved person to prosecute a claim to trial. It is a mechanism which attempts to ensure that the disputes between the parties are firmly established before the hearing and that at trial no party can be taken by surprise. The procedures have not been designed with medical negligence cases especially in mind. The court can only award compensation; it cannot change practice or admonish doctors. This means that the doctors do not have to say sorry or explain what happened. The law only requires that the injured party be compensated. Nothing more, nothing less.

PRELIMINARY INVESTIGATION

The first steps

Lawyers tend to 'pigeon hole' everything. In medical negligence the case is divided into two steps. The first step is known as the 'pre-action or the preliminary investigation', which is intended to cover the 'finding out' phase. The outcome of this investigative phase will determine whether legal proceedings are to be issued. The second step covers the process from issue of court proceedings to trial.

This section is intended to set out all matters which the solicitor needs to cover before proceedings are issued. The overall aim of the solicitor is to investigate the evidence to ascertain whether the claim has a reasonable chance of winning in court. In other words the whole basis of the claim is determined during this phase. The investigation and gathering of evidence must be as thorough as possible. Many more cases are rejected by negative legal advice at the conclusion of the preliminary investigation phase than by judges at trial! It is vital to get it right. No case can ever be taken to court without a proper preliminary investigation.

The main steps taken by the solicitor are:

- to arrange an initial interview to obtain a statement from the patient;
- to arrange how the costs of the investigation and the subsequent legal case are to be paid;
- to obtain all the evidence including disclosure of the medical records;
- to obtain reports from the appropriate and independent medical experts.

Meeting the solicitor

The patient need not worry about the first meeting with the lawyer. Most solicitors are sympathetic and used to dealing with clients who have suffered personal trauma. The main objectives for the solicitor are:

- to introduce himself and to establish a good working relationship with the client;
- to ascertain the facts as far as possible so as to make an informed decision as to whether the case merits further investigation;
- to establish how the costs of the initial investigation will be funded.

Preparing for the meeting

All this has to be achieved relatively quickly. The client can assist the solicitor before the meeting by:

- preparing a short statement which will include the important dates and events surrounding the allegations of medical negligence;
- listing the name and address of *all* the hospitals and doctors that he has attended;
- having available all relevant financial information (including national insurance number) so that a decision can be made as to whether or not to apply for Legal Aid.

The first meeting

During the initial interview the solicitor should cover the following topics.

INFORMATION TO ASCERTAIN THE FACTS

By the time most victims of a medical accident enter a solicitor's office they are feeling very aggrieved. The fact that they have decided to seek legal advice is an indication of this.

Many patients do not have the full facts for a variety of reasons e.g. in surgical cases the patient may have been under an anaesthetic! Understandably patients do not have the medical expertise to know precisely what went wrong. They do know what they have suffered and they question whether it was the doctor's fault. Nevertheless the solicitor will skilfully try to obtain as much information as possible, so that an informed assessment can be made as to the strength of the case. Subsequently a statement, in the patient's name, will be prepared setting out the known facts, the medical history and the potential claims of medical malpractice. This statement is not sent by anyone at this stage except the patient's lawyers and medical experts.

EXPLANATION OF THE LAW

It is important for the solicitor to explain to the client the stringent legal tests as to negligence and causation. The law may be difficult and perceived to be unfair but the lawyers have to work within the system.

The solicitor will draw attention to the basic test for medical negligence in its simple terms (See in *Bolam v Friern Hospital Management Committee* (1957) 2 All ER 118) and apply it to the known facts of the case.

It will also be important for the patient's statement to cover the consequences of the alleged negligence (e.g. the pain and suffering, the loss of earnings or the extra care and attendance required).

WHETHER THE CASE CAN BE BROUGHT IN TIME

Sadly, some clients wait a long time before they seek legal advice. There are many reasons for this. Often they are related to the conduct of the doctors in the first place. It is essential for the solicitor to establish from the outset how the time constraints established by the Limitation Act 1980 will affect the case. This is explained in more detail in Chapter 17. In broad terms legal proceedings cannot be commenced more than three years from the date of knowledge of the act of negligence. There are exceptions to this rule and the court has the knowledge of ability to override it in special cases (see Chapter 17).

TO ESTABLISH HOW THE CASE WILL BE FUNDED

The solicitor will clearly explain the risks on legal costs and the magnitude of those risks (see Funding below).

THE MEDICAL BASIS OF THE CLAIM

In most cases, at this early stage, the solicitor will be unable to tell the client whether or not there is a medical basis for a medical negligence claim. The solicitor is unlikely to be medically qualified. Much depends on what is contained in the medical records. A considered view can only be given once all the medical records have been reviewed by an independent expert. However the solicitor should be able to indicate whether or not he thinks the claim merits independent medical investigation by medical experts.

TO OBTAIN SIGNED FORMS OF AUTHORITY FOR THE RELEASE OF THE MEDICAL RECORDS

Although Health Authorities and their solicitors now generally accept their duty to allow patients and their legal representatives the right to see and copy their medical records, such disclosure will never be given without a signed form of authority from the patient. It is essential that the solicitor obtains copies of *all* the client's medical records (whether or not he thinks they are relevant) and he will therefore need a list of all the medical practitioners which the patient has attended so that the forms of authority can be prepared and signed.

TO GIVE GENERAL ADVICE ON THE LEGAL PROCEDURE

Most clients will have heard on the grapevine that medical negligence cases are especially difficult and they take 'a long time'. The solicitor will advise the client specifically about the procedures and the time taken to complete the case. Good advice at this stage will avoid unjustifiably high expectations.

ALTERNATIVES TO LEGAL PROCEEDINGS

Recourse to litigation may not be the correct advice in every case. The solicitor may advise the client to make a complaint through the NHS Complaints Procedure (this unified system was established on 1 April 1996; for more detail, see Chapters 5–8). Where there has been serious professional misconduct the matter should be reported to the General Medical Council or the UKCC (Nurses and Midwives). Dentists are regulated by the General Dental Council. The Health Service Ombudsman investigates complaints of maladministration in the provision of health services within the NHS (See Chapter 9). Since April 1996, the Health Service Ombudsman also investigates complaints about all doctors, dentists (and their staff), including actions taken wholly or partly as a result of their exercise of clinical judgment. In effect, the Health Service Ombudsman is now at the apex of the NHS Complaints Procedures.

Often clients will be advised to take up these extra legal rights in tandem with civil litigation. Other clients, even at this early stage, will be advised that their best course lies within the NHS Complaints Procedures or with the relevant professional body. Some patients are urged to pursue their rights with the NHS Complaints Procedure as a prelude to litigation. Sometimes this tactic can produce evidence to make the legal claim stronger. A warning: watch the limitation period!

THE PURPOSE OF LITIGATION

It needs to be said again and again. The only purpose of legal action is to obtain compensation for a person harmed by the consequences of a medical mishap which is negligent. No matter how gross the act of negligence, the civil courts can do nothing more. They cannot strike off, imprison, fine or admonish the 'guilty party'. They can only award the victim money. It is important that the solicitor and the client decide together what it is that the client hopes to achieve. That may not be compensation.

THE VALUE OF THE CLAIM

Giving a realistic value of the potential claim is no easy matter. The process and investigation can take as much, if not more time, than the one for medical negligence. At the initial meeting, the solicitor will have nothing like enough information to give a proper valuation of the claim. Nevertheless, he or she will be able to give a broad outline of how damages are assessed by the courts and state how he or she intends to progress this, most important area of the case. Since the fundamental question will be 'can the patient recover damages?' the lawyer will be probing to make sure that the compensation recoverable will outweigh the legal costs of so doing. If the patient has been receiving benefits from the State, these will have to be taken into account in assessing the likely value of the claim (for more detail, see CRU Benefits Chapter 19). A significant number of cases founder on the rocks of economic justification.

FUNDING

No legal action can commence without proper consideration of funding, for lawyers and experts expect to be paid; they will not work for nothing. The winner's costs are paid by the loser. The risk of losing and paying both sides' costs deters many careful people from contemplating legal action.

The prediction of victory is not easy in any legal case; it is unusually difficult in medical malpractice cases. It cannot be done 'on the hoof'. Proper advice needs proper investigation. Proper investigation may involve a significant expense.

There are a number of options for funding a case, as follows.

LEGAL AID

Civil legal aid will be granted to those who qualify on financial grounds where as a matter of law there are reasonable grounds for taking or defending proceedings. The Legal Aid Board will also consider whether in the particular circumstances of the case it is 'unreasonable' that legal aid should be granted (part of this test will be whether the benefits to be obtained in the proceedings do not justify the likely costs). The Legal Aid Board accepts that in medical negligence cases it is difficult to form a clear view on prospects of success when Legal Aid is being applied for. It still insists that applicants must show that there is a prima facie claim in medical negligence (not just the investigation) particuarly in small cases worth less than £10,000. "In smaller cases, if there is little prima facie evidence of negligence, legal aid may be refused on the merits on the basis that the NHS Complaints Procedure may be a more appropriate avenue for the applicant to pursue." (Legal Aid Handbook 1997/8). This is a direct reference to the new NHS Complaints Procedure which came into force on 1 April 1996 (see below). This approach by the Legal Aid Board has been condemned by plaintiff's lawyers, and the jury is still out as to its long term implications. The message is however clear: in medical negligence cases legal aid will become increasingly difficult to obtain. At the time of writing the Labour Lord Chancellor has announced an intention to abolish legal aid from virtually all civil actions.

Financial limits for legal aid

The financial limit to qualify for legal aid for medical negligence cases for the year April 1998–9 is a lower income rate of £2563 up to £8370 per annum and a lower capital limit of £3000 up to £8560. Persons who are above these limits will not qualify for legal aid no matter how strong the case is. A financial contribution must be made by the applicant for legal aid where his means are between the lower and upper income and capital levels. Payments of the contribution are made on a monthly basis throughout the life of the case. Persons on income support automatically qualify financially for legal aid free of contribution.

Children

Children are assessed on their own means (not their parents') and almost always qualify for legal aid.

The statutory charge

Subject to any contribution and the statutory charge (see below) the Legal Aid Board will pay the legal costs of the legally aided person if he loses the case.

Although the defendant's costs are sometimes paid by the Legal Aid Board, more usually the defendant pays his own costs in a legally aided case. He may obtain 'an order for costs against the plaintiff, not to be enforced without leave of the Court' if the plaintiff loses. In practice, the defendant is unlikely to recover his costs unless the plaintiff wins the lottery or the pools.

If the claimant (the plaintiff) wins the case, the defendant pays the majority of the costs though the Legal Aid Board may be able to recoup any unrecovered costs from the damages. This recoupment is called the Statutory Charge.

LEGAL EXPENSES INSURANCE

Several commercial insurers offer legal expenses insurance for a premium. The policy is usually not limited to medical negligence actions. It will cover legal fees up to a stated amount (say £25,000) and for claims arising within a specified period (usually 12 months). Such policies are often, though not always, combined with other insurance (e.g., household or motor). It is a feature of this type of insurance that it cannot be purchased 'after the event' i.e., after the medical accident. In other words, to be used, the medical accident must have occurred when a policy was already in place.

PRIVATELY FUNDED

Few people are wealthy enough to litigate a medical negligence case on the basis of their own means. Many people (too 'rich' for legal aid) are therefore denied justice. Even relatively simple medical negligence cases can eat up £40,000 of fees for both sides. In difficult cases the sky's the limit!

CONDITIONAL FEES

Since July 1995, lawyers have been allowed to conduct medical negligence cases on a conditional fee basis. This is essentially a 'no win no fee system' in respect of the plaintiff's lawyer's fees. If the case is won, the lawyer charges 'basic costs' (his normal fees for taking the case to trial) most of which are recoverable from the defendant. There may be a shortfall which the client has to pay (see Costs below).

Success Fee

The 'success fee' is an additional amount which will be added to the legal bill if the case is won. This is not recoverable from the defendants (and will therefore usually be paid from the damages). It is calculated by adding a percentage uplift to the basic costs (e.g., if the basic costs are £10,000 and the uplift is 25%, the success fee will be £2,500). The success fee is intended to reflect the level of risk the solicitor takes because if the case is lost he will not be paid.

Whilst the case proceeds, the client is usually expected to pay all the disbursements such as court and expert fees as soon as they become due. If he wins, these costs will generally be recovered from the defendant.

In the event that the case is lost the client is still liable to pay for:

- his own disbursements including barrister's, expert's and court fees which are not covered by the conditional fee agreement;
- the defendant's full legal costs including solicitor's, barrister's, expert's and court fees.

Conditional Fee Insurance

To overcome this, the concept of 'after event insurance' has been developed. For a premium, conditional fee insurance can be purchased *after* the medical accident has occurred. This will reimburse the patient for his own disbursements and for the defendant's legal costs up to a stated amount. The cost of such insurance is at present very high and will only be provided if the patient has reasonable prospects of success. The cost of this insurance policy is not yet recoverable in the action against the defendant as a disbursement in the action.

AVMA Conditional Fee Insurance

A recent development in this area has been a joint venture between AVMA and an insurer (Litigation Protection Ltd) to provide conditional fee insurance at discounted rates. The details of the scheme are as follows:

- it is available only to clients of solicitors who are members of the AVMA Referral Panel;
- all cases will have to be vetted by a caseworker from AVMA and be monitored by AVMA caseworkers;
- AVMA will receive a fee from Litigation Protection for its services;
- the insurance will cover the defendant's costs and disbursements as well as the plaintiff's disbursements including retrospectively the disbursements incurred in investigating the case prior to the signature of the CFA and acceptance of the insurance.

Cost of Insurance

- The premiums payable are as follows:

Liability for costs (any one action)	*Indemnity Premium £*
Up to £10,000	850
Up to £25,000	1,652
Up to £50,000	3,100
Up to £100,000	6,000
Above £100,000	by negotiation

Payment in 10 instalments can be arranged.

At the end of the first meeting with the solicitor

In practical terms the client should come out of the initial interview with some information on the law (including the limitation period), details of the mechanics of investigation, the prospects for funding the legal claim and a knowledge of the time scale and legal procedures involved. Information will have been given as to the alternatives to litigation and the personal burdens imposed by taking court action. In short, the client should have sufficient information to decide whether or not he should pursue a claim for medical negligence.

The solicitor will have established the strength of the case (albeit to a limited extent), obtained enough information to prepare a statement and advised on how the case is to be best funded.

Advice not to proceed

Even at this stage, in some cases, the correct advice will be not to proceed, e.g.:

- there is no medical basis for the claim;
- the patient has not suffered any harm that can be compensated;
- the extent of the harm does not sound sufficient in damages to warrant further action;
- the case is best dealt with by the miscreant's professional body;
- there is no realistic method of funding the case;
- the case falls foul of the time limits prescribed by the Limitation Acts;
- fighting the claim would impose too much of a burden on the victim and his relatives;
- the victim's purpose is not to obtain damages but to achieve some alternative goal.

In practice, it is a combination of the above which prevents sensible patients and cautious lawyers from taking further action in many cases. It can be seen that even some strongly based cases can fall by the wayside.

OBTAINING THE MEDICAL RECORDS

Once the decision to investigate a claim has been made, one of the first steps the solicitor will need to take is to obtain copies of all the client's medical records.

Obtaining all records before claiming

Both the prospective plaintiff and defendant(s) in a medical negligence claim are entitled under the law to obtain copies of documents held by the other parties before legal proceedings have commenced. The legal process used by solicitors to obtain copies of documents is termed 'discovery' or 'disclosure of documents'. In a medical negligence action, discovery normally happens twice: once before the court proceedings commence, i.e., during the preliminary investigation, and this is termed 'pre-action discovery', and once after the defence has been served (see *discovery* below).

The importance of obtaining the medical notes before proceedings are issued cannot be overstated.

Legal rights to obtain the records

The patient may have been receiving treatment over many years from a number of different hospitals or doctors and the solicitor will first need to identify what records may be available and which organisation currently holds them. The approach used for obtaining the records will depend on who holds the records, the form in which the records are held and when the records were made:

- records held by potential defendants: request voluntary disclosure and if this is refused, obtain an order for pre-action discovery;
- records held by non-defendants: request voluntary pre-action disclosure and if this is refused obtain an order for disclosure following commencement of the proceedings;
- records made after November 1991: apply for access under the Access to Health Records Act 1990;
- computer held records: apply for access under the Data Protection Act 1984.

In most cases, it is usually possible to obtain copies of the records on a voluntary basis from both defendants and non-defendants. It is only where there has been a refusal to release the records that the solicitor would need to enforce entitlement to pre-action disclosure from potential defendants. This is done by obtaining an order from the court. For records held by non-defendants, the appropriate method is an application under the Access to Health Records Act 1990.

The law governing pre-action discovery

In the High Court the position is controlled by Section 33(2) Supreme Court Act 1981 and the implementing rule, RSC Order 24, Rule 7A.

In the County Court, the authority is given by Section 52(2) County Courts Act 1984. By virtue of Order 13, Rule 7(1)(g) of the County Court Rules 1981, RSC Order 24, Rule 7A also governs the procedure in the County Court. This means that the same rules apply to both courts.

The rules allow discovery of documents limited to personal

injury cases where 'the parties are likely to be parties' to a further action in court.

Therefore a prospective plaintiff (or defendant) in a medical negligence or other personal injury claim is able to inspect and obtain copies of documents *before* the proceedings have commenced. In other areas of law, it is only possible to obtain disclosure after proceedings have commenced.

In order to obtain pre-action disclosure, the documents must:

- be relevant to the issues of the potential claim;
- be or have been in the prospective defendant's possession;
- not be protected by privilege.

In other words, the plaintiff is only legally entitled to pre-action discovery if there is possibly a case and if the person who holds the records is likely to be a defendant in the action. There is no entitlement to pre-action discovery if the record is held by someone who is not a potential defendant although it may be possible to obtain these records under the Access to Health Records Act 1990.

To whom should the records be released?

Section 33(2)(b) and Section 52(2)(b) detail to whom the records can be released. Under no circumstances should the claimant's solicitor consent to disclosure to his medical advisers only. The Form of Authority (completed at or after the initial interview) will specify that the records be sent to the solicitor (a) because he needs to check the records himself and (b) to prevent the defendant identifying the name of the patient's expert witness early on.

Refusal to disclose – application for pre-action discovery

Nowadays, it is rare that a prospective defendant will refuse to supply the medical notes. If he does, the patient, through his lawyer, will apply to the court for an order for production of these documents, which save in very exceptional circumstances will be successful.

Although the defendant is usually aware of his duty in law, administrative failures often lead to a delay in the disclosure of medical records. The plaintiff's solicitor is obliged to allow a reasonable time for such discovery. In one case (*Hall v Wandsworth Health Authority* (1985) 129 Sol Jo 188), the court said that six weeks was reasonable. In practice, a court would accept about two months' delay as reasonable.

Application to court

The application to the court is made by way of an 'originating summons' supported by an affidavit (sworn statement). Sadly, even where there has been a delay caused by the defendant's inefficiencies, it is likely that the court will order that the costs of the application be paid by the patient (see *Costs* below).

Pre-action discovery and problems with limitation

It should be noted that even though the three year limitation period may have expired (and even if an application to disapply the limitation period may be extremely unlikely to succeed) an application for pre-action discovery can still be successful. See *Harris v Newcastle upon Tyne Health Authority* (1989) 2 All ER 273. In other words the fact that the claim is or could be time barred is not a reason for the defendant to say that the medical records are not disclosable.

Proceedings issued before pre-action discovery

There may well arise a situation in practice when it becomes necessary to commence a court action before the medical records are obtained, because the limitation period is due to expire shortly. In these circumstances the problems on limitation will have to be balanced against the requirement for early discovery of the medical records. A consequence of issuing proceedings is that the plaintiff can no longer make an application for pre-action discovery pursuant to Section 33(2) of the Supreme Court Act 1981 (or the similar provision in the County Court). The application for discovery will have to be founded on Order 24, Rules 3 and 7 (see *discovery* below). Discovery can still be obtained before the foundation document (the Statement/Particulars of Claim) has to be sent to the court.

Documents required to be disclosed

The authority to make an application for pre-action discovery does not make all the defendant's documents discoverable. So, for example, section 35(1) of the Supreme Court Act 1981 allows a defendant to refuse to disclose documents which may be injurious to the public interest or may cause harm to the applicant. Similarly, a document arising only because of contemplated litigation is protected from such disclosure. See *Lee v South West Thames Regional Health Authority* (1985) 2 All ER 385. This is important. It means that if a Health Authority or Trust has investigated an incident which may result in future legal proceedings, the fruits of that investigation are not disclosable to the other side (e.g. witness statements, reports etc.). This is sensible because it allows each party to conduct a private investigation in an uninhibited way. For the same reason, the patient's initial statement to his solicitor is not disclosable to the Health Authority at this stage.

Computer records

The pre-action application allows discovery of information stored on computer disk. See *Alliance & Leicester Building Society v Ghahremani* (1992) TLR 313. For example, medical information relevant to the proceedings held on computer must be disclosed (e.g. MRI scans) if requested under these provisions.

Costs

The Health Authority or Trust which is ordered to disclose the records is entitled to the legal costs of the application and of complying with any order made, *unless the court otherwise directs.* If it can be shown that the Health Authority is at fault, e.g., where there has been a delay in disclosing documents, the court may refuse that party the costs or, in exceptional cases, order the Health Authority to pay the patient's costs. See *Hall v The Wandsworth Health Authority* (1985) 129 Sol Jo 188 where the court ordered the defendants to pay the costs when they delayed disclosure for six months.

Disclosure against non negligent parties

Often the patient would like to obtain medical notes and records from medical practitioners or institutions who are not likely to be defendants in the subsequent proceedings. This is almost always necessary to conduct a full investigation into the complaints. Unfortunately, there is no special authority to allow this and the plaintiff will have to wait until *after* commencement of the proceedings to make such an application (see Section 34 and Section 53 of the Supreme Court Act 1981 and the County Courts Act 1984). The Access to Medical Health Records Act 1990 is increasingly making this defect less significant (see below). In practice disclosure by 'non-parties' is given voluntarily on provision of a signed form of authority, an undertaking to pay copying fees and confirmation that no action is intended against that party.

Access to Health Records Act 1990

The Access to Health Records Act 1990 provides a statutory basis for the patient to obtain copies of his or her own records generated after 1 November 1991. The healthcare provider (GP, Trust, private consultant etc.) must allow inspection of the record and supply a copy if this is requested within 40 days. The advantages of this procedure are:

- disclosure must be given quickly (40 days);
- an explanation of medical terms should be given by the healthcare provider;
- it is usually cheaper because a solicitor need not make the request;
- the Health Authority, Trust etc. need not be a party to the proceedings.

The downside is that the Act only covers 'health records' (which may exclude important administrative records) made after 1 November 1991. Another important limitation is that section 5(1) restricts access to records which can or are likely to cause physical or mental harm to the patient or other individual. (See summary in Appendix 6)

Data Protection Act 1984

An application can be made for access to computer held records under the Data Protection Act 1984 but there are restrictions in relation to the health records similar to those under the Access to Health Records Act 1990 (see above). In practice, the Data Protection Act is not often used to obtain discovery of medical records.

The Practice

In practice, Health Authorities now accept that there is a duty to disclose where the claimant is likely to have a *prima facie* case. It is essential that the letter of claim (sometimes called a letter before action) should show that there is this *prima facie* case by setting out potential allegations of negligence.

Lack of disclosure usually means inefficiency on the part of the Health Authority or their solicitors rather than an objection to disclosure in principle. Nevertheless the patient's lawyer should be strict with his or her interpretation of reasonable time and if necessary apply to the Court where the delay is more than two months.

Summary

In summary, the procedure adopted by the claimant's lawyer should be as follows:

- arrange for Forms of Authority to receive medical records to be signed by the client;
- write a 'letter before action' to the potential defendant which will set out the likely allegations of negligence, ask for an explanation and request disclosure of the medical records;

- write letters to other holders of medical records for voluntary disclosure of those records;
- if no voluntary disclosure is given by the potential defendants within two months, issue an application for pre-action disclosure or apply under Access to Health Records 1990 for formal disclosure;
- if no voluntary disclosure is given by non-defendants, make a formal application under Access to Health Records 1990 for disclosure of records created after 1 November 1991.

It is only in exceptional cases that this pre-action discovery process should take more than six months.

Law Society Protocol

In August 1995 the Law Society launched a protocol for obtaining hospital medical records to standardise and streamline the disclosure of these records. This requires the applicant's solicitor to complete a prescribed form containing all the relevant information available to enable the hospital to identify and copy the notes. The solicitor must also indicate whether there is a potential claim against the hospital and the 'grounds' for such a claim. The aim of the protocol is to save time and costs for the benefit of the patient.

WHAT TO DO WITH THE NOTES

The medical notes will be the keystone to any medical negligence action. The judge at trial is likely to prefer the contemporaneous notes over any oral evidence given at trial where there is a factual dispute. It is crucial, therefore, that from an early stage the notes are easily deciphered and ordered. It is incumbent upon the plaintiff's solicitor to organise and paginate the notes from the outset. Good practice is to organise the notes as follows.

Hospital Notes

- clinical notes (including accident & emergency notes);
- operation notes, consent forms and anaesthetic notes;
- nursing/midwifery notes (including care plans etc.);
- laboratory test reports (including x-ray reports & EEG reports);

- correspondence;
- drug notes and prescription forms;
- temperature charts and fluid balance charts;
- administrative notes.

This list is not exhaustive. Specialist areas in medicine tend to have notes describing particular functions. The best examples are the Cardiotocographic Tracing Record (CTG) in Obstetrics and the Intensive Care Unit charts in head injury cases.

GP Records

- Lloyd George cards (some more modern GPs are now using A4 sized clinical notes);
- test reports;
- correspondence.

All the notes should be placed in chronological order and paginated.

Once the records have been paginated, they should be read and checked for legibility and missing notes. The notes are paginated so that each page can be easily identified (e.g. when in correspondence with the client, the defendant's solicitors, the experts and Counsel).

In obstetric cases where negligence is alleged during labour, it is essential that a continuous copy of the CTG record is obtained. In orthopaedic and head injury cases, the plaintiff should obtain copies of all the relevant x-rays including MRI scans and CT scans (preparing a schedule of x-rays is often helpful).

It is increasingly useful to obtain colour photocopies of documents like anaesthetic records, partograms and the labour records in relevant cases.

Sadly, and all too often, there are medical notes and x-rays etc. missing but a careful organisation of the disclosed documentation often helps identification and retrieval of the missing notes earlier.

Missing records

Regrettably there are some occasions when crucial medical records are never found and are said to be missing. There is very little that can be done by the claimant's lawyer in this situation other than to obtain a court order for the responsible officer for the Health Authority to provide a sworn statement describing the steps taken to find the missing notes and a declaration that the notes are in fact missing. It is almost impossible to pursue a case where all the medical records are missing. In many cases some notes are missing. Each case must be looked at individually as to whether the missing record is crucial to the prosecution of the case.

CHOOSING AND INSTRUCTING AN EXPERT

What type of expert?

Remember it is the plaintiff who has to prove that there was negligence and that this negligence caused or 'materially contributed' to the injury or loss.

One legal test of negligence is set out by Edmund-Davies LJ in *Whitehouse v Jordan* (1981) 1 All ER 267:

> '. . . is the standard of the ordinary skilled man exercising and professing to have that special skill.'

In other words an expert must be prepared to say that the medical practitioner has been negligent (i.e. tested against someone who has the same qualifications and experience as the defendant). In other words, a doctor of the same standard would not have made the same mistake.

Doctor's specialisms

Medical science, like the law, is becoming much more specialised. It is essential that the instructed expert specialises in the relevant field. For example if a general surgeon carries out a varicose vein operation which goes wrong then a general surgeon should be asked to prepare a report (not an expert vascular surgeon). If the general surgeon reports that the operation was appropriate only to be undertaken by a vascular surgeon (e.g. because of history of recurrent varicose veins) thereafter the solicitor is justified in seeking the opinion of that specialist (if only to ask the question what would have been the result if the specialist had carried out the surgery).

The expert must have been working in the relevant field at the time when the alleged negligence took place. (See also Assessing the Quality of the Expert below)

The role of AVMA

Instructing the correct expert is fundamental to the progress of any case and the lawyer should tap as much experience as possible. Unfortunately the pool of experts available to the plaintiff is relatively small. He should make it a rule never to instruct an expert unless he has heard something positive about him from a reliable source. AVMA (Action for Victims of Medical Accidents) have been identifying suitable experts on an individual case basis for many years. New and established experts are evaluated and monitored by medically qualified caseworkers employed by AVMA.

The Law Society

The Law Society runs an Expert Witness Register which is based on applications from experts supported by references provided by lawyers practising in the personal injury and medical negligence fields.

It is not appropriate to consult the treating doctor(s) as expert(s) on liability or causation in the majority of medical negligence claims. This is because the treating doctor is unlikely to be genuinely independent.

Instructing an expert

Many experts practising in this field are vastly experienced and can produce excellent reports with little guidance. Others are not.

Contents of expert's report

A good report should deliver the following:

- a forensic reconstruction of the events using the notes and the patient's recollections;
- a statement as to whether any medical records are missing;
- an explanation of the medical and scientific terms used in the notes and in the report;
- an opinion on whether or not the medical practitioner has acted or failed to act in accordance with the standards of a responsible body of medical opinion. Here the expert should consider each possible sin of omission/commission and give reasons for his opinion;
- reference to the published medical and scientific material in support of his opinions (with copies supplied);
- whether any acts or omissions of the medical practitioner concerned have caused or materially contributed to the injuries;
- whether any issue in the case falls outside his expertise.

The report need not be in a form for disclosure to the hospital at this stage but it will, if positive, form the basis of the claim when proceedings are eventually drafted.

Theoretically the expert's primary duty is to the court, but he is also a member of the plaintiff's team.

The solicitor's instructions to the expert should aim to maximise the expert's fraternity (though the worst expert is the 'hired gun') and therefore courteousness and presentation are important. The letter of instruction needs to include a chronology (referring to the paginated notes) and specific questions on the areas of concern so that the expert understands the basis of the complaint. It should also ask the expert to apply the legal tests of negligence (Chapter 15) as evidenced by sub-standard treatment and causation as evidenced by 'material contribution' to the injuries.

The solicitor should involve the expert in the case as early as possible and communicate with him regularly.

All experts should refuse instructions (rightly) if they have any connection with the potential defendant.

Assessing the quality of an expert

The ultimate function of an expert witness is to explain to the court facts and opinions based on medical concepts which are likely to be unfamiliar to the judge at trial. An expert must be independent, objective, cogent, consistent and truthful. If the expert fails in any of these attributes his evidence will be rejected. It is the duty of the lawyer to ensure that the expert's opinion is based on the correct factual basis.

Matters of opinion are for the expert alone, but it may be necessary for the lawyer to challenge the opinion on the basis of the criteria set out above (see 'Instructing an Expert') and on the legal tests for negligence and causation. It is unusual to run a key issue of negligence in any case with one expert only.

Meeting the expert

It is vital in every case for the lawyers to meet the expert face to face to test his mettle as early as possible and before the expert gives his evidence to the court.

Analysing the report

The basis of every expert's report will be his view as to whether there has been an act or omission on the part of the healthcare professional which constitutes lack of care. This will be based on the expert's medical knowledge and experience. It is essentially a subjective test which is the major reason why two experts should be instructed in most cases. There is a clear distinction between 'best practice' and whether an act or omission is 'responsible'.

In a case called *Loveday v Renton* (1990) 1 MLR where the medical opinion was deeply divided, the judge said of the medical issue:

> 'The question has to be determined on all the evidence in the case, which is primarily the oral evidence of the witnesses tested in cross examination. The court cannot simply accept the opinion or belief of a witness, however eminent, that such is or is not the case. The basis for the opinion must be examined, tested against other evidence, for consistency and logic and the validity of the reasoning.' (Stuart-Smith LJ)

AVMA also run a service where their medically qualified caseworkers will analyse medical reports to establish that:

- all the relevant medical issues have been addressed;
- whether in their medical experience and according to their bank of medical information the expert's views on liability and causation are tenable.

If a client is unhappy with his solicitor's assessment of a medical report, AVMA will review the report free of charge for the client.

Liability and causation reports

It is often necessary to have separate expert opinions on liability and causation. The classic example is in obstetric cases where the patient has suffered cerebral palsy. The lawyer requires a report from an obstetrician on the question of negligence and a paediatrician on causation of injury.

Medical examinations

It is inevitable that the claimant will have to undergo medical examinations both with his own experts and the experts instructed by the defence. Not all those experts considering the issue of negligence require to see and examine the plaintiff (though this is often wise). All experts asked to report on causation of injury and condition and prognosis will have to examine the plaintiff. It is not necessary for the plaintiff to be accompanied by the lawyer to these medical examinations. The expenses in attending the examination are recoverable. (The solicitor will claim these after the examination from the defendant's solicitor – payment should be received within a few weeks.)

The defendant's lawyer does not have to send any medical

report he obtains to the plaintiff's lawyer if he does not want to rely on it in court.

Refusing a medical examination

The principle is that the defendants must be entitled to ask the claimant to undergo a medical examination where he or she has suffered an alleged personal injury, subject to the test of reasonableness. The balance is between this and the claimant's right to privacy. If the claimant refuses to undergo such an examination, he must have good reasons which must be disclosed to the court and the defendant. It is not enough to show that the plaintiff is nervous or does not like the defendant's choice of doctor. A reasonable refusal might be that e.g. the defendant's expert wants to perform an invasive test (e.g. MRI carried out under a general anaesthetic).

If the plaintiff refuses to have a reasonably requested medical examination, the legal proceedings will be suspended and may later be struck out.

Quantum reports

The lawyers must instruct appropriate experts so that the judge at trial can assess the amount of compensation (quantum of damages) which is to be paid to the plaintiff. In modest cases, quantum reports will be limited to medical opinions on condition and prognosis. In large cases, where the claimant has suffered significant physical and mental injury a variety of experts may be instructed. These can include nurses (to comment on extra care and attendance), physiotherapists, occupational therapists, speech therapists, computer and technology experts, architects (housing needs) and employment consultants (loss of earnings).

Medical and scientific literature

All expert reports should be supported by reference to medical literature published at the time of the alleged complaint. The more supportive the published material, the more likely it is that the expert's view will represent a responsible body of medical opinion.

Prudent lawyers also ask their experts to provide a list of published material which does not support the case in readiness for the defendant's assault.

ASSESSING THE EVIDENCE AND THE DECISION TO COMMENCE PROCEEDINGS

Abandoning cases after expert advice

Once all the evidence is obtained and the independent experts' reports have been received, the solicitor and the client consider what to do next. It is now that the strength of the case is assessed and the decision is made whether to commence legal proceedings. Ultimately, this is the decision of the client who will receive advice from his or her solicitor based on the evidence of the independent expert. Sometimes, it will be necessary for a barrister to advise if the case is complex. We have already seen why some cases are abandoned after the first interview. At this stage, many more cases are lost. The main reasons are:

- lack of documentary or other quality evidence that there has been a negligent act or omission;
- that there has been an 'error of judgment' which does not amount to negligence according to the legal test;
- lack of convincing evidence that the negligent act or omission has caused damage that can be compensated;
- no satisfactory method of funding has been developed.

The decision whether or not to institute and continue proceedings is alive throughout the life of the case as each new piece of evidence is obtained. It is, however, at this point that the most careful analysis should be undertaken.

The bottom line is that no case can be taken further without the support of an independent expert and the lawyer.

It is also important to note that a decision to proceed now does not mean that the case will win or inevitably go to trial. There are many more hurdles to jump!

Choosing Counsel

It is often now that the client receives further legal advice and the solicitor will instruct Counsel (also called a barrister) who should be experienced in medical negligence litigation. This is important for only practitioners who have been properly trained in medical negligence and have undertaken similar cases learn the techniques to avoid the many pitfalls.

The barrister is independent of the solicitor and is a specialist in evidence and advocacy. It is the barrister who will represent the client in court and argue the case before the judge at trial. Although solicitors have some rights of audience in the High Court and full rights of audience in the County Court, it is rare for a solicitor to advocate his own case in either court.

Strength of case

By the time of receipt of the expert report(s), the solicitor will have, at the very least, a detailed Proof of Evidence, all the medical notes and records and the expert's report(s) on negligence and causation.

This probably constitutes the first opportunity for a proper analysis of the strength of the case. Sometimes this can be carried out by a barrister in conjunction with the solicitor.

The options for the solicitor and the client at this stage are as follows:

- strongly positive expert report: advise client and instruct the barrister to prepare the formal court documents;
- positive report: advise client and arrange a meeting with the experts and Counsel to discuss further progress. Consider whether further expert evidence is necessary;
- negative report: obtain a further expert opinion and/or consider the matter with Counsel and the experts in a meeting;
- strongly negative report: advise the client and consider whether further expert evidence is necessary. Consider whether a meeting with Counsel and the experts is economically justifiable.

It goes without saying that there may be a considerable dialogue between the solicitor, client and the expert(s) at this stage. It is also very important and absolutely necessary for the client to be part of the dialogue and allowed access to the expert via the solicitor. The client should be kept well informed and should be an integral part of the decision making process.

Role of Counsel

A barrister (also known as Counsel) is self-employed but operates from 'chambers' which is an association of practising barristers within a chamber (an office building). These chambers in London are situated in or near the Inns of Court. There are usually sets of chambers at every High Court Centre throughout the country. Only a few practising barristers have experience in medical negligence cases.

Meetings with barristers are called consultations or conferences. The barrister appears in court to advocate on the case on the client's behalf.

The barrister also produces:

- the formal paperwork which is sent to the court and to the defendants (see Statement/Particulars of Claims below);
- opinions/advices (written or verbal) in relation to the strength or otherwise of the case. These advices will often cover additional evidence required and other matters such as advice on the law, the value of the claim and tactics.

The primary purpose of instructing a barrister is (at this stage) to advise on strength of case and to draft the paperwork necessary to commence an action in court. This document is called the Statement of Claim (confusingly, in the County Court it is called the Particulars of Claim). In medical negligence actions it is normal (though not mandatory) to have a conference (meeting) with Counsel and the experts in order to prepare this statement of claim.

Meeting Counsel and the experts

If there is a conference with the experts present, the lawyers (and the client) should take that opportunity to question the expert and to knock their reports into shape taking into account the significance of *Bolam* (1957) 2 All ER 118 and *Maynard v West Midlands RHA* (1985) 1 All ER 635 and that the standard of proof in civil proceedings means that the claimant has to prove his case on the balance of probabilities.

The lawyers will address in detail the question of what harm the negligent treatment has caused the patient. Once liability is established this issue, causation, is often the single most important feature of the use. It is easy to see why. Many patients are having treatment from the doctor because they are unwell. Not only do the medical experts have to establish what harm the negligence directly caused, but also the likely extent of recovery had the patient received appropriate treatment. A good example is where a hospital doctor fails to prescribe the appropriate drug and the patient dies. The expert concludes that this failure was negligent. However, he goes on to say that even if the appropriate drug had been prescribed the patient would have died anyway because the cause of death was not related to the failure to prescribe the drug.

COURT PROCEDURES – FROM ISSUE OF PROCEEDINGS TO TRIAL

Court proceedings

What is meant by legal proceedings? Everyone has heard that so and so has 'issued a writ'. This means that he or she has commenced legal proceedings. It is the first step in the process which ends with a full blown trial.

The effects of issuing a writ (in the County Court it is called a summons) are as follows:

- the case becomes a matter of public record;
- the limitation clock stops.

The effects of serving the writ or summons are:

- the defendants e.g. the Health Authority/Trust/doctor etc. now know that there is a serious risk that the case will be pursued and will step up their own legal investigations;
- the procedural clock starts because the courts apply a strict timetable to get the case to trial;
- the legal costs start to increase considerably;
- if the case is later withdrawn, the plaintiff will be responsible for the defendant's costs.

COMMENCING THE LEGAL CASE

The following tables set out the milestones in a typical High Court and County Court case.

An average case takes about 24 to 30 months to complete after the issue of proceedings.

Writ/ summons

In both courts the legal action is commenced by issuing (for a fee) a document which names the parties and sets out the broad nature of the claim. It is dated and endorsed with a court seal (which gives it authority and validity). In the High Court this is called a writ. In the County Court this is called a summons. Both must be served on the named defendant(s) within four months from the date of issue.

An Acknowledgement of Service will be served with the writ

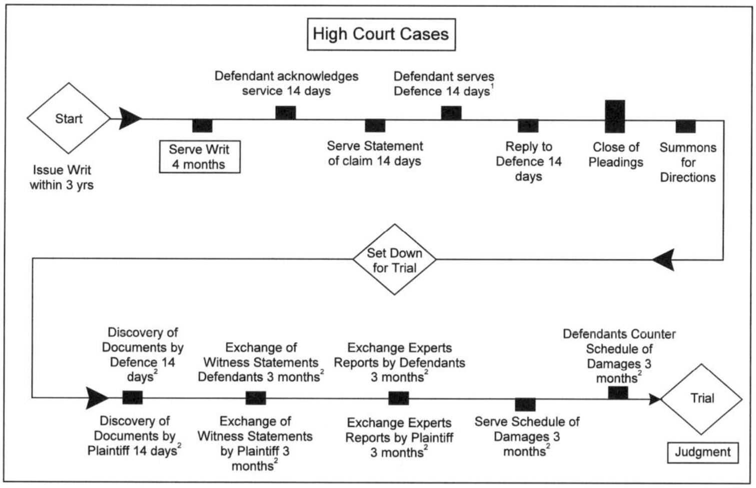

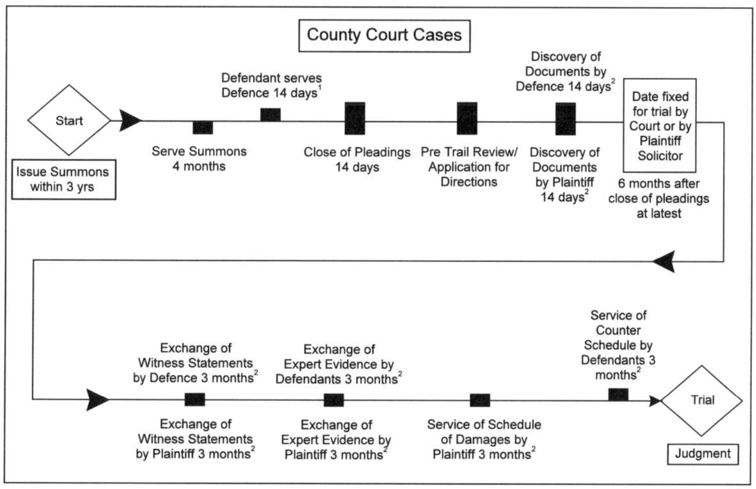

Notes:

1. Extension of time normally granted.
2. Subject to variations by the court or the parties in any particular case. See also the diary of an actual case at the end of the chapter.

whilst a Form N.9 will be served with the summons. Both documents require the defendants to confirm receipt of the writ/summons and indicate whether a defence is likely to be served.

Statement/ Particulars of Claim

This is the formal document which sets out in detail the plaintiff's case to the defendant(s). Although it can be amended (changed) at any time up to the judgment, the lawyers, the client and the experts should (as far as possible and on the evidence available) consider it to be the unalterable foundation on which the case is fought. It should therefore set out the full case and all the allegations of negligence and causation which are supported by the experts. Every Statement/Particulars of Claim in a medical negligence action will claim for compensation (damages) and interest on damages pursuant to the relevant statutory provisions.

The elements of the Statement/Particulars of Claim are as follows:

- the names of the parties to the action;
- a brief chronology containing relevant dates and a brief factual history;
- a resume of the acts or omissions alleged to constitute the negligence (what went wrong);
- identification of the consequences which have flowed from those acts or omissions (causation);
- identification of the injuries suffered;
- the setting out of financial loss and damage up to that time.

Support of the experts

It cannot be over emphasised that the expert's report must support the allegations of negligence set forth in the Statement of Claim and it is therefore wise to let the experts see and approve it before it is served on the defendants.

Documents to be served with the Statement of Claim

The rules require that the following documents be served with the Statement/Particulars of Claim:

- medical report on condition and prognosis (not liability or causation;
- Schedule of Losses (e.g. loss of earnings etc.).

In Legal Aid cases, a Notice of Issue of Legal Aid Certificate should also be served.

Medical report on condition and prognosis

In any case which claims compensation for personal injury the Statement/Particulars of Claim must be accompanied by a medical report which sets out the injuries suffered, the present condition and the prospects of improvement (see Chapter 19). It will therefore be essential for a medical examination of the patient to be undertaken and this report produced *before* any court action commences. In some cases, more than one report will be required if the damage caused by the alleged negligence crosses two medical specialities (e.g. plastic surgeon for facial scarring and psychiatrist for psychological trauma).

Schedule of losses

The same court rules require that the plaintiff serve a Schedule of Special Damages with the Statement/Particulars of Claim. This is a document which sets out the plaintiff's financial losses. Since the court can only award compensation (a sum of money), the plaintiff is obliged as far as possible to set out what he has lost in financial terms because of the injury caused by the negligence. Typically this will include loss of earnings, cost of prescriptions, medical expenses, extra travelling expenses and so on. The principle is that the plaintiff can claim for losses and additional expenses incurred as a result of the defendant's negligence (see Chapter 19).

CONSIDERING THE DEFENCE

Time limits

The defendant must acknowledge that he or she has received the court papers 14 days after receipt and indicate whether he or she intends to defend the action.

Technically the defence (i.e., the formal response from the party against whom the claim is made) is due 14 days after service of the Statement/Particulars of Claim (or 28 days if this is served with the writ/summons). Inevitably, the defendant's lawyers will seek further time to prepare this defence as they will need to obtain their own independent expert evidence on the allegations made by the plaintiff. The plaintiff's solicitor must balance the desire to encourage the defendants to get on with the action quickly, against the risk of their making an application to the court for further time. Each case is different but save in exceptional circumstances the Defence should be served within two months of the date of service of the Statement of Claim.

The defence

Just as the Statement of Claim is the foundation of the plaintiff's claim, so the defence should be the bedrock of the defendant's case. Lamentably, the defence is often no more than a regurgitation of the medical records and a bare denial of the claims of negligence, causation and injury. The defence will follow the same format as the Statement of Claim (numbering and paragraphs, etc.) so much so that it is not possible to understand it without reading it alongside the Statement of Claim.

Defence to client and experts for comments

As soon as the solicitor receives the defence, he will send a copy to the client and to the experts. The experts will comment on what, if anything, gives rise to concern and whether there are any matters upon which the defendant should be asked to elaborate. If any factual matters are raised within the defence which are inconsistent with the client's case, then these should be carefully reviewed with the client and expert in order to ascertain the implications for the case.

Consideration of a request for further information

Theoretically, the issues between the parties should now be clear, but often more detailed information is required at this stage.

Two methods, the Request for Further and Better Particulars and Interrogatories, can be useful weapons to the plaintiff, particularly when the defence filed is little more than a bare 'holding defence'.

Request for further and better particulars

The former is an opportunity to seek to request further information (Request for Further and Better Particulars of the Defence) which is unclear from the defence.

Interrogatories

With Interrogatories, the plaintiff is entitled to ask searching, relevant questions going to the root of the case at this and any later stage. To provide answers to the Interrogatories an individual witness from the defence must depose on oath. This can on occasion elicit an admission of conduct which cannot really be defended.

The courts are increasingly reluctant to order any party to answer any Interrogatory until the process of discovery is complete and factual witness statements have been exchanged.

Both the Request for Further Particulars and the Interrogatories can be used to great effect where there may be an inconsistency between the pleaded defence and the medical notes, and the witness statements.

Reply to the defence

A plaintiff is deemed to deny all matters contained in a defence, except in so far as the same are admitted or not admitted. The Reply to the Defence (a further pleading) can be utilised for the situation in which the plaintiff admits an allegation contained in the defence but can explain it away so as not to damage or destroy the case. So, for example, assume a plaintiff alleges lack of informed consent to a surgical procedure. The defence states that the plaintiff had been supplied with a booklet on the morning of the operation. The plaintiff may then in his Reply admit that a booklet was given but say he was not given sufficient time to read it or, that it did not contain the requisite information. A Reply is also used where the issue of limitation is raised (for the first time) in the defence.

TACTICS

Which court? In most cases, the choice of court is determined by the amount of damages recoverable but there are borderline cases. In those cases, it is advisable to choose the High Court. Not only does this indicate to the defendants that the claim is worth at least £50,000, but it also gives the plaintiff's lawyer much more control over listing and other procedural matters. Further it is more likely that the case will be tried by a judge with experience of medical negligence cases.

Split Trials The rules of the court (RSC Order 33) allow any issue of fact or law 'to be tried before, at or after the trial'. This means that the parties have the capability of deciding (with the consent of the court) whether they want some issue decided before (e.g. the question whether the case is statute barred due to limitation) or after (e.g. the full assessment of damages) the main trial (on negligence) has taken place. In medical negligence cases, the most common choice is between a trial on negligence and causation and a later trial of quantum issues or a trial on all issues at once. In cases where negligence and causation are strong, it may be advantageous to go for a split trial because it is likely that the narrow issue will take less time to come to court.

The decision on whether to split the trial is usually taken at the Summons for Directions, but may be taken at any time during the course of the case.

Payments into court This is the most effective weapon in the defendants' armoury. It is a mechanism which forces the plaintiff to consider carefully the value of his claim. At any time the defendant can pay a sum of money into court, in effect to offer to settle the plaintiff's claim.

The plaintiff's solicitor is notified of this 'payment in' and has 21 days from the time of notification to decide (with his client) whether or not to accept it in settlement of the claim.

If the 'payment into court' is accepted the case will end. The client will receive the amount paid in and the defendants will be required to pay all the legal costs up to the time of acceptance, on a standard basis.

If the payment into court is not accepted then, in the absence of a better offer, the case will proceed to trial. The judge at trial is not told of the payment into court and he will decide the case on the merits of the evidence put before him. If he awards damages equal to, or less than the payment in, then the plaintiff will be responsible for all legal costs (including those of the defendants) from the date of payment in, up to and including the costs of the trial. It is likely that these costs will be very substantial in any contested medical negligence case.

If the judge awards compensation of more than the amount paid into court, then the plaintiff receives that sum and the defendant pays all the costs on the standard basis.

In legally aided cases, all payments into court must be reported to the Legal Aid Board. Legal aid will be withdrawn if the client decides to proceed against his own lawyer's advice.

A payment into court need not be accompanied by an admission of liability (indeed mostly it is not). The plaintiff will not recover his costs in successfully proving liability if he fails to beat the payment into court (even where liability is tried separately).

It goes without saying that all payments into court should be considered very carefully.

Payments into court can put enormous pressures on the plaintiff's legal team, particularly if they are well judged by the opposition. For this reason alone, wise defendants make payments into court early in the proceedings. Each payment into court must be considered on its own merits. In some cases a payment in can be made to exert economic pressure, in others it can be seen as the opening bid in negotiations but the claimant will never know. The risk on costs therefore means that no payment into court can be refused lightly.

Interim payments

The plaintiff may at any time after the writ or summons has been served apply to the court for an interim payment on account of damages. The application must be supported by a sworn statement containing details of the medical evidence, the losses to date and any special needs or hardship being suffered by the plaintiff. The court must be satisfied that the plaintiff will win the case and therefore substantial damages.

Speedy trial

In medical negligence cases, there are often doubts about the likelihood of success and interim payments are only applicable in exceptionally strong cases or where liability has been admitted or already decided in the plaintiff's favour (see Split Trials above). Where hardship is very acute the plaintiff can apply for a Speedy Trial.

Summary judgment

The plaintiff can apply to the court for judgment for damages to be assessed (once the Statement/Particulars of Claim has been served on the defendant) on the grounds that the defendant has no defence to the action. This application must be supported by a sworn statement setting out why there is no defence.

This procedure is only very rarely utilised in medical negligence litigation. Such applications must be made with caution, for it usually requires the plaintiff to disclose his expert medical evidence early in the action and therefore before the defendant. Moreover any form of expert evidence from the defence is usually enough to defeat the application.

Settlement

The majority of cases settle before trial. In order for a particular claim to settle pressure must be maintained on the defendants by adhering to the Order for Directions. The best way is to obtain an early trial date. Many cases settle in the two months leading to trial.

THE SUMMONS FOR DIRECTIONS

Fourteen days after the defence (or any Reply) has been served, the court says that 'the pleadings are closed'. It does not matter whether there in fact has been a request for subsequent pleadings (e.g. Further and Better Particulars of the Claim or Defence). It is now the duty of the plaintiff's solicitor to prepare the case for trial (even though the trial date is still likely to be a long way off.) This is where the plaintiff's solicitor can take control and exercise initiative. He must draw up a timetable setting out the various procedural steps to steer the case to trial. This is called a Summons

(Request) for Directions which must be sent to the court which will issue the summons and give a hearing date.

High Court

In the High Court, the plaintiff needs to apply to the court for this because a medical malpractice case does not fall within the procedure in personal injury actions known as automatic directions (see Order 25, Rule 8(5) – the automatic directions apply to any action for personal injuries except where the pleadings contain an allegation of a negligent act or omission in the course of medical treatment).

County Court

In the County Court the automatic directions *do* apply in medical negligence actions (see CCR Order 11, Rule 17). However those automatic directions are not suitable for the conduct of medical negligence actions and an application should be made to the court pursuant to CCR Order 11(4) for further or different directions.

Summons for directions

Whether the case be proceeding in the High Court or the County Court the substance of the Request for Directions should be the same and should deal with the following matters:

- any defects in the defence, e.g. an outstanding Request for Further and Better Particulars;
- any unanswered Interrogatories;
- whether the action is to be tried separately on limitation/liability/causation/quantum;
- disclosure and inspection of the relevant documents by both parties – these documents are not just the medical records, but also all documents relevant to the proceedings (e.g. the plaintiff's financial records or the defendant's policy documents);
- mutual exchange of statements by witnesses of fact;
- mutual exchange, discipline and number of medical expert witnesses on liability, causation and quantum issues;
- mutual exchange of published/unpublished medical and scientific material;
- setting down and fixing the date for trial;
- time estimate for the trial;
- experience of judge at trial;
- issues on quantum of damages – exchange of medical evidence on condition and prognosis, updated schedule of loss with supporting evidence, counter schedule of loss with

supporting evidence. Number of expert witnesses to be called on quantum issues.

If the case is proceeding in the County Court, the lawyers should also consider whether or not the action should be transferred to the High Court on the grounds of medical or legal complexity.

Hearing for directions

In the absence of agreement by the parties' lawyers, the court (if necessary at a hearing) sets a date by which each direction (e.g. disclosure of witness statements) must take place.

After the hearing/agreement of the parties, a document known as the Order for Directions will be drawn up (usually by the plaintiff's solicitors) and be sealed by the court. This sealed document is the timetable and authority for getting the case to court. No medical negligence case can get to court without such an Order. Pressure must be maintained by the adherence to the Order for Directions. If the defendants flout the Order (as they often do) then the plaintiff's solicitor should without hesitation seek assistance from the court by the use of 'unless orders'. These are orders issued by the court to enforce compliance with the Order for Directions. They are termed 'unless orders' because unless the failure is remedied by the defaulting party a drastic consequence will follow.

The new Practice Direction – High Court

Since 1 November 1996, (following the publication of Lord Woolf's report 'Access to Justice' in July 1996), there has been a change in the High Court rules in medical negligence cases. In order to pave the way for a case management system likely to be imposed in April 1999, the following rules now apply in medical negligence cases where the pleadings close after 1 November 1996. The Practice Direction was amended 1 January 1998.

- A summons for directions *must* be issued within 28 days of close of pleadings, and the plaintiff must send this and the following documents to the other side:
  - a description of the case limited to 250 words;
  - a chronology of events;
  - a list of initial witnesses.
- The defendant *must* within 14 days produce:
  - a list of outstanding issues limited to 250 words;
  - before the hearing the defendant must send comments on the plaintiff's chronology and a list of initial witnesses.

- All these documents must be lodged with the court 48 hours prior to hearing.
- The parties are no longer able to agree a timetable without the court's input, and there will almost always be a hearing at which each party will produce a list of potential witnesses and experts (including number and discipline).
- It is also specified that the plaintiff should serve a letter before action at least three months before the writ is issued, setting out the fullest information available. This is so that the defence have full notice of the claim and begin investigating the claim.
- The lawyer dealing with the claim must attend this hearing.

The court will also consider the other matters set out above (see the Summons for Directions above).

The court will also fix a second hearing for directions closer to the trial date to make sure that all the timetabling requirements have been complied with.

Obtaining a trial date

To fix a date for trial, it is necessary to set the case down for trial.

High Court

In the High Court (in London) the solicitor should 'set down' the case for trial shortly after the Order for Directions has been made. This involves lodging the pleadings (Writ, Statement of Claim, Defence etc.) with the court and paying a fee. The case will then go into a trial list and be given a fixed date for hearing or 'KP' date. As there are usually a number of medical experts in medical negligence cases this KP system is not appropriate. Usually in medical negligence cases the court will allow a fixed date for trial because of the need for attendance by medical experts who may have many other commitments.

High Court delay in obtaining a date

The length of delay between the date of fixing the trial and the actual trial is variable depending on:

- completion of the timetable set out in the Order for directions;
- the availability of the medical experts;
- the number of other actions in the court list;
- the projected length of the trial;
- the availability of the parties' barristers.

In most cases the trial is fixed about 9–15 months after the application to fix date. It is therefore important to set the case down for trial at the earliest opportunity after the hearing of the Summons for Directions.

County Court

The procedure for setting down for trial in the County Court is much more difficult because of the varied listing arrangements adopted by each local court. However there has been a dramatic change to the County Court Rules which prescribe that the plaintiff *must* apply for a hearing date six months after 'the close of pleadings' (14 days after receipt of the defence). If the plaintiff *fails to apply* for a trial date within 15 months of the close of pleadings then the claim against the defendant will automatically be struck out (i.e. the claim will no longer be able to proceed). It is the date of this application that is important, not when the case is tried. It is therefore extremely important that the plaintiff's solicitor seek a trial date as soon as possible after the close of pleadings. In most County Courts the delay between trial listing and trial hearing is 9–12 months, enough time to allow compliance with the timetable by all parties.

Discovery

The first step in the timetable is to ensure that all the relevant documents to the case have been disclosed by each party. The plaintiff and the defendant must produce a list of all the documents in their possession, custody or power relevant to the case. This will include documents relevant to the case on quantum as well as liability and causation. In most medical negligence cases, the defence will have disclosed the medical records before the case has commenced. Once proceedings are on their way, the obligation for disclosure is much more onerous. It may be that there will be other documents held by the defendants which are relevant, e.g.:

- policy documents in relation to how a particular medical procedure is to be carried out;
- other administrative documents;
- any non-privileged investigation file including any Independent Professional Review;
- any documents, medical records, etc., where there has been a similar act of medical negligence.

Either party can request disclosure of a particular document which he thinks the other may have. If the party refuses, then an application can be made to the court.

Discovery of particular documents

It is also during this discovery phase that the plaintiff should obtain disclosure of any documents withheld by any non-party pursuant to Section 34 and Section 35 of the Supreme Court Act 1981. On application to the court, this allows the plaintiff or the defendant to obtain disclosure of any documents held by someone who is not a party to the litigation (e.g. non-party Health Authorities or the plaintiff's employer or former employer).

It is very important that full disclosure of all the relevant documents is achieved at this stage.

DRAFTING AND EXCHANGE OF WITNESS STATEMENTS

The modern development of 'cards on the table' litigation has been a boon to medical negligence solicitors, for the rule is disclosure of the factual evidence early in the proceedings.

It is fundamentally important that the exchange of expert medical reports on negligence and causation takes place *after* witness statements are exchanged. This is because the experts need to know *all* the facts before committing to a final opinion.

When the plaintiff receives treatment from a medical practitioner in the ordinary course of things he leaves the clinical judgments to that practitioner. In many cases the plaintiff cannot give any significant evidence as to what went wrong and apart from the notes (which are sometimes inadequate) the defence witness statements are the only way in which the plaintiff can ascertain the true facts.

Contents of witness statement

A good witness statement should be expressed in the first person.

- It should state the full name and address and occupation or description of the person making the statement.
- It should represent the evidence following a chronological order and be divided into numbered paragraphs with double spacing and wide margins.
- It should always be signed, and must end with the words: 'the above statement is true to the best of my knowledge and belief'.

The plaintiff's factual witnesses are likely to include the plaintiff himself, members of his family and friends who have information about the facts in issue including the effects of the injuries sustained by the alleged negligence. The defendant's witnesses *should* include *all* the relevant witnesses to the facts involving the complaint made by the plaintiff. Usually, the Order for Directions will contain a provision that no factual witness can give evidence at trial unless his statement is disclosed to the other side at the appropriate time.

A recent protocol issued by the court (known as a Practice Direction) states that a witness statement is to stand as the main evidence of that witness and can be expanded on only with express permission of the trial judge. As the plaintiff may not get the opportunity to say anything more at trial, it is therefore important to make the statement as full as possible and in the correct form.

In *Letpack v Harris* (1996) *The Times* 6 December this modern practice was recently underlined by the Court of Appeal in which it was stated that a plaintiff who failed to disclose a witness statement in the time specified by the Order for Directions was at risk of not being able to rely on that evidence, unless such action was justified in all the circumstances.

Experts' views on witness statements

It is always necessary to send the opponent's witness statement(s) to the expert for his comments *before* exchange of his report. Often the defendant's statements will contain 'new' information which may alter the expert's opinion.

The client will also want the opportunity to comment on the defendant's witness statements.

Consideration of the evidence

The next and vitally important stage is the exchange of expert medical report(s) on negligence and causation. Some considerable time will have elapsed since the case has been fully appraised by the solicitor, client, the barrister and the experts together at a meeting. By this time the factual chronology will be complete.

Now is the moment for the lawyers to check that the case is in order, and that:

- negligence can be established;
- causation of injury can be established;
- the experts are still supportive and convincing;
- as a consequence of the negligence some compensationable injury occurred;

- the schedule of loss and damage is complete and up to date;
- the experts' reports on quantum are ready for exchange.

Meeting with Counsel

The barrister is the authority to advise on the way the case is to be presented at trial and he therefore should have the opportunity to consider *all* the experts' reports prior to disclosure to the other side. The experts' reports must be considered extremely carefully so that there are no inconsistencies:

- between each expert and the primary facts set out in the Notes, Statement of Claim, Defence and Witness Statements;
- between each expert instructed in the claim;
- between any expert instructed and the available scientific and medical published material.

All material inconsistencies must be resolved by discussion. It is not appropriate for the lawyers or the expert to impose a view on another expert (it will only lead to tears at a later stage!)

This meeting with Counsel also affords the opportunity for Counsel to review what further evidence is necessary to advance the case at trial.

EXCHANGE OF EXPERTS' REPORTS

After full consultation within the plaintiff's team (the defendant's team will be performing a similar analysis) and once all are satisfied that the experts' reports are in a form which properly represents the plaintiff's case, the exchange of reports must take place. Although this is likely to be the most fundamental 'procedure' in the case, there is no sorcery about how it is done. The parties' solicitors speak on the telephone and agree to exchange the reports in the post.

PREPARING FOR TRIAL

In all medical negligence cases, the trial date will be known well in advance so that all the preparation can be geared towards this.

No case ever runs exactly in accordance with the time schedule for the case set out in the Order for Directions. There are always delays in exchanging evidence and completing the other formalities. There are often features which cannot be predicted at the outset which lead to delay.

In the High Court in London, the trial date will remain fixed save in exceptional circumstances. The trial list is controlled by the judge in charge of the lists whose job is to decide whether to allow cases to be postponed. Any application for adjournment must be made to him; it will be refused (even if the other side consents) unless there are very good reasons which make a fair trial impossible.

In the County Courts, postponement of the trial is far more frequent because pressure on judicial time is much more acute (Circuit judges have a wide range of disputes to resolve).

The final step on the Order for Directions is exchange of published medical and scientific material and again this should be done well before the date fixed for trial.

In addition the experts' CVs should be obtained to be included in the trial bundle.

The patient's solicitor should also check the copy records against the original medical records. Invariably, the patient will have been receiving further treatment and those notes, if relevant, will be needed at trial.

Trial bundles

It is incumbent on the plaintiff's solicitors to prepare the bundles of the relevant documents (usually in lever arch files) for trial which include:

- pleadings and expert reports;
- witness statements;
- the medical records;
- the published/unpublished scientific and medical material;
- schedule of damages and documents in support;
- counter schedule of damages and documents in support.

It is also helpful to the judge (and to the lay clients) if the trial bundles include a glossary of the medical and scientific terms.

Pre-trial conference

Medical practice can be both mystifying and seductive to lawyers. From the day of receiving instructions until the conclusion of the trial, the lawyers have to aim to ensure that the judge at trial will see 'the wood for the trees'. The pre-trial conference is the final opportunity to make sure what is necessary for the court to fully understand the case. All the experts should be seen for the final time. It is better to ask important questions now than be embarrassed at trial. Similarly, it is crucial that the lawyers restrain the experts from dealing with extraneous or irrelevant matters. The experts and the clients must be made to understand and accept the legal requirements in the case. This is the final opportunity to thrash out any problems within the team.

Within reason the defendant's case should now be known, and it should be possible to anticipate how the experts and the client will be cross-examined and the appropriate preparation be made.

THE TRIAL PROCESS

The trial is the culmination of any litigation process, yet the reality is that most plaintiffs' cases do not even get 'to the doors of the court'. The vast majority of cases settle either because they have no reasonable prospects of success and have been dropped on the way or the defendants make an offer of compensation which the sensible plaintiff decides to accept.

Trial by judge

Every medical malpractice trial is conducted before a judge (without a jury). Each party will be represented by Counsel (in substantial and complex cases there will be two Counsel — leading and junior) and have factual and expert witnesses prepared to give evidence in support of the claim and denial.

The opening

The case is 'opened' by the plaintiff's Counsel i.e. he gives a short explanation of the remaining disputes between the parties.

These may be one or a combination of the following:

- dispute as to the facts and chronology of the material events;
- whether the allegations of medical negligence are well founded on the basis of the medical evidence and the law;
- whether the claimant has suffered any harm as a result of any proven act of negligence. This will be a dispute of medical evidence;
- the value of the claim (this can be a very substantial dispute);
- whether the claim is time barred.

The judge will have had an opportunity to read the trial bundles (and each party's skeleton argument) before the trial (unfortunately because of time pressure on the judiciary this pre-trial reading is often not as full as it might be). The modern practice is to keep the opening speech short in the interests of saving time and costs.

Plaintiff's evidence

The plaintiff then calls his evidence, factual witnesses first and then the experts (in practice the parties often agree that the factual witnesses on both sides give evidence first followed by the expert evidence). Each witness gives his or her evidence and then is cross examined by the opposing Counsel.

The plaintiff will be expected to attend (if he or she can) the trial and will be allowed to hear all the evidence for and against him or her. Usually, contested cases take more than one day to resolve and the plaintiff should make the appropriate arrangements. Often, it is better to attend with a friend or family member.

The plaintiff and members of his or her family will have to give evidence to the judge at trial about what they remember and how the mistake has affected his or her life. Most of this evidence will be contained in the statement already disclosed to the defendants and the judge.

The defendant's Counsel will be allowed to ask the plaintiff questions as will the judge.

The judge listens to and notes the evidence and can also ask questions of each witness and of the parties' Counsel. It is on the basis of the evidence adduced at trial that the judge must make his decision. The onus is on the plaintiff to prove his case on the 'balance of probabilities'.

Defendant's evidence

The defence will also call its factual and expert witnesses and the plaintiff's team is given similar opportunities to test the evidence.

Closing speeches

At the end of the evidence the respective Counsel (the defendants go first) have an opportunity to address the judge (the closing speech) where the final attempt is made to persuade him of the salient points of the evidence and the law which supports the case.

Judgment

The judge will give his judgment (often after some further consideration which will result in a short delay) either in written form (which he reads) or delivered like a speech (from his notes) in open court with the claimant and the defendant present. He will make findings of fact (indicating which witnesses' evidence he prefers), decide whether there has been negligence and what, if any, injuries have been caused by that negligence. If appropriate, he will also calculate (usually in considerable detail) the amount of compensation, if any, which is due to the plaintiff.

The plaintiff's solicitor will usually write to the plaintiff after the judgment hearing giving a summary of the findings of the judge and a breakdown of how the damages have been calculated (if appropriate).

JUDGMENT AND COSTS

Ultimately, the judgment will be reduced to a short form document (with a court seal) which will name the winner of the case, the amount of damages awarded and the amount of costs to be paid. The winner's solicitor must draw up this judgment (in the County Court the court does it) and serve it on the loser. Normally the damages are payable within 14 or 21 days. In most medical negligence cases there is little problem in recovering the damages since the defendant is insured. To encourage speedy payment of the damages, interest runs at a punitive rate (the judgment rate) from the date of judgment until actual payment (presently 8% per annum).

The legal costs

Who pays the legal costs is ultimately a matter for the judge at trial, but the usual rule is that the loser pays the winner's costs. However, in practice the loser seldom has to pay all the costs of the winner.

Assessment of costs

Costs are covered in detail in a separate chapter (see Chapter 21). The rules have now been simplified, the paying party pays costs either on an:

- *indemnity basis*: where costs recovered are allowed except where they have been unreasonably incurred and any doubts will be resolved in favour of the receiving party (the winner); or a
- *standard basis*: where reasonable costs are allowed and any doubts are to be resolved in favour of the paying party (the loser). Where the court makes an Order for costs without

indicating the basis of the assessment, then the standard basis will be applied.

The latter basis is almost always ordered.

Taxation of costs

The courts have a long established system for dealing with disputes over the amount of costs. The receiving party (the winner) must draw up a formal bill (there is a particular format) and serve it on the paying party (the loser) and the court. After the disputes between the parties have been further defined, the court fixes a hearing before a taxation master (or in the County Court a district judge) who determines what will be paid.

The formal bill must be lodged with the court within three months of the date of judgment, and interest will be payable on costs from the day of judgment at the judgment rate.

LEGAL AID CASES

Successful cases

The legally aided party recovers his 'standard basis' costs from the defendant. Any unrecovered legal costs are recouped from the plaintiff's damages and contribution (if any). This is called 'the statutory charge'.

Unsuccessful cases

The plaintiff's costs are paid by the Legal Aid Board from public funds and the contribution paid by the client. The defendant's costs are sometimes paid by the Legal Aid Board but more often than not, their costs remain unrecovered.

APPEALS

All *initial* decisions by the court can be the subject of appeal as follows:

- interlocutory[1] decisions in the High Court to a single High Court Judge;
- interlocutory decisions in the County Court to the County Court Circuit Judge;

[1]An interlocutory decision or judgment is a decision made by the court prior to the trial and which only deals with part of the matter in dispute.

- final decisions of the High Court Judge to the Court of Appeal;
- final decisions of the County Court Judge to the Court of Appeal;
- decisions of the Court of Appeal to the House of Lords.

There are strict time deadlines as to the submission of an appeal. In interlocutory matters this is five days. In final decisions it is 28 days from the date judgment is perfected.

The burden of showing that the original judge was wrong, either on the facts or the law, lies on the person bringing the appeal. The duty of the court of Appeal is to rehear the case but it does so 'on paper', that is it does not hear evidence and relies on the transcript of the proceedings in the court below. It only overturns judgments if (i) the judge has erred in principle or (ii) his judgment is manifestly wrong on the facts.

WHAT IF THE LAWYER GETS IT WRONG?

Doctors make mistakes, so do lawyers. The solicitor owes a duty to the client to provide a service with reasonable care and skill in accordance with the standards of a reasonably competent solicitor. If the client does not think that the solicitor has achieved that standard then he should seek the advice of another lawyer (who should be experienced in medical negligence cases). The client should not lose out because all solicitors are insured to cover the costs of such claims.

The lawyer is immune from an action in negligence when he acts as an advocate in court. This immunity now extends to pre-trial work which is intimately connected with how the case is conducted in court.

If a solicitor acts in accordance with advice given by Counsel (who has been properly instructed) he is unlikely to be held liable for negligence. The lawyer will also not be liable for carrying out the client's instructions, providing he has advised about the hazards of continuing on the basis of those instructions.

The value of the damages in any claim against the solicitor is the amount which the client would have received if his medical negligence case had been conducted properly.

Solicitors

A solicitor must operate a complaints handling procedure which states who in the organisation will investigate complaints and what action will be taken when the complaint is investigated. If the client is not satisfied, he will be given information about the Office for the Supervision of Solicitors (OSS). This is the Law Society's independent complaints handling area. It takes action on:

- professional misconduct; and
- inadequate professional services.

If a client is not satisfied by the way the OSS has handled the complaint, he can ask the Legal Services Ombudsman to examine the treatment of the complaint. The Ombudsman can recommend that the OSS or the solicitor pay compensation to the client.

Barristers

The Courts and Legal Services Act 1990 designated the Bar Council as the authorised body for the profession. All barristers must be members of the Bar Council and are obliged to comply with the Codes of Conduct produced by the Bar Council. Any failure to do so will amount to professional misconduct.

In the first instance all complaints of professional misconduct should be addressed to the Professional Conduct Committee of the Bar Council. The Secretary of the Committee will carry out a preliminary investigation into the complaint. If there are sufficient grounds the matter will be referred to the Summary Tribunal (less serious matters) or the Disciplinary Tribunal. The disciplinary tribunal has the power to: disbar (strike off); suspend for a prescribed period; fine up to £5,000; order the barrister to repay or forego his or her fees; or, in the least serious matters, reprimand. The summary tribunal may not disbar or suspend and can impose fines of up to £500.

If a person is dissatisfied with the Law Society's or Bar Council's handling of the matter he or she may bring the complaint to the attention of the Legal Services Ombudsman.

Useful addresses:

Office for Supervision of Solicitors
Victoria Court
8 Dormer Place
Leamington Spa CV32 5AE

General Council of the Bar
3 Bedford Row
London WC1R 4DB

Legal Services Ombudsman
22 Oxford Court
Oxford Street
Manchester M2 3WQ

CONCLUSION

Medical negligence cases are often complex, but most should be investigated and brought to trial within about three years of first seeing a solicitor. Each case is different and the outline above sets out the major steps on the journey from initial investigation to trial.

Example of a timetable in a real case

Flynn v Maidstone Health Authority

Victoria Flynn was born with cerebral palsy on 3 November 1988. The cerebral palsy was caused by the negligence of the consultant obstetrician in failing to expedite delivery. The following sets out the major milestones in the legal case. The trial which was held in October 1992 was on liability only.

1st Interview	16.12.89
Legal Aid application	09.03.90
Legal Aid received	03.05.90
Application for pre-action discovery	17.06.90
Medical records received	14.07.90
1st expert's report received (obstetric)	02.10.90
Counsel's advice received	03.11.90
2nd & 3rd experts' reports received (obstetric/paediatric)	May '91
Meeting with Counsel	26.07.91
Issue of writ	12.07.91
Service of writ	18.07.91
Service of defence	11.10.91
Summons for directions	13.12.91
Set down for trial	19.12.91

Defendant's list of documents	24.04.92
Exchange of witness statements	May '92
Meeting with Counsel and experts	19.06.92
Meeting to approve experts' reports	27.07.92
Exchange experts' reports	09.09.92
Pre-trial meeting	15.09.92
Trial [5 days]	19.10.92
Judgment	26.10.92

Judgment was given in Vicky's favour and damages were assessed at a later hearing.

Chapter 19

QUANTUM

Caroline Jenkins

Once a plaintiff has established that there has been a breach of duty, and has shown that damage has resulted from that breach, the question of the amount of financial compensation to be paid has to be considered. In this chapter we describe how damages are calculated including the effect of interest, deductions from damages and the Compensation Recovery Unit.

TYPES OF DAMAGES

Restitutional damages

The principle underlying the payment of damages is to pay to the plaintiff a lump sum to compensate for the pain, suffering, loss of amenity and financial losses caused by the negligence of the defendant. In order to establish the amount of compensation to be paid, the court will look at the nature and extent of the injury, how the plaintiff's life has been affected by it in the past, and how it will be affected in the future. The point of the exercise is an attempt, (however crude), to put the plaintiff in the position he or she would have been but for the injury. The size of the awards given to plaintiffs are governed not only by the facts of the particular case but by awards given to other plaintiffs in similar circumstances in decided cases.

GENERAL DAMAGES

General damages are awarded to compensate the plaintiff for the past and future pain, suffering and loss of amenity caused by the negligence. Such damages are naturally difficult to quantify as they depend very much upon the impact of the negligence on each individual plaintiff: an intensely personal matter. It is important for the lawyer to present not only the plaintiff's situation following any injury, but also the way of life before the injury.

Pain, suffering and loss of amenity

Damages for pain can be claimed to compensate a plaintiff for the actual pain caused at the time of injury itself, the continuing pain arising from the injury and any pain that will be caused in the future by any complication of the injury or any necessary repair operation arising from the injury.

Suffering includes such things as the fright or terror leading up to or arising from the injury, any fear of future disability because of the injury, humiliation, embarrassment and/or sickness resulting from the damage and any disfigurement caused by the injury. It can also include the suffering and distress caused to a plaintiff who, as a result of the injury, is made aware that his or her life expectancy has been reduced.

The court can take account of such matters as an interference caused by the injury to the plaintiff's leisure or sporting activities, recreations or hobbies; this is called loss of amenity. It may also include the loss to the plaintiff of enjoyment of family life, their loss of prospects of marriage and any sexual dysfunction caused by the injury. Given the broad nature of loss of amenity, it is vital for the lawyer to obtain from both the plaintiff and the plaintiff's friends and relatives clear statements detailing both the social and psychological profile of the plaintiff prior to the injury, and post injury, in order to establish the nature of the resultant loss.

Loss of congenial employment

This head of damage is to compensate a plaintiff who can no longer carry out the employment of his or her choice. For example in the case of *Chapman v London Fire and Civil Defence Authority* (1989), a fireman who was injured during his work was unable to pursue his career and had to take up another job which he did not enjoy as much. He was awarded damages for his loss of job satisfaction. If a claim is to be made under this head, as with loss of amenity claims generally, it is important that full evidence should be obtained not only from the plaintiff detailing the pleasure of the former employment, but also a clear statement from the former employers and workmates confirming the position.

Bereavement damages

Please see Chapter 20 on Fatal Cases.

Unconscious patients

Defendants may argue that a plaintiff cannot be compensated for pain, suffering or loss of amenity in circumstances where the patient is unaware of such loss – e.g. when the plaintiff is in a coma. The courts have held that a claim is sustainable and in

Anwar v Wandsworth Health Authority (1990), three weeks of unconsciousness between the negligent administration of an anaesthetic and death resulted in an award of £900. Higher awards are made to patients who remain in a persistent vegetative state for months or years.

Evidence

All claims for pain, suffering and loss of amenity must be supported by medical evidence from the relevant discipline, e.g. orthopaedic complaints by an orthopaedic consultant, scarring by a plastic surgeon etc. The report should be obtained from an independent source and not from the treating doctor. It will almost certainly require an examination by the reporting doctor. Except in unusual cases the defendants will obtain their own evidence and are entitled to insist on a separate examination. The costs of attending the defendant's doctor are recoverable.

Psychiatric illness

In the field of medical negligence litigation, perhaps more than in any other field of personal injury litigation, questions of psychiatric injury often play a large part. Where vulnerable patients are let down by their medical advisers, especially where death or serious injury result, psychological trauma may occur. Where a claim is made in circumstances where no physical injury is suffered by the plaintiff, but psychiatric illness has been sustained, special rules apply. [See *Alcock v Chief Constable of South Yorks Police* (1992) 1AC 310, *Sion v Hampstead Health Authority* (1994) 5 Med LR170, *Tredget v Bexley Health Authority* (1994) 5 Med LR178 and *Page v Smith* (1995) 2W LR 644.]

To succeed in claiming damages the plaintiff must show:

- *recognised psychiatric illness*

In all cases (i.e. whether or not physical injury has also been suffered) where a claim for psychiatric injury is contemplated, in order for the claim to succeed, psychiatric evidence must be produced to show that the plaintiff has suffered a psychiatric injury. This must go beyond the ambit of a normal reaction to a shocking event or sequence of events, such as grief, fear, sorrow, anger or distress.

- *primary victims*

In cases where the plaintiff suffers no physical injury but e.g. is a direct victim of the shocking event which caused psychiatric injury, the route to recovery of damages is relatively straightforward.

Assuming that the plaintiff can establish liability and that he or she is suffering from a recognised psychiatric injury due to the defendant's act, the next step is to show that the defendant owed him or her a duty of care. In the 1995 case of *Page v Smith* it was held that, if it can be shown that the defendant should have reasonably foreseen that his or her conduct would expose the plaintiff to the risk of personal injury – whether or not the resultant injury was physical or psychiatric – the relationship between the plaintiff and the defendant was sufficiently proximate so that a duty of care would arise. The court held that the duty of care applied to primary victims who included close relatives of persons injured.

- *secondary victims*

In cases where the victim is not directly involved in the incident giving rise to the claim but is a witness or bystander, the courts have set strict limits on the circumstances in which claims may be made. It has been established that in such cases the plaintiff must satisfy the following criteria.

- That the plaintiff has suffered a recognised psychiatric illness as a result of the negligence and has not merely experienced the normal grief, distress or sorrow that can be expected witnessing the distressing experience.
- That the particular psychiatric illness resulted from the shock of the event itself. 'Shock' has been defined as a sudden and direct appreciation by sight or sound of a horrifying event or series of events. This can be clearly distinguished from the stress, strain, grief and sorrow which result from a gradual or retrospective realisation of the events themselves.
- That the plaintiff was sufficiently close to the events that are alleged to have caused the injury in both space and in time.
- That the injury was reasonably foreseeable and that the relationship between the plaintiff and the defendant was sufficiently proximate.
- That there is a proximity of relationship between the 'primary victim' and the plaintiff to allow foreseeability.

Evidence

It is often very difficult for plaintiffs to discuss the nature of the psychological damage that they and their families have suffered. To prove such damage it is essential that a psychiatric report be commissioned as early as possible to identify and consider the nature and extent of any psychological trauma. The psychiatrist instructed must understand the legal tests to be applied, and must be provided with a clear and detailed statement from the plaintiff (and from close friends and relatives). He or she must also be given a full set of the plaintiff's medical notes. It is very likely that if such a claim is made the defendants will instruct their own psychiatric expert which will mean a further examination.

SPECIAL DAMAGES AND FUTURE LOSS

Special damages comprise the calculable losses and expenses that have been incurred by the plaintiff since the injury up to the date of the trial. Future losses are those which the plaintiff will incur in the future. It is very important that both the client and the lawyer appreciate the variety of claims that can be made under this head. Since awards for general damages are relatively modest the bulk of any award will comprise special damages and future loss. The basis of the award of special damages and future loss is a precise calculation; it is therefore important that the client understands the necessity for keeping careful records and receipts from the outset. It is of considerable assistance to the lawyer when preparing the schedule of special damage to be able to attach to that schedule supporting receipts in relation to all the items claimed. It is often very helpful for the client to keep a daily diary, not only detailing expenses incurred, but also gratuitous care afforded. In practice it is more difficult for the defendant's solicitors to attack a schedule if each item is supported by documentary evidence.

- **Loss of Earnings – Past and Future**

A loss of earnings claim will cover a plaintiff's temporary, partial or total inability to work as a result of the injury. The plaintiff can recover the value of the lost wages or, if self employed, lost profits, net of tax and National Insurance contributions. In addition claims may be made for such things as loss of promotion prospects, pension rights and other benefits – e.g. a company car, private medical care, company loans, etc.

Duty to mitigate loss

It is important to remember that a plaintiff has a duty to take all reasonable steps to keep his losses to a minimum. The defendants will always raise this. It is important to ensure that documentary evidence is provided of any attempts made to find work or limit losses. It may even be necessary to obtain a report from an employment consultant about the difficulties in finding employment on the labour market. This will enable the plaintiff to establish that he or she has carried out her duty to mitigate his or her loss and substantiate the reasons why he or she has failed to obtain employment.

Loss of earning capacity

It is possible to claim an amount for loss of earning capacity as a result of the injury even where no precise figure can be placed on loss of earnings. This arises in circumstances where the plaintiff has any continuing disability that could put him or her at a disadvantage on the open labour market in the future. It is difficult to value such claims as restrictions on employment opportunities are notoriously difficult to estimate. Again it may be advisable to obtain the advice of an employment expert who can more readily identify trends in particular occupations which may put a particular plaintiff more at risk of such a disadvantage. The award that is made is usually referred to as a Smith and Manchester award, named after the case of *Smith v Manchester Corporation*. The award can be a substantial item: its importance should not be overlooked.

Lost years

In some cases a severe injury may reduce the life expectancy of a plaintiff and, in these cases, a claim can be made for the loss of earnings in years when the plaintiff will be dead but, had it not been for the injury, would have been alive and working. The amount paid for under this head will be subject to deduction of the living expenses that the plaintiff would have incurred during the period.

Evidence

In all cases involving past and future loss of earnings, it is important to obtain as much documentary evidence as possible of the plaintiff's employment history. Any medical reports on present condition and prognosis should be updated regularly. The medical experts should be made fully aware of any deterioration in the plaintiff's condition and the impact that this might have upon employment prospects. In complex cases a forensic accountant may be employed especially when the plaintiff was self employed or a director of a small company and significant future profits may have been lost.

- **The Use of Multipliers in Future Loss Claims**

Multipliers

The approach adopted by the court when looking at future losses is to consider the nature and extent of the plaintiff's disability and the period over which the losses will be incurred. Taking loss of earnings as an example, if a plaintiff is so disabled as to have no prospects of future employment, then he or she will be entitled to all wage losses, pension losses and any fringe benefits until retirement age. The loss is calculated at the date of the trial. It is based upon the plaintiff's annual income and employment benefits, net of tax and National Insurance. This amount, termed the multiplicand, is then multiplied by a figure based upon the number of years during which the inability to work will persist (i.e. date of trial to retirement). However, this figure is then adjusted to take into account such factors as the contingencies of life e.g. premature death, sickness and the fact that the plaintiff will recover a lump sum figure now to compensate for a loss to be spread over a number of years in the future e.g. if a seriously injured plaintiff is a male and is 45 at the date of trial he has 20 years of working life remaining. Using the conventional discount rates applied by the court he will receive a multiplier of between 10 and 12. The calculation of the multiplier is not an exact science (even when actuarial tables are used) and judges tend to use their discretion.

Using the same example, if the plaintiff needed care to be provided for the remainder of his life, the multiplier to be applied to the annual cost of care would be 11.5 to 14.5.

These examples are based on normal life expectancy. Where life expectancy is reduced lower multipliers will be applied.

The theory behind the use of multipliers is that at the end of the day the plaintiff should be provided with a lump sum which, when invested, will produce an annual income comparable to the losses incurred.

It should be noted that there is a significant debate between lawyers and the courts as to what rate of investment the plaintiff will achieve. This is to be considered by the House of Lords in 1998.

- **Expenses**

Expenses incurred up to the date of the trial are special damages. The plaintiff is entitled to recover all expenses reasonably incurred, up to the date of the trial. Thereafter the plaintiff can claim as future loss all expenses which foreseeably arise out of the injury suffered and which will be incurred in the future. Below is a list of some of the items that have successfully been claimed against defendants.

Travelling and transport

Potential claims include:

- attending medical consultations past and future;
- travelling and incidental costs of relatives visiting the plaintiff in hospital;
- increased travelling and car costs in the future as a result of disability e.g. the adaptation of a manual car to an automatic car for a disabled driver, or the purchase of a completely new vehicle adapted and designed for the plaintiff's particular wheelchair needs;
- an allowance for transport by taxi (or other means) for a plaintiff who can no longer drive or the provision of a car for a partner;
- driving lessons for partners or spouse where the plaintiff can no longer drive;
- additional mileage and insurance because of disability;
- cost of recovery service;
- cost of car telephone.

Medical expenses

A claim can be made for private past and future medical care including the cost of future remedial operations required as a result of the negligence; it is irrelevant that the treatment is available on the NHS (see Law Reform (Personal Injuries) Act 1948).

Therapies

The cost of any physiotherapy, speech therapy, occupational therapy, counselling and certain types of complementary medical treatments; the cost of drugs purchased, prescription charges paid and any other general medical expenses arising as a result of the injury. The test applied by the court is whether such expenses are or will be reasonably incurred.

A claim can be made for a sum to recompense relatives and friends for care afforded to the plaintiff in the past, even though no charge was made for this at the time. Many injured patients rely on relatives to provide care and assistance when they suffer injury.

Where paid nursing care has been provided in the past it can be claimed if properly supported by receipts and documentary evidence as a special damages item. Where it is needed in the future it can be claimed as a future loss and in such cases it is helpful to obtain an expert nursing report to set out the basis of the claim and its likely amount. In cases where the injury is severe the future cost of care is likely to be the most expensive item.

Domestic help

Where a plaintiff has had to employ additional help in the home in the past or is likely to do so in future this item can be claimed as a item of special damage or future loss. Even where in the past care has been afforded gratuitously by relatives and friends, if this could be provided reasonably by the employment of a domestic helper in future it can be claimed as a future loss. Again documentary evidence needs to be provided to establish the amount of the help required and its likely cost. This is something that can be provided by a specialist occupational therapy report or by a report from a general rehabilitation expert.

Accom-modation

Where the plaintiff needs a 'live in carer', extra space for aids and appliances and the plaintiff needs accommodation on one level, the plaintiff can claim for:

- the increased capital costs of the new accommodation over and above that which he or she would have spent in any event;
- the cost of adaptation;
- removal expenses including legal fees, stamp duty, surveyor's fees, estate agent's fees and furniture removal;
- the extra cost of furnishings for the additional rooms;
- the extra cost of maintaining and insuring the property.

Accommodation claims are always complicated because of the legal principles involved. It is always necessary to obtain a report from an expert architect if such claims are contemplated.

Aids and appliances

In cases of utmost severity, and in cases where the plaintiff has lost a limb, an occupational therapy report can be invaluable for identifying aids and appliances necessary to enable the plaintiff to carry out normal activities more readily and to enable him or her to regain some independence. Such reports will deal with such matters as the installation of a stair lift and the provision of wheelchairs, hoists, special baths, chairs, beds and ramps. This list is not exhaustive.

Technological equipment

In cases where the plaintiff has suffered brain damage or other injury which has reduced mobility and the ability to communicate, a claim for technological equipment may be sustained. It involves the provision of powered mobility, communication aids, computers and environmental controls. Often such items are indispensable to maximise the plaintiff's potential. Again it will always be necessary to instruct a technological expert to prove such claims.

DIY and gardening

A claim can be made to recompense a plaintiff for an inability to undertake household repairs, general housekeeping, home decoration and gardening.

Holidays

Disabled people need holidays; often they are more expensive because carers need to come and specialised facilities are required. These costs are recoverable.

Miscellaneous costs

A claim can be made in respect of clothing and bedding soiled or destroyed; for associated laundry costs and additional bedding and clothing required because of disability. A claim can be made for increased charges in relation to gas, electricity and telephone either because the plaintiff is at home more or because his or her accommodation is bigger.

Court of Protection fees

Persons who are incapable of looking after their own affairs can claim the fees of the Court of Protection. This organisation has been set up specifically to protect the interests of people suffering from such a disability and in all cases involving significant brain injury the damages will be paid into the Court of Protection.

PROVISIONAL DAMAGES

Usually damages are paid on a once and for all basis. Provisional damages provide an exception to the rule. Where a provisional damage award is made the plaintiff can return to recover further damages later if a specified risk of further injury actually occurs:

e.g. epilepsy after a head injury. The difficulty with provisional damages is that it is necessary for the expert evidence to specify that a serious deterioration or disease will occur and to indicate within what period of time the second application for damages may be made. The right to recover further damages arises only when the stipulated disease or serious deterioration occurs. By and large provisional awards are restricted to complicated cases, where there is a clear and foreseeable risk of a different condition developing in the future.

INTEREST

Interest can be awarded on damages. Different rates of interest apply to general and special damages. No claim for interest can be made in respect of future losses.

Interest on general damages

Interest on general damages is awarded at 2% pa from the date that the proceedings are served upon the defendant. In a case where the general damages are likely to be high, delay in serving the proceedings reduces the interest recoverable.

Interest on special damages

Interest on special damages is awarded at the Court Special Account Rate (currently 8% pa) between the date the special damages started (usually the date of the medical accident) and the date of hearing. Because the losses accrue over this period, conventionally lawyers apply half the rate for the whole period. However, the half rate is not always appropriate, for instance where a substantial loss has been incurred and paid by the plaintiff immediately after the accident (e.g. medical expenses or a large loss of earnings) there being an appreciable lapse of time between the incurring of the expense and the date of trial. In such circumstances it is more appropriate to claim at the full rate. A ready reckoner table is provided annually in the Law Society's Gazette compiled by Rodney Nelson-Jones and most practitioners use this extremely useful table for calculating the interest to be applied.[1]

[1]Rodney Nelson-Jones has now published 'Computing Personal Injury Damages': a comprehensive set of 48 software programmes

COMPENSATION RECOVERY SCHEME

Since the Social Security Act 1989 the Government has been able to recoup social security benefits paid to citizens injured as a result of medical (and other) negligence. The system had many critics and has recently been reformed by the Social Security (Recovery of Benefits) Act 1997 which came into force on 6th October 1997. The Act is retrospective and now applies to all cases. Schedule 2 of the Act sets out the benefits and from which head of compensation they are deductible as follows:

Head of Compensation	Benefit
Compensation for earnings lost during the relevant period	Disability working allowance Disablement pension and gratuity Incapacity benefit Income support Invalidity pension and allowance Jobseeker's allowance Reduced earnings allowance Severe disablement allowance Sickness benefit Statutory sick pay Unemployment benefit
Compensation for cost of care incurred during the relevant period	Attendance allowance Care component of disability living allowance
Compensation for loss of mobility during the relevant period	Mobility allowance disability living allowance Mobility component of disability living allowance

No deduction of benefits can be made against general damages. Any benefits which have been paid but which are not reducible from the plaintiff's damages must be paid back by the defendant in any event. For example the plaintiff only recovers general damages of £10,000 but has received Attendance Allowance of £5,000. The defendant will have to pay the plaintiff £10,000 and the DSS £5,000.

The benefits to be taken into account run from the date of the injury to the date of settlement or judgment or to the date five years from the injury, whichever comes first.

STRUCTURED SETTLEMENTS AND TRUST FUNDS

Structured settlement

Structured settlements result when both parties agree that the plaintiff should receive an annual payment instead of a conventional lump sum. The advantages and disadvantages are discussed in Chapter 21.

Trust funds

In certain circumstances the court or the plaintiff's advisers may suggest that the damages are paid into a Discretionary Trust. Again this is discussed in Chapter 21.

EXAMPLES OF AWARDS OF DAMAGES

- *Janardan v East Berkshire Health Authority (1990)*

Boy aged five at the date of trial. Seriously brain damaged at birth because the obstetricians failed to expedite delivery in the face of foetal distress. The total award comprised:

Pain, suffering and loss of amenities:	115,000
Special damage (agreed):	33,000
Future medical and therapeutic needs (agreed):	53,000
Future care and attendance:	280,000
Loss of earning capacity:	75,000
Costs associated with home (agreed):	62,500

Computer aids, appliances and misc (agreed):	75,000
Transport and travel (agreed):	15,000
Total award:	708,500

Interest was awarded of £14,619

- *Ellinger v Riverside Health Authority (1992)*

During a minor operation, under a local anaesthetic, to remove a lump on her neck, Mrs Ellinger negligently suffered damage to the nerves in her left shoulder. This caused limitation of movement and acute pain. Married five months before the surgery, sexual relations with her husband were now painful. She needed two operations to repair the damage. She could no longer play squash nor participate in winter sports. Her ability to work was not affected. She found it difficult to care for her baby, especially tasks involving lifting and carrying. A nanny was required because of her disabilities to undertake domestic chores (e.g. ironing, vacuuming, cleaning etc.) She was awarded general damages of £30,000; special damages of £1,980 and future costs of nanny and home help of £115,410.

- *Wrigglesworth v Doncaster Health Authority (1996)*

General damages of £12,500 were awarded to Mrs Wrigglesworth because of medical negligence when the hospital failed to diagnose internal bleeding after a hysterectomy. Mrs Wrigglesworth suffered a pelvic abscess and small bowel obstructions which led to a midline laporotomy and small bowel resection. She still had a scar on her abdomen which aggravated her bowel problems, and suffered some psychiatric trauma at the time of her injury.

CONCLUSION

It will be seen that the calculation of damages is an art in itself. It is important that the lawyer and the client treat this aspect of the claim seriously. Although English law may not be able to put the plaintiff precisely in the position he or she was before the medical accident, with care, skill and supportive documentation much can be done to improve the plaintiff's life by obtaining the maximum amount of compensation available.

Chapter 20

FATAL CASES

Rodney Nelson-Jones

This chapter explains how damages are calculated in cases where the patient dies as a result of medical negligence. It also sets out who can claim and in what circumstances.

TWO TYPES OF CLAIMS

Where a victim of medical negligence dies, two types of claims may arise:

- a claim on behalf of the deceased's estate (pursuant to the Law Reform (Miscellaneous Provisions) Act 1934)[1]
- a claim on behalf of the deceased's dependants (pursuant to the Fatal Accidents Act 1976)[1]

The two claims are not alternatives. Where both arise, they are additional to each other. For example, £10,000 damages on behalf of the estate plus £90,000 damages on behalf of the dependants produces a total award of £100,000.

THE ESTATE'S CLAIM

When a person dies, any claim for damages that he or she may have survives for the benefit of his or her estate e.g. where anaesthetic negligence caused brain damage during an operation in 1969 but death only ensued in 1972 (*Gray v Mid Herts Group Hospital Management Committee*[2]).

Any court action must be brought by the personal representative of the deceased: the executor of the will or, if the person died without making a will (intestate), by the administrator of the

[1] As amended by the Administration of Justice Act 1982
[2] (1974) 118 Sol Jo 501

estate. The damages form part of the estate and are distributed in accordance with the terms of the will or the laws of intestacy, as the case may be.

THE DEPENDANT'S CLAIM

When a person dies due to medical negligence, in respect of which he or she could (if still alive) have recovered damages, his or her dependants can pursue a claim arising out of the death e.g. where a surgeon left a towelling pack in a patient's body during an operation for removal of gall stones, and the pack set up a fistula from which the patient died (*James v Dunlop*[3]).

It is essential that the deceased had not already lost his or her right to recover damages. Therefore, if he or she had already received such damages during life, or if his or her claim had been pursued and lost, his or her dependants would not be entitled to sue after the death.

It is also essential that the medical negligence caused the death. Consequently, where casualty doctors negligently failed to treat a vomiting night watchman who died a few hours later due to arsenical poisoning, his widow's claim was dismissed when it was held that he would have died of the arsenic even if timeously treated. (*Barrett v Chelsea and Kensington Hospital Management Committee*[4])

WHO CAN CLAIM ?

Under the Fatal Accidents Act 1976, the right to recover damages is restricted to certain specified categories of dependants. These include:

- a surviving spouse, a divorced spouse, or a 'common law spouse' who had been cohabiting with the deceased for at least two years immediately before death;

[3] (1931) 1 BMJ 730
[4] (1955) *The Times*, 1–2 November

- any parent, any person whom the deceased treated as a parent, or any other ascendant (e.g. grandmother);
- any child or other descendant of the deceased, or any child of a family whom she had treated as hers whilst married (including an adopted child);
- any brother, sister, uncle, aunt, nephew, niece or first cousin;
- any stepchild, illegitimate child, or in-law or half-blood relative within the above categories.

Mere friends do not qualify. Nor do homosexual partners. Nor does a fiancé(e), unless there has been at least two years' cohabitation immediately before the death.

NEGLIGENCE

The principles of negligence are the same as in cases of surviving patients. The acts and omissions of doctors and nurses are judged by the same criteria. Only the ultimate outcome is different. Examples of successful fatal claims include:

- a general practitioner's failure to consider the possibility of pneumonia, from which the patient died two days later (*Bova v Spring*[5]);
- a failure to give an anti-tetanus injection after the patient's finger had been severely crushed by a lump of coal, with the result that he died of toxaemia due to tetanus infection (*Cole v Reading and District Hospital Management Committee and Another*[6]);
- a woman's death three weeks after giving birth, as a result of lung infection caused by anaesthetic mismanagement during a caesarean section (*Corbett v Barking Havering and Brentwood Health Authority*[7]);
- a hospital doctor's failure to diagnose appendicitis in an 11 year old girl who was ill with abdominal pains and

[5] (1994) 5 Med LR 120
[6] (1963) 107 Sol Jo 115
[7] (1990) 1 Med LR 433

vomiting (*Elder v Greenwich and Deptford Hospital Management Committee*[8]);

- the negligent administration of pentothal anaesthetic by an inexperienced junior doctor (*Jones v Manchester Corporation*[9]);
- the death of the actor Roy Kinnear in a Madrid hospital which negligently failed to provide immediate treatment for hypovolaemic shock caused by blood loss from a riding accident whilst filming (*Kinnear v Falconfilms NV and Others*[10]);
- the death of a baby boy eight weeks after birth due to brain damage sustained in a horrifically mishandled caesarean section (*Kralj v McGrath*[11]);
- a hospital doctor's failure to detain for observation and examination a man with a badly bruised abdomen due to a kick from a horse, where the patient subsequently died due to general peritonitis (*Payne v St Helier Group Hospital Management Committee*[12]);
- a general practitioner's diagnosis of a common cold in a one month old baby who was icy cold, displayed mauve colour and breathed irregularly, prior to dying of staphylococcal pneumonia (*Riddett v D'Arcy*[13]);
- a masseur's treatment with ray lamps which severely burned the back of the patient who died of toxaemia (*Snell v Carter*[14]);
- a works doctor's failure to provide check-ups and warnings to toolsetters whose midriffs frequently became covered with cutting oil, one of whom died due to epithelioma of the scrotum (*Stokes v Guest, Keen and Nettlefold Ltd*[15]);
- a nurse's administration of six ounces, instead of six drachms, of paraldehyde to a patient who died without recovering consciousness (*Strangeways-Lesmere v Clayton*[16]);

[8] (1953) *The Times*, 7 March
[9] (1952) 2 All ER 125
[10] QBD transcript
[11] (1986) 1 All ER 54
[12] (1952) *The Times*, 12 November
[13] (1960) 2 BMJ 1607
[14] (1941) 2 *Lancet* 321
[15] (1968) 1 WLR 1776
[16] (1993) PIQR P262

- a hospital's failure to diagnose and treat serious heart disease, resulting in a fatal heart attack (*Taylor v Somerset Health Authority*[17]);
- a hospital's failure to supervise a patient with known suicidal tendencies who hanged himself by a rope from a pipe in a disused building on a hospital site (*Waller v Canterbury and Thanet Health Authority*[18]):
- a casualty officer's discharge without treatment of a man who had been pinned to the ground by a wheel of a lorry. Post-mortem examination after his death a few hours later disclosed a broken collar bone, 18 fractured ribs and badly congested lungs (*Wood v Thurston*[19]).

However, liability was not established in respect of:

- a school medical officer who rather underestimated the gravity of a 15 year old pupil's infective hepatitis, leading to his death three years later from cirrhosis of the liver (*Holland v Devitt and Moore Nautical College Ltd*[20];
- a general practitioner who called at the old address of a patient who had moved without notifying him and, after ringing the doorbell of an adjoining flat left to pay other urgent visits, following which the patient died due to bronchitis a few days later (*Kavanagh v Abrahamson*[21]);
- a newly qualified hospital doctor who examined a patient complaining of chest pains for nearly an hour before discharging him, only for the patient to die in the street of a massive coronary thrombosis quarter of an hour later (*Parkinson v West Cumberland Hospital Management Committee*[22]);
- a general practitioner who after thoroughly examining a 26 year old patient initially concluded that she had acute hysteria, only for her to die of meningitis after he eventually arranged for her admission to hospital (*Sadler v Henry*[23]);

[17] (1993) 4 Med Lr 34
[18] 1993 CLY 1453
[19] (1951) *The Times*, 25 May
[20] (1960) *The Times*, 4 March
[21] (1964) 103 Sol Jo 320
[22] (1955) 1 BMJ 977
[23] (1954) 1 BMJ 1331

- a dentist who extracted 28 teeth in one operation from a patient with pyorrhoea, and the referring doctor who administered the anaesthetic, when the patient bled profusely and died of the rare condition of acute leukaemia (*Warren v Greig; Warren v White*[24]);
- a general practitioner who first saw in September 1983 a patient complaining of deafness and referred him to an ENT specialist in September 1984; an acoustic neuroma was discovered by cranial scan in February 1985, and the patient died after an operation to remove it (*Richardson v Kitching*[25]);

This last case illustrates the importance of causation. The issue was not only:

- whether the doctor had been negligent; but also
- whether the delay had made any ultimate difference.

On the negligence issue, it was held that the delay had not been proved to be the result of the doctor's acts or omissions, as opposed to the patient's reluctance to seek specialist advice. On the causation issue, the judge held that the widow had failed to prove that the delay caused the death.

Where medical negligence causes pain and suffering but is not responsible for the patient's subsequent death, the estate can claim damages under the Law Reform Act 1934 but that is all. Only when the negligence has caused death can the dependants claim damages under the Fatal Accidents Act 1976 as well.

LIMITATION

As seen in Chapter 17, court action arising out of a death cannot be successfully pursued if the deceased himself or herself had become barred from proceeding. If, therefore, the deceased had not commenced court proceedings within three years of acquiring

[24] (1935) 1 *Lancet* 330
[25] QBD 28 March 1995

the relevant knowledge, his or her heirs/dependants will be *prima facie* statute barred.[26]

Example One

Deceased's knowledge 1989. Death 1993. Court action started in 1995 would be statute barred.

However if the deceased's three year limitation period had not expired by his or her death, an entirely fresh three year time limit arises which runs from the date of relevant knowledge of personal representative(s) in the estate's claim under the Law Reform Act 1934, or of dependants in a claim under the Fatal Accidents Act 1976. This fresh limitation period applies, even where it results in court action being started four to five years after the deceased's date of knowledge.

Example Two

Deceased's knowledge 1990. Death 1992. Court action started in 1994 is not statute barred.

All the above limitation periods, which are contained in Sections 11–14 of the Limitation Act 1980, are subject to the court's discretion to disapply them under Section 33. Therefore judges are empowered to temper justice with mercy in suitable cases.

Example Three

Husband dies due to preventable heart attack in 1991. Medical records are retained and defence witnesses are still available. Owing to severe and prolonged grief reaction, widow only commences court action in 1995. Although her case became *prima facie* statute barred in 1994, a judge might well allow it to proceed to trial.

VALUE OF THE CLAIM – LAW REFORM ACT

With one major exception, the value of the estate's claim under the Law Reform Act 1934 is the value that the deceased's own

[26] This section is a short and simple summary of complex law. Readers wanting to study it in detail are referred to Chapter 6 of *Personal Injury Law* (Butterworths, 1994)

claim would have had, if judgment had been given the minute before his death. It therefore consists of:

- general damages for the deceased's pain and suffering caused by the medical negligence;
- interest on general damages;
- special damages i.e. the deceased's financial losses and expenses resulting from the negligence, including the value of care provided by relatives. Funeral expenses may be added if the estate has paid these;
- interest on special damages.

The exception to the above principle is that the estate's claim cannot include a claim for the deceased's loss of earnings during the 'lost years' of his life. Consequently the effect is that damages recovered under the Law Reform Act cover the period up to the death but not (apart from interest and funeral expenses) beyond it.

Example Four

Owing to a negligent failure of diagnosis, the deceased suffers from cancer for one year before dying of it. He was forced to give up work and lost £7,500 net earnings, his wife gave him care to the value of £5,000 and funeral expenses were £1,250.

General damages for pain and suffering	£20,000
Interest	£600
Special damages	£13,750
Interest on special damages	*£2,200*
Total Law Reform Act award	**£36,550**

VALUE OF CLAIM – FATAL ACCIDENTS ACT

Bereavement damages

The first item is bereavement damages. These are only payable to:

- the wife or husband of the deceased; or
- where the deceased died unmarried before the age of 18, to both parents if he or she was legitimate or to his or her mother alone if he or she was illegitimate.

A divorced or 'common law' spouse cannot recover bereavement damages. Nor can a child in respect of a parent's death.

The amount of bereavement damages has been fixed by Parliament at:

- £3,500 for deaths up to March 1991; and
- £7,500 for deaths from 1 April 1991 onwards.

Loss of Dependency

The rest of a fatal accidents claim belongs to the dependants. It is divisible into dependency on the deceased's net income (the income dependency) and dependency on his or her various familial services (the services dependency).

In an adult case where the deceased was working and the dependent spouse was not, the income dependency tends to be two-thirds of the deceased's net earnings where there are no dependent children or three-quarters of these earnings if there are two such children. From the future multiplier is deducted the period between death and trial. Additional allowance may be made for dependency on the deceased's pension after retirement.

The services dependency is designed to compensate the family for the deceased's:

- domestic services e.g. painting, decorating, maintenance, repairs, house adaptations, window cleaning, cooking, laundry, housework, and looking after children;
- gardening e.g. mowing lawns, planting flowers, building huts or ponds, repairing fences;
- driving, which may have been an invaluable resource (specially in rural areas) to a dependant unable to drive;
- other services of value e.g. repairing and servicing cars.

The best measure of the value of these services is the labour plus VAT cost (excluding materials) of their being performed professionally.

Example Five

Facts as in Example 4. Death at age 55. No dependent children. Hearing two years later. Deceased husband was earning £13,500 per annum net and would have retired at age 65. Dependent spouse did not work. Deceased's pension in retirement would have been £5,400 per annum. He was moderately useful around the house and garden. Surviving spouse used to drive herself. But for the negligence, the deceased would have lived to age 72.

Bereavement damages	£7,500
Interest on bereavement damages (8% p.a. × 2 = 16%)	£1,200
Income dependency to hearing: £9,000 p.a. × 2	£18,000
Services dependency to hearing: £750 p.a. × 2	£1,500
Interest on special damages (16% ÷ 2 = 8%)	£1,560
Future earnings dependency: £9,000 p.a. × 5	£45,000
Future pension dependency: £3,600 p.a. × 3	£10,800
Future services dependency: £750 p.a. × 7	*£5,250*
Total Fatal Accident Act award	**£90,810**

Examples Four and Five Summary

Estate's claim under Law Reform Act	£36,550
Dependant's claim under Fatal Accidents Act	£90,810
Total damages	**£127,360**

The position is more complicated where the surviving spouse also works. In such cases, the income dependency is apt to be abated to take account of the second income. The formula for calculating this was set out by the Court of Appeal in *Coward v Comex Houlder Diving Ltd.*[27]

It will be apparent from the above that the assessment of fatal damages is very financially orientated. In this respect, the law has progressed little since Lord Wright commented in *Davies v Powell Duffryn Associated Collieries Ltd*[28] that 'it is a hard matter of pounds, shillings and pence'. Grief is recognised only by the fixed and limited method of bereavement damages.

---

[27] Unreported, but included in Kemp & Kemp on Damages

[28] (1942) 1 ALL ER 657

This may lead to broad justice in cases where there is a substantial financial dependency. In other cases, equally tragic, grieving relatives may receive an award that is not only derisory but almost derisive. Few personal injury lawyers relish explaining to the parents of an instantaneously killed four year old that even with negligence proved, their only compensation for the death (apart from funeral and associated expenses and interest) is the bereavement damages of £7,500.

DAMAGES FOR PSYCHIATRIC INJURY

An offshoot of this deeply undesirable state of affairs has been an increase in claims by parents for damages for their own psychiatric injury resulting from the death. These are only allowed in special circumstances, and usually attract only modest awards. In *Tredget and Tredget v Bexley Health Authority*[29], however, the devastated parents of a baby boy born black and mauve after a chaotic delivery, only to die of brain damage two days later, recovered a total of £300,000 damages.

PROCEDURE

Where the deceased has left a will, the executor's title derives from that. Therefore it is unnecessary to obtain a grant of probate before starting court action. Nevertheless a grant should be obtained before damages become payable, so that defendants may have the security of paying on the basis of a valid will.

If there is no will, there is initially no entitlement to sue. The administrator's authority only derives from the grant of letters of administration which accordingly should be obtained before court proceedings are commenced. Where time constraints make this impossible, the appropriate amendment of the proceedings will in general be allowed when the grant becomes available.

[29] (1994) 5 Med LR 178

At the end of a fatal case, due to the potentially different beneficiaries from an award, the total damages must be allocated:

- between the estate's claim under the Law Reform Act 1934 and the dependant's claims under the Fatal Accidents Act 1976; and
- when there is more than one Fatal Accidents Act dependant, between those dependants.[30]

Where one of the dependants is a minor (i.e. aged under 18) or is unable due to mental disorder to manage and administer his or her affairs, any settlement must be approved by a court at least in so far as it affects that dependant.[31]

CONCLUSION

The law in relation to fatal claims is complicated and governed to a large extent by statute. Claims can be initiated on behalf of the estate of the deceased or for the dependants of the deceased. The law defines who the dependants can be fairly narrowly; for example, friends do not qualify even if they were co-habiting for up to two years. Parliament has also restricted the damages for bereavement to £7,500 which are only claimable by parents and spouses. These rules apply to all actions for personal injury and death, not just medical negligence claims.

[30] RSC Ord 22 r4, CCR Ord 11 r4
[31] RSC Ord 80 r10, CCR Ord 10 r10

Chapter 21

THE END OF THE CASE – PREPARING FOR THE FUTURE

Claire Fazan

In this chapter we look at various aspects of the end of a case including sorting out costs and compensation, the effect of the Legal Aid Board statutory charge, the administration of the award of compensation and how the end of the case can mean preparing for the future.

Medical negligence cases end in a variety of ways and at very different stages. Whether or not the end of the case is synonymous with a successful conclusion will depend upon what the individual plaintiff sought to achieve by seeking the services of a lawyer and whether the legal process is capable of providing such a result.

Thus, for example, the end of a case may not be successful in terms of recovering compensation, but the individual plaintiff may be satisfied because the investigation has for the first time provided an explanation of what happened, and how and why it happened.

COSTS

When the case ends, the question of costs will have to be resolved. This can be a slow, confusing and frustrating process for the plaintiff. It is nevertheless, an important stage because until costs are paid, the plaintiff may not receive all the money to which he or she is entitled. For the client who has Legal Aid, the receipt of the damages may be delayed. The privately funded litigant who has had to pay costs will be out of pocket until costs are paid by the opponent.

Medical negligence cases are undoubtedly expensive cases to litigate. This is because the issues are often complex and thus require more time from the lawyer than other less complex cases. It is also because it is essential to involve the medical expert(s) throughout the case. For these reasons it is not unusual for the costs to be equal to or exceed the recoverable compensation in claims of smaller value.

Information available to clients

Solicitors should now be advising clients both at the outset and throughout the case what the likely level of costs will be and the level of costs should no longer come as a surprise to the client at the end of the case. In the case of a legally aided plaintiff, if the solicitor holds a legal aid franchise, information on the level of costs should be given on a six monthly basis. The private client should be kept informed regularly about the level of costs. Disbursements of more than a nominal amount (i.e. experts and counsel's fees) must be agreed by the client in advance. Some firms will bill regularly throughout the case and many will require money on account of costs.

Who pays the costs?

The normal costs provision in all civil cases is that once proceedings have been commenced, the loser pays the winner's reasonable costs. This means that if a plaintiff successfully recovers compensation from a defendant (either as a result of settlement or judgment at trial), the reasonable costs of preparing and running the claim should be recoverable against the defendant. However, it is important to appreciate that the opponent rarely has to pay all of the successful plaintiff's legal costs. There will inevitably be work which it is reasonable and necessary to undertake but for which it would not be reasonable for the defendants to pay. For example, if the plaintiff has been treated by a number of doctors, time may have been spent obtaining evidence and advice in order to assess which doctor, if any, was negligent. The costs of this work will not necessarily be recoverable against the defendant if the claim is run on the basis that some but not all of the doctors involved were negligent. Another example is when a lawyer has to repeatedly write to a plaintiff who fails to respond to correspondence or phone calls; the costs involved in doing so may not be recoverable from the defendants. The prudent plaintiff should assume that something in the region of 75–80% of costs will be recovered from the defendant in the event of the claim being successful.

Costs if no proceedings are issued

If a case ends following the investigation (and, therefore, no proceedings have been issued), the defendant Health Authority or doctors will not be responsible for the client's potential costs of the investigation. It also means that the client will not be responsible for any costs the potential defendant has incurred as a result of the investigation (except where there has been an order for costs on a pre-action application: see Chapter 18).

Unsuccessful claims

The unsuccessful plaintiff who has the benefit of a legal aid certificate does not feel the impact of the normal costs order. If at the end of court action the plaintiff loses the case, all the legal aid costs incurred by her (apart from any contribution paid to the Legal Aid Board) will be paid by legal aid. In these circumstances, the court usually makes an order that the plaintiff should pay the defendant's costs, but the court then says that these cannot be enforced without leave of the court. This is what lawyers call a 'football pools' order because it means that if at any time in the future the plaintiff suddenly becomes immensely wealthy (such as by winning the pools or national lottery) and if the defendant finds out about it, he or she can return to court and seek leave to enforce the costs order.

Taxation of costs

If costs cannot be agreed between the parties, there is a hearing called 'taxation' at which a court official decides how much of the plaintiff's legal costs the opponent should have to pay. Despite attempts to speed up the taxation process there are still delays of many months in getting taxation hearings listed in both the County and High Courts. This can mean that it is common for there to be a delay of as much as a year between the damages being decided and costs being resolved. Where the client was legally aided there will then be a further administrative delay after payment of the costs before the Legal Aid Board authorises the payment of full damages to the client.

WHEN COSTS ARE *NOT* RECOVERABLE FROM THE DEFENDANT

Legal aid cases

Costs will be paid by the legal aid fund in those cases where no substantive proceedings have been issued against the potential defendant or where the plaintiff has been unsuccessful in proceedings.

If costs are to be paid by the legal aid fund, there will have to be an assessment by the Legal Aid Board or a taxation by the court of those costs before the lawyer can be paid. The purpose of this process is to ensure that only those costs properly incurred under the terms of the legal aid certificate are recoverable and that the rates charged by solicitor, counsel and expert are at a level which it is deemed should be paid by the fund.

In a case in which no proceedings have been issued, the certificate of discharge of legal aid is the authority to assess costs or to tax in a medical negligence action where a pre-action application has been issued, but no substantive proceedings have been commenced.

Discharge of legal aid certificate

If the lawyer advises the client that there is no reasonable prospect of succeeding on a claim, he or she must then report this advice to the Legal Aid Board. The Board will send the client what is called a 'show cause' letter and unless the client is able to show that there are reasonable grounds for continuing, the certificate will be discharged. (Civil Legal Aid (General) Regulations 1989, Reg. 81.) Where the client accepts the lawyer's advice, the quickest and most efficient way of getting a certificate discharged is for him or her to sign a form consenting to discharge of the certificate and for this form to be sent to the Legal Aid Board.

Privately funded cases

If a privately funded litigant does not pursue a claim after the initial investigation and there has been no order for pre-action costs against him or her, then all that will happen is that her lawyer will render a final bill for all unbilled work. The client has the right to require the solicitor-client costs to be taxed (Section 70, Solicitors Act 1974).

Defendant's costs

If, the plaintiff loses the case and is ordered to pay the defendant's costs, then the defendant will serve a bill on the plaintiff for his or her costs. If those costs are not agreed the plaintiff can require them to be taxed.

WHERE COSTS ARE RECOVERABLE FROM THE DEFENDANT

Legal aid

It is often possible to agree costs with defendants without the need to tax. That said, agreement on costs is less common than in ordinary personal injury claims probably due to a combination of factors, in particular, the time intensive nature of medical negligence cases, the numbers of experts required and pressures on Health Authority funding. If costs can be agreed and no claim is to be made on the legal aid fund then, following payment of the agreed costs, the lawyer notifies the Legal Aid Board of the payment of costs on a legal aid form (CLA26), and any balance of damages due to the client will be paid.

In cases where party and party costs are agreed and the certificate was granted on or after 25th February 1994, the plaintiff's solicitor can apply for an assessment of legal aid costs if it is believed that they amount to less than £1,000 (Civil Legal Aid (General) Regulations 1989, Reg 106A), or where the legal aid costs will exceed £1,000 may apply for a taxation of legal aid only costs (Reg. 107A(2)). These costs are deductible from the damages as a result of the Legal Aid Board's statutory charge.

Privately funded cases

If costs are not agreed in full, any compromise on costs agreed with the defendants will have to be approved by the client or funding body (e.g. legal expenses insurer) because it will, inevitably, increase the costs payable by the client. If costs are not agreed, it will be necessary to tax.

The client has the right to have the solicitor-client costs taxed (Section 70, Solicitors Act 1974).

Persons under a disability – minors or patients

Order 62, Rule 16 of the Rules of the Supreme Court requires the taxation of any costs payable by the plaintiff in cases involving minors and those acting under a disability. In such cases, the normal order when a settlement is approved by the court is for party and party costs to be taxed if not agreed, with the plaintiff's solicitor waiving any further costs in the event of agreement.

STATUTORY CHARGE

When compensation is paid, any part of the plaintiff's legal costs which the defendant does not have to pay will come out of the damages. This share of costs is called the 'statutory charge'. It is important because it reduces the amount of compensation which the plaintiff actually receives. For this reason, the plaintiff has the right to attend the taxation of costs and to make representations relevant to the costs which will be borne out of damages. When lodging the bill of costs for taxation, the plaintiff's solicitor has to certify that the client has been informed of this entitlement and whether he or she wishes to attend the taxation.

The Legal Aid Board will take account of any contributions paid by the plaintiff towards legal aid in assessing how much the statutory charge should be.

Example of the effect of the statutory charge

Compensation recovered	£50,000
Total plaintiff's costs	£23,000
Costs recovered from the defendants	£20,000
Total of legal aid contributions made by plaintiff	£1,000
Statutory charge to be deducted from the plaintiff's compensation after taking account of total contributions	£2,000
Net amount received by plaintiff	£47,000

CONDITIONAL FEE AGREEMENTS

Lawyers are now allowed to undertake medical negligence claims on a conditional fee basis. Such an agreement does not in any way affect the plaintiff's liability to pay the defendant's costs in the event of losing. (See Chapter 18 for information on Conditional Fees)

Example of the effect of the conditional fee agreement

Damages	£50,000
CFA success fee 25%	
Plaintiff's costs	£20,000
Plaintiff's disbursements	£3,000
Defendants pay costs and disbursements of £20,000	£20,000
Calculation:	
Damages	£50,000
Less solicitors' success fee (25% of £20,000)	£5,000
Unpaid costs	£3,000
Balance due to client	£42,000

The plaintiff will always be advised to purchase insurance to provide payment of the defendant's costs in the event of losing (see Chapter 18). This is an additional cost to the plaintiff. Assume that the plaintiff purchased £25,000 worth of cover, which costs about £2,100, the actual amount the plaintiff would receive in damages is £39,900.

THE AWARD

When can the damages be paid?

Where the client has been in receipt of legal aid, the compensation cannot be released to him or her until the costs have been recovered and any statutory charge has been calculated and deducted from damages (Civil Legal Aid (General) Regulations 1989, Reg.90).

The effect of this is that receipt of compensation by the plaintiff can often be delayed many months or even in excess of a year in those cases where costs have to be taxed. It is something which understandably many people find hard to understand and hard to bear following the stresses of the litigation.

It is possible for the impact of the delay to be eased if the solicitor is able to give an undertaking to the Legal Aid Board that costs will not exceed a specified amount and that in the event of their doing so, no claim above the specified amount will be made on the fund. If the solicitor is able to do this, then the Board will authorise release to the client of any compensation in excess of the specified amount (Regulation 90 of the General Regulations referred to above). Where the costs exceed the damages, it is unlikely that the solicitor will be able to make such an undertaking.

Investing the award

For some plaintiffs, an award of compensation is the source of much anxiety because they will not have managed sums of money of the size of their award before.

Any plaintiff who receives compensation should appreciate that the award is intended to cover both past and future expenditure and the importance of obtaining investment advice. Advising clients on how to invest compensation is not something which any lawyer should enter into without appropriate experience and expertise. However, the lawyer will probably be able to suggest potential sources of such advice.

Preparing a will

Where there is a substantial award, the plaintiff should be reminded of the importance of preparing a will.

The Court of Protection

Where an award is for a child or adult who will never be capable of managing his or her own affairs, it will be administered by the Court of Protection and a Receiver will be appointed. The Receiver will normally be a member of the family. If there is no one suitable, a professional receiver will be appointed.

The application to the Court of Protection is made by submitting the appropriate Court of Protection forms. These include a form which has to be completed by a doctor who knows the plaintiff and who must certify that he or she is and will continue to be unable to manage his or her own affairs.

The court then considers both the application for it to administer the plaintiff's affairs and the suitability of the proposed Receiver. If it is satisfied on both counts, an order will be made appointing the Receiver. The court will then either meet or correspond with the family about the administrative arrangements and how income will be paid and the award invested will work. Useful information packs about Court of Protection procedure can be obtained from the Public Trust Office.

Impact of receipt of award on Social Security Benefits

Where the plaintiff has been relying on means-tested social security benefits such as income support or family credit, the award or settlement will mean that a substantial capital sum is received by way of damages. Capital of £8,000 or more will mean that the client will cease to be entitled to income support (Income Support (General) Regulations 1987, Reg. 45).

Discretionary trusts

However, if the capital sum is paid into a discretionary trust, the plaintiff may still be entitled to income support (see Schedule 10, paragraph 12 of the Regulations). Care must be taken to ensure that the trust is in place before any money is paid out of court or by the defendant. The money must be paid directly to the trustees. If money is paid to the plaintiff's solicitor, it is treated as the plaintiff's capital (*Thomas v Chief Adjudication Officer* R(SB) 17/87).

The income from the trust fund is taken into account as income for the purpose of calculating income support (Income Support (General) Regs. 1987, Schedule 9, paragraph 22).

Such arrangements are not very flexible, and the client and lawyer will need to discuss whether it is appropriate for the individual concerned.

STRUCTURED SETTLEMENTS

Lump sum

Almost always, compensation is paid by way of a lump sum. By this method the plaintiff receives a cheque for the entire sum of damages due to him or her (after deduction of the Legal Aid Board statutory charge). It is then for the plaintiff to ensure that the money lasts as long as necessary by being prudent and by investing any funds not required immediately in order to maximise the return on the money. Whilst the award of damages is tax free the interest on the investment of the money is subject to income tax.

Awards of damages are based on a number of assumptions, including projected (and therefore uncertain) life expectancies. Because of the way in which awards of damages are currently assessed, they are unlikely ever to meet the projected annual lifetime needs even if a plaintiff lives only as long as anticipated. That shortfall is obviously much increased when the plaintiff lives longer than expected. There can be no further claim on the defendant, unless the award was of conditional provisional damages (see Chapter 19) even if the damages run out.

Structured settlements

With a structured settlement the plaintiff will receive a *tax free annuity* from the fund on monthly, quarterly, biannual or annual basis for the rest of his or her lifetime regardless of how long or short that is. Whilst such security can be very attractive, it has to be weighed against the major disadvantage of structured settlements, namely their inflexibility. Once set up, a structured settlement cannot be varied. This means that if the plaintiff's circumstances change unexpectedly and a large sum of money is required immediately, the money is not available in the way in which it would be if the entire sum had been invested. It also means that there is no large fund of money to form part of the plaintiff's estate on death.

Structured settlements are not appropriate for small awards of damages. They can be advantageous in certain circumstances where substantial damages are expected. It is essential to obtain specialist advice from forensic accountants in order to weigh up the relative financial and practical merits of a structured settlement as against a lump sum award. If this is to be done, it must be done before any final order is made. Otherwise the tax benefits of a structured settlement will not be reaped.

Almost all structured settlements that have arisen from medical negligence cases are funded out of Health Authority and Department of Health funds, rather than being funded by the purchase of insurance annuities. Such arrangements are attractive to Health Authorities because cash is paid out over a long period and therefore helps cashflow.

A structured settlement cannot be imposed upon a party. If one is to be entered into, it will have to be approved by the Department of Health and the Inland Revenue. Where the award is in favour of a minor or someone acting under a disability, it will also have to be approved by the court and in the latter case, the Court of Protection. It is essential that before any adjournment to consider a structured settlement, the defendants agree to pay the costs of investigation and implementation of the structured settlement. Any costs that are not recovered will further reduce the award of compensation.

Example of structured settlement

- Compensation conventionally agreed in the sum of £1,100,000.
- £400,000 used to provide for the plaintiff's immediate needs such as purchase and adaptation of a house and to provide a fund to meet unexpected contingencies in the future.
- £700,000 used to purchase annual payments for the plaintiff for the rest of the plaintiff's life.

- The amount that £700,000 will provide by way of annual payments will vary depending upon the prevailing long term interest rate, competition in the insurance market and the plaintiff's own circumstances (e.g., life expectation, immediate and deferred needs). On this example, depending on the circumstances, the return might be in the region of £30–35,000 per annum.

THE END OR THE BEGINNING?

We have seen that medical negligence cases can end at different stages and for different reasons. The case may end because, following the initial investigation, the lawyers advise that there is no reasonable prospect of succeeding or because the client decides that he or she does not wish to pursue the case. It may end during the case because, e.g. after disclosure of witness or expert witness evidence, the lawyers advise that there is no longer a reasonable prospect of the claim succeeding. It may end after judgment at trial either in favour of, or against, the plaintiff.

Regardless of the stage at which a case ends or how it ends, the conclusion is often a time of conflicting and powerful emotions for the plaintiff and family.

It has been explained earlier in this book (Chapter 15) that in order to succeed in recovering compensation, a patient must be able to prove through expert medical evidence that medical care was of a negligent standard and that the identified negligence caused the injury and financial losses. We have also seen the different stages of a case when its strength and value are assessed.

In those cases in which the legal advice at the conclusion of the investigation stage has been that there is no claim which can be pursued, the plaintiff may feel both that there has been a thorough investigation of the issues and that the independent medical experts have been able to explain satisfactorily what happened and why. This may be important not just for individual plaintiffs, but also for their families. For example, where a child has been injured, it can be a great help to the family in explaining what has happened both to the child as it gets older and to its siblings.

However, he or she and the family may feel quite differently when the legal advice has been that, although there is evidence of negligence, the negligence cannot be shown to have caused injury or that the potential compensation is so low that the cost of proceedings cannot be justified. In such cases, the plaintiff may well feel very disappointed. That disappointment may turn into anger and bitterness, if the limits and constraints of the legal process and the legal aid system have not been clearly and fully understood.

The client who loses at trial will obviously be extremely disappointed but, having witnessed and been part of a rigorous and public examination of the quality of care provided, his or her disappointment may be tempered by the sense of a battle well fought.

It is not only in unsuccessful cases that the client may experience an emotional 'crisis' at the conclusion of the case. During the litigation any one of a number of concerns and emotions may have been the motivating force for the client: anger, concern to prevent a recurrence or a pressing need to provide a certain future in the form of financial security for a disabled child or surviving family. It is often only at the point of settlement that the client or family will experience fully the harsh reality that no money can compensate for injury and the consequent months and years of physical and psychological pain; for disfigurement, disability and associated practical and financial problems. It is not uncommon for clients to experience the process of settlement as a price being placed on their life or the life of a loved one. Thus, at this stage, the client who has apparently come to terms with what has occurred may once again experience great pain and/or anger about what has happened.

The end of the case is also the point at which the lawyer/client relationship comes to an end. Where the client has found the relationship with the lawyer (or the whole medico-legal team) very supportive, this change will need to be prepared for.

OTHER PROBLEMS AND REFERRALS TO OTHER AGENCIES

The end of the case may reveal other problems. Some of these will require advice from the lawyer, others will require referral to other agencies. For example, where the negligently caused injury has affected a child's educational needs, advice may be needed about how to ensure that appropriate provision is provided or the client who has had a stillbirth may want and need support from either an individual counsellor or from an agency such as the Stillbirth and Neonatal Death Society (SANDS). (See Appendix 6 for addresses of appropriate agencies)

Both during and after a case (and perhaps especially in unsuccessful cases) a client may need advice on what benefits he or she will be eligible for. If the lawyer is unable to provide this, he or she should be able to provide the name of a local agency who can help.

CONCLUSION

In exactly the same way that the lawyer should prepare for trial from the outset, the client must prepare for the end of the case and what happens once it is over.

The emotions which a claimant brings to the lawyers' office and thus into the claim will range from rage, anger, pain, loss, grief, humiliation or a mix of all of these. The legal process is a blunt tool and one which was not designed (nor is it appropriate) for dealing with emotions that go to the very core of an individual's sense of self and well-being. If the legal process and this end stage is to be part of the healing process, it must help the individual to put the tragedy of the injury and how it happened in the past, thus enabling her to prepare for the future. If the claimant has not fully understood the limits of what can be achieved through the legal system and the constraints of the system, there is a danger that the recourse of law will leave the person feeling disempowered and abused. The result of this may then be that the medical accident that began the whole process will continue to be the dominant feature of life rather than a tragic event that occurred in the past.

Chapter 22

SMALL CLAIMS COURT AND LITIGANTS IN PERSON

Patrick Allen

Many claims for compensation for injuries arising from medical negligence are small and often the claimant will be advised not to instruct a lawyer and to proceed through the Small Claims Court. This chapter explains the procedure and warns of the pitfalls.

INTRODUCTION

Most people, apart from the very poor and children, are not eligible for legal aid or cannot afford the high level of contributions required for a certificate. Medical negligence litigation is complicated, expensive and uncertain so most litigants other than the poor or wealthy are effectively denied access to the courts for these claims.

More and more people are resorting to conducting their own cases as litigants in person, but this is not feasible for most medical cases. Without a lawyer to guide the plaintiff through the legal and procedural minefield, many claims will fail, and the plaintiff may then face a large bill for the defendant's costs.

SMALL CLAIMS PROCEDURE

The small claims procedure of the County Court has been devised to enable claimants to litigate claims quickly, in an informal setting and without fear of costs if they lose. The normal rules of procedure and evidence do not apply. Claims are arbitrated by a District Judge at a single hearing.

No costs are awarded to the successful party against the loser apart from the cost of issuing the summons and up to £200.00 for the report and attendance of an expert witness.

The 'small claims court' is not a separate court but a separate procedure within the County Court structure. Small claims are issued and tried under the rules laid down in Order 19 of the County Court Rules ("CCR") 1981.

The procedure was originally intended for simple debt-type claims under £100. The jurisdiction has been raised in various stages, in 1991 to £1000 and in January 1996 to £3000. Personal injury claims (which include most medical and dental claims) are exempted from the latest rise. Therefore the procedure is only available for medical or dental claims which do not exceed £1000. If the claim is purely for the cost of treatment or expenses with no personal injury damage alleged, it is possible to argue that the new £3000 jurisdiction will apply.

WHICH KINDS OF CLAIMS?

While most medical claims will exceed £1000, the small claims procedure may be useful for the following:

- minor dental negligence e.g. causing temporary numbness of the tongue or gums which gets better in a short time;
- dental negligence which can be put right with modest additional treatment;
- claims for the cost of modest medical treatment required as a result of negligence but where there has been little pain and suffering or long term injury;
- a claim where the plaintiff decides to limit the total damages to £1000 even though the damages are worth more than this;
- a defence and counterclaim for modest damages for suffering or the cost of treatment e.g. where the patient is being sued for unpaid private treatment.

PROBLEMS WITH SMALL CLAIMS PROCEDURE

Although the amount involved in a medical claim may be small, complex issues of law and evidence will arise. To succeed the plaintiff must prove:

- that the defendant was negligent i.e. that advice or treatment complained of fell below the standard to be expected of reasonably competent doctors/dentists; and
- the negligence caused the loss complained of; and
- that he or she has evidence to support the claim for pain and suffering and consequential expenses.

All this requires evidence from suitable witnesses, probably medical consultants.

It is impractical for plaintiffs (i.e. patients) to employ a solicitor to prepare and present such claims. The cost of doing so would swallow up the damages. Even so, defendants in medical cases (i.e. doctors, dentists and hospitals) are likely to be represented by a lawyer or experienced claims manager. The issue for them is not simply one of costs but professional reputation. Thus the plaintiff will always be at a disadvantage to the defendant

It is not easy for a claimant acting in person to obtain medical reports from consultants and if necessary bring them to court. Even if the doctors are prepared to cooperate with the claimant, the cost of their services may be unrecoverable and obliterate the damages.

The court may decide, in all but the most trifling claims, that the case is not suitable for arbitration because 'a difficult question of law or question of fact or complexity is involved' (Order 19 Rule 3(2)(a) CCR 1981). This could be said to apply to every medical negligence case.

Thus a claimant who begins what he or she believes is a simple case with no cost risk may find that the court transfers the case to full trial procedure where the claimant is liable for the defendant's costs (from the date of transfer out of arbitration) if he or she loses.

On the other hand, most proceedings are settled without the need for a hearing and the threat or issue of a small claim may be enough to persuade a Health Authority or insurer to buy off the claim for around £1000 rather than face the extra costs and delay of fighting the case.

PRACTICAL STEPS IN A SMALL CLAIM

The plaintiff must first obtain the medical records. This can be done by writing a letter or sending the Law Society/BMA approved form to the GP, dentist, consultant or hospital concerned (copies of the form may be obtained from the Law Society). Most defendants now hand over medical records without a struggle but the claimant will have to pay administrative and copying charges which may amount to £75. Where the defendant refuses to release the records, an application can be made to the court for an order for disclosure under Section 33 Supreme Court Act 1981. The procedure for this is described in Chapter 18.

It is simpler and cheaper to obtain the records under the Access to Health Records Act 1990. The same Law Society/BMA form should be used. The records disclosed will only go back to 1st November 1991 so this will be insufficient if earlier records are relevant to the claim. A fee of £10 plus the cost of photocopies will be payable.

The plaintiff must then obtain a medical report, preferably from a doctor of consultant status, confirming that the treatment was negligent *and* that this has caused the injury or loss complained of. A separate report may be required to show precisely what injury the plaintiff has suffered as a result of treatment, what will be the permanent damage, if any, and how much it will cost to have corrective treatment if this is relevant.

It is vital that the reports, while proving the essential elements of the claim, are not over long and expensive. Doctors are used to charging well over £300 for medical negligence reports. Here the plaintiff needs a succinct opinion and a fee not exceeding £75 if the claim is to be viable.

DRAFTING PROCEEDINGS

The plaintiff should obtain county court Form N2 – 'Default Summons (amount not fixed)' from the court or a legal stationer. This requires the plaintiff to state the names and addresses of the parties and the particulars of the claim against the defendant. The particulars should be set out on a separate sheet in numbered paragraphs, signed and dated. The particulars should be brief but state the date and place of the treatment, by whom it was carried out, why the treatment was negligent, and what losses the plaintiff has suffered. The plaintiff should state that the claim is limited to £1000 and that arbitration is sought.

The plaintiff must draft a schedule of damages showing the

expenses which are being claimed in addition to damages for pain and suffering. These can include the cost of private treatment, prescriptions, the cost of travel to treatment, loss of earnings for any time off work caused by the initial treatment or the subsequent corrective treatment, and interest on these expenses.

LIMITATION

The Limitation Act 1980 applies to small claims. Court action shall usually be commenced within three years of the date of the treatment or advice complained of. There are exceptions to this rule and the court has a discretion to disapply the three year period. However for simple small claims we may assume that three years from the treatment is the deadline to issue a claim. (See Chapter 17)

ISSUING THE CLAIM

To issue the claim, the plaintiff can go to any County Court and should produce three copies of the Form N2 and particulars of claim, the medical report(s), the schedule of damages and a cheque for the plaint fee. The fee payable is around 10% of the damages claimed, e.g. £500 claim – £50 fee. For claims not exceeding £1000 the fee is £60. In most cases, the plaintiff will not know precisely how much the claim is worth. Therefore it will be safer to limit the claim to £1000 and pay the £60 fee.

Once the claim has been accepted, a summons will be prepared and served by the court by post on the defendant. If the defendant decides to fight the claim, a defence must be filed within 14 days.

On receipt of the defence, the court sets a date for the arbitration hearing. The parties are required to send each other copies of any documents that they intend to rely upon. If the medical evidence has not been agreed, the plaintiff must decide whether to bring the expert to the hearing or attempt to rely on the report. Bringing the expert will almost certainly be too expensive and impractical. However the plaintiff runs the risk of not proving the case without having the witness at court.

The plaintiff should prepare a chronology of events and an

indexed and paginated bundle of documents which he or she intends to use at the hearing. This would include the particulars of claim and the defence, the medical reports, relevant medical records and receipts or estimates for treatment. Three copies should be taken to the hearing – one for each party and one for the judge.

THE HEARING

The hearing of a small claim arbitration is informal and in private and evidence is not given on oath. The plaintiff should present the case, taking the judge through the chronology and referring at each stage (by page number) to the documents in support. The plaintiff must prove the case 'on the balance of probabilities' (rather than the criminal law test of 'beyond all reasonable doubt'). (See Chapter 15)

Surveys have shown that litigants in person frequently underestimate what is needed to present their cases to a court. It is not enough to tell the story or call for justice. Litigants should appreciate the elements (set out above) which must be proved to establish their claim. The importance of obtaining good medical and documentary evidence to back up the claim cannot be overemphasised.

If the claim is proved, the arbitrator will make an award to cover general damages for pain and suffering and expenses and the limited costs allowed under the rules. The award is final and generally can only be set aside if there has been an error of law.

If the defendant fails to file a defence, the plaintiff can enter judgment with damages to be assessed. A hearing will then be fixed for the assessment. The court will only be interested in how much the claim is worth rather than the issue of negligence. The plaintiff must still produce evidence to link the damages to the negligence and to substantiate the damages.

COUNTERCLAIMS

If a patient has a grievance over private treatment and decides not to pay the bill, he or she will very likely be sued. If the claim is under £1000, then the patient can defend it under the small claims procedure and counterclaim if appropriate using the form sent by the court. The Defence and Counterclaim is likely to allege that the treatment was negligent and therefore the fees are not recoverable. Medical evidence in the form of a report from a consultant will be needed if the Defence and Counterclaim is to succeed.

LITIGANTS IN PERSON – BIGGER CLAIMS

It would take many chapters to detail the procedure for running a medical claim through the High Court or County Court without a solicitor. Litigants in person should at the very least have access to the Rules of the Supreme Court or the County Court (called the White Book or the Green Book respectively). These books may be found at the public library. Claimants might benefit from advice on evidence and procedure from a solicitor from time to time for a specific fee. Citizens Advice Bureaux and Law Centres will give free advice. There is a branch of the CAB at The Royal Courts of Justice in London. Many of the practical steps and difficulties set out above are applicable to bigger claims. The main difference is the risk of costs if the claim fails.

CONCLUSION

Pursuing a claim for damages for medical negligence may seem daunting. However the courts are helpful to litigants in person and with determination and organisation it is possible to succeed.

Chapter 23

THE WOOLF INQUIRY AND THE FUTURE OF MEDICAL NEGLIGENCE LITIGATION – 1998

Sarah Leigh

This chapter explains the recent initiative taken by Lord Woolf to reform civil justice and discusses the impact on medical negligence claims.

SUMMARY

The recent report by Lord Woolf into the Civil Justice System made the following recommendations:

- to encourage systems for resolving cases without litigation;
- to use mediation to resolve disputes;
- to involve clients more closely in litigation;
- to reduce costs;
- to reform the use and work of experts;
- to ensure court control of litigation;
- to introduce new slimline systems for resolving smaller claims;
- to introduce new mechanisms for eliminating out weak cases or defences.

The inquiry stimulated discussion and work on reform which still continues and both the preconditions for litigation and its practice have been affected. In London a new practice direction has been implemented (see Chapter 18) as a direct result of the Woolf recommendations.

Reformed techniques for resolution of issues, like the instruction of single experts in quantum issues and liability expert's meetings, are beginning to creep into practice. Efforts are being made to encourage mediation with the NHS.

At present it is not clear to what extent Lord Woolf's recommendations will be implemented.

THE WOOLF INQUIRY, ITS WORK AND RECOMMENDATIONS FOR THE REFORM OF MEDICAL NEGLIGENCE LITIGATION

In 1994 Lord Woolf was commissioned to propose reforms of the whole civil justice system (the High Court and County Court system excluding family cases).

Civil Justice Council

He recommended that the system be comprehensively reformed and that a Civil Justice Council be formed to monitor and support the civil justice system. In 1996 the Court Proceedings Act was passed, to enable some of these reforms to be carried out and a Civil Justice Council and a new Rules Committee to be established. This chapter is written in the transitional period between the formulation of the proposed reforms by Lord Woolf and the full implementation.

Medical negligence

Lord Woolf's view of medical negligence is that it is very expensive, very inaccessible, very difficult to understand and very slow. Litigation is a considerable endurance test both to the injured patient and to any doctor or nurse involved in the claim.

In the spring of 1995 Lord Woolf decided that medical negligence was an area of 'peculiar difficulty' and committed a lot of his time and energy to it.

NHS changes

Lord Woolf spent a great deal of time talking to claims managers and other NHS management staff about record-keeping and witness statements, about incident reporting and communication with patients. He was keen to see much franker explanations being given to patients and improvements in resolving actions without litigation.

Doctors

From doctors Lord Woolf heard of the stress and depression that the long litigation process caused them, their immense frustration at the system, its slowness and the way it interfered with their clinical work. He heard complaints about medical experts, mainly about the minority of very partial experts who wrote unreliable reports which patients were then using to pursue unrealistic claims or hospitals were defending claims which could not in the end be defended. The doctors were almost as angry about poor defences holding up compensation to patients as they were about unmeritorious claims wasting their time.

The message to doctors (from patients and lawyers) was that they needed to involve themselves in making the medical dispute system work.

Patients

From patients he heard about lost or allegedly forged records, bad communication systems, bad lawyers and a host of other problems.

In July 1996 Lord Woolf's final report was published and it contained general proposals for the reform of litigation together with a chapter on medical negligence specifically.

CHANGES IN THE CULTURE

Resolving claims without going to court

The first principle was that we needed to change our attitude to litigation so that it would be more open, less adversarial, less antagonistic, more tailored to patients' needs. There had to be efforts to resolve claims without going to court. Changes in the culture could be made by the operators of the system (the lawyers and experts) talking to the consumers (the patients, doctors and administrators) and working out ways to make it more user-friendly and more effective.

Patients and healthcare professionals

Doctors and managers should 'demonstrate their commitment to patients' wellbeing by adopting a constructive approach to claims handling'. Patients 'must recognise that some degree of risk is inherent in all medical treatment'. Every effort should be made to *prevent* disputes by improving patient/doctor communication. The General Medical Council should reconsider defining more closely the doctor's duty of disclosure. Every patient who has suffered an adverse outcome is entitled to an explanation and where appropriate 'an apology'.

Avoid litigation

Woolf's view is that we should try much harder to avoid litigation by discussing the complaint with the other party before resorting to it. Patients and their representatives must play their part by giving the defendant at least three months' notice of the allegations of negligence before serving proceedings. Defendants in turn must respond fully – Woolf suggested the NHS should improve its systems for tracking staff who have moved on. Unreasonable behaviour by either side should be taken into account by the court later in setting timetables and awarding costs.

Client's involvement

A critical feature of the Woolf approach is that involving clients on both sides improves litigation. He recommended that the client always attend the important hearings during the course of the case (case management conferences). He thought it wrong that a client can go through a whole legal action without ever seeing anyone connected with his or her case other than their own solicitor and barrister (as at present).

At present the parties feel distant from the issues; Lord Woolf felt it was necessary to get people together as early as possible, always thinking of the legal costs incurred to date and for the future.

Access to justice

It costs perhaps an average of £3000 to investigate a medical accident and the total cost of a case can be astronomical. There is no way of estimating or limiting the cost of conducting a claim. The real costs of dealing with the litigation, including the time of doctors, other healthcare professionals and clients' families, are far higher. Achieving justice is expensive – so the problem was how to reduce and control the cost while at the same time maintaining a fair system.

One reason why medical negligence litigation is expensive is that there is no check on what lawyers spend time on; no one to say it is not worth doing that or having a second expert there. Woolf suggested that *the court should assess* what work was worth doing. This was to be called 'case management'.

Case management by the court

He also felt that having the parties involved at the case management hearings would lead to economies because the lawyers would have to say how much had been spent and what future costs were likely to be incurred.

Standard payments

Lawyers charge by the hour; there is little incentive to do the work faster and more efficiently. Lord Woolf suggested standard payments for each stage of a case. The problem with that (the lawyers say) is that you win cases by spending time on them, and if you pay lawyers irrespective of whether or not they spend the time, then you are putting a premium on bad work.

COURT CONTROL

Paul McNeil's chapter on how litigation works (see Chapter 18) makes it clear that at present it is for the parties to run the action. The court has a very limited opportunity to affect the procedural course. In any event, it exercises relatively little influence at present. Cases are run by solicitors to suit solicitors.

The Woolf prescription for this was that the court should control litigation, setting timetables, examining issues, making decisions about what evidence was needed. He recommended:

- training for procedural judges;
- better computer technology;
- allowing the judges much more time for procedural work;
- the solicitor in the case (instead of a clerk) should always attend hearings before a procedural judge;
- hearings or 'case management conferences' should be used by the court to control the case and to seize opportunities for settlement and/or mediation.

Training judges

Lord Woolf's strong contention was that judges need to be trained in court case management in general and in medical negligence in particular. There should be judges who specialise in medical negligence work and 'a medical negligence list', staffed by experienced procedural and trial judges. Medical negligence cases should only be heard at specialised trial centres. Judges should be given sufficient support staff and computer technology.

Experts

Partisan, dishonest or incompetent experts are the plague of medical negligence litigation.

Lord Woolf's contention was that experts should be more answerable to the court, and not to any particular party. Their instructions and deliberations should be transparent to the court and unaffected as much as possible by their clients' demands. He proposed a revolutionary recommendation: that no expert report should be admissible unless the instructions for the report are annexed. He would have liked to see single experts appointed, but there was huge resistance to this among lawyers (on behalf of their clients) and doctors alike.

Opposing experts to meet

The Inquiry's work resulted in a strong vote of confidence in a hitherto little used mechanism in this area: meetings between each sides' experts *before* the trial. Getting experts together to discuss identified issues was recommended as something which should happen in every case and at as early a stage as possible.

Smaller claims and proportionality

A large proportion of medical negligence claims are for less than £10,000, but there is no limit on the amount of money spent contesting them. A claim worth only £1,000 may cost 20 or even 30 times that to prosecute or defend. This breaks the Woolf rule that claims must be litigated for a reasonable proportion of their value if justice is to be done.

Strict proportionality of costs to damages cannot be applied but 'disproportionate use of resources in this area is unsustainable'.

A number of new models of litigating smaller claims were considered, from variants of the general 'fast track' procedure (recommended by Woolf for litigation in general) to a slimmed down 'best practice' model. The modified fast track (involving only one expert) found very little favour with lawyers and experts and the general view was that a modified fast track would be best. The report suggested that smaller claims models should be piloted (so far none have been apart from the Birmingham Pilot which was already in place before the Inquiry finished).

Mediation

Lord Woolf was keen to see more medical negligence cases mediated. This is a method of 'managed negotiation', with the parties meeting privately at a place and time of their choice to hear each other's point of view and to work out a solution which suits. The patient would attend and have direct contact with those who have injured him (instead of hearing of them only in letters and reports from his lawyers). The doctor or manager would also be there to offer the patient remedies such as:

- acknowledgement of the injury and its causes;
- an apology;

- information about what has been done since the accident to stop it happening again.

These outcomes are not available in the present system.

The mediator is not a judge. Each party puts its point of view (and the client as well as the lawyer for each side gets the chance to do this). The mediator then manages negotiation between the parties who are in different rooms, trying to convey each party's opinions safely to the other, and help them work out a solution.

Eliminating weak claims and weak defences

Lord Woolf proposed new summary judgment procedures which will allow parties to apply for judgment or to strike out a claim (depending on which party is applying) on the ground that the opposite party's case has no reasonable chance of success. At present judgment is only available against the defendant on the technical ground that there is no defence to the action.

This would enable the judge on a summary judgment application to look at the evidence in the case. It is a vital remedy to appease those who claim that far too many weak cases are litigated almost to the point of trial (at huge cost to both sides) whereas in other cases money is wasted by weak defences being maintained for too long.

Plaintiffs suffer at present from the payment into court scheme, whereby defendants can make a low payment in and avoid paying the costs from then on if the plaintiff is unlucky enough not to recover more at trial – but there is no corresponding weapon at present for the plaintiff against the defendant.

Under the Woolf recommendations the claimant will be able to 'offer to settle' a case for a particular sum. The intention is that there will be penalties by way of interest on damages and costs if the defendant does not accept the offer and more is then recovered at a subsequent time.

Experts' meetings should also be a useful tool for testing and eliminating weak cases on both sides.

OTHER DEVELOPMENTS AFFECTING THE SYSTEM BETWEEN 1995–8

Other developments have occurred to complicate the picture of the operation of Lord Woolf's recommendations in medical negligence litigation.

NHSLA

Since the summer of 1996 the National Health Service Litigation Authority (NHSLA) has attained control over all defendants' operations. The NHSLA must approve all settlements involving more than £10,000 in costs and damages.

This is combined with the increasing standardisation of NHS risk management systems. This was introduced and developed by the Clinical Negligence Scheme for Trusts, under which NHS Trusts (which may provide hospital or community care) may join a scheme which provides for their indemnity against claims, in return for standards of record keeping and risk management generally.

Defendant's solicitors

There has been a shift of NHS legal services from the public to the private sector. There are now no legal departments left in Trusts or Health Authorities in England to carry on litigation. The work is now concentrated in the hands of fewer larger firms of solicitors who have the resources to provide legal services at ever more competitive rates. The effect is that the work is more efficiently conducted at a lower cost.

Following the Woolf Inquiry the Healthcare Lawyers Association (of which most of the big defendant firms are members) has been established. The effect of this is likely to result in a more united defence strategy.

Plaintiff's solicitors

The Law Society's Medical Negligence Panel identifies solicitors with sufficient experience to conduct such cases. AVMA has a specialist solicitors' referral panel and will remain in close contact with such solicitors during the conduct of a case.

Legal aid franchising

The Legal Aid Board has now devised a franchise system for legally aided work. Franchised firms of solicitors have been audited by the Legal Aid Board and are recognised as being providers of a quality service.

The NHS mediation pilot

This scheme, which will run to the end of 1997, will pay towards the cost of mediating a successful medical negligence claim. Only nine cases have been mediated since the pilot started but there are more in the pipeline.

THE IMPLEMENTATION OF WOOLF

The Government's role

The Inquiry was instigated by a remarkable legal reformer, Lord Mackay of Clashfern, the Lord Chancellor until May 1997. Following the Labour landslide victory of May 1997 the Government has to consider whether to implement the Woolf proposals. Some of the proposals require changes in the court rules or legislation, others investment in training, information technology or other support. These changes are badly needed if the Woolf prescriptions are to work.

The Woolf reforms were always intended to be consensual – the most important changes in this area were to take place in people's hearts and minds rather than within the statute or rulebooks. Some reforms can be achieved by simply developing and relying on the existing rules. The new Practice Direction 49 (see chapter 18) is a demonstration of what can be achieved without legislation.

To some limited extent the cultural changes are taking place because their driving force is a combination of the demands of clients, on both sides, and the paymasters – the Legal Aid Board and the NHSLA. These two latter bodies could in fact achieve much of the Woolf reform programme without any legislation, simply by requiring the lawyers they pay to observe reformed principles as a condition of funding.

The Clinical Disputes Forum

One group continues to exist to carry on the consultation and co-ordination work of the Inquiry throughout the whole field of medical negligence.

The Forum brings together the key senior people from the clinical, legal and lay stakeholder organisations. These people work together to achieve by consensus practical ways of improving the system and of underpinning the programme of reform set in motion by the Woolf Inquiry *Access to Justice*. The Forum is the meeting ground for every interest group involved in medical negligence claims and complaints. Membership is individual. The Forum develops ideas and solutions which members think they can 'sell' to their constituencies. This approach to a constituency membership rather than mandated representation gives members freedom to express their views and act as experts on what is needed on each front. At present there are only 26 members. Forum projects are developed through working parties. The first such working party has completed work on a Protocol for Clinical Disputes Resolution. Others are working on the use of experts, incident reporting, the interface of complaints and litigation and the constitution of the Forum.

Pre-litigation protocols

One of Woolf's most important developments was to encourage interchange of views and common investigation as soon as possible after the medical accident. There was very general agreement that plaintiffs should abandon the ambush principle and be more open about the nature and value of their case before legal proceedings were commenced.

The costs regime and case management system are important factors here; if pre-action work is well paid for but little time is left for work after the issue of the claim then the parties will concentrate more on a resolution of the claim.

Generally this development is hard on defendants, who traditionally have not investigated claims until long after proceedings have begun.

The Clinical Disputes Forum's most important task for 1998 will be the wide dissemination and discussion of this Protocol and putting it into general practice. Clients must understand at the beginning of the process, before they are referred to solicitors, that what they should expect are strenuous efforts to resolve the claim without court action.

New Practice Direction

The Senior Master, Master Turner (one of Lord Woolf's Assessors in the Inquiry) formulated a draft practice direction designed to develop the reform of practice in the High Court and a users' group was set up to discuss this with the Masters. As a result a new Practice Direction was issued in October 1996 (and amended in January 1998) headed 'Medical Negligence' which was the joint creation of the court and the users and which brought in a new era of litigation in this field. (See Chapter 18) At present all medical negligence cases are assigned to Master Foster or Master Murray.

Expert Witness Institute

The Expert Witness Institute is a new body formed to develop systems for training experts in the court process and their duty to the court and to accredit them.

CONCLUSION

Up to now medical negligence litigation has been very inconsistent. The training, personality and personal style of the litigator has dictated very different styles of operation. Every medical negligence specialist is an individual with his or her own practices and habits. In future the drive of the paymasters towards the twin aspirations of value for money and higher standards in solicitors' services will lead to more consistent practices. Information technology and computer case management systems will reinforce this effect.

With the right tools (e.g., dispute resolution procedures) more cases will be resolved pre-action with less cost and anguish for the consumers (patients and doctors). Cases will be much better prepared. Case management (even under the present arrangements) will be organised specifically to narrow the issues, save wasted costs and speed up the litigation process.

Mediation will probably be more used in future, and will provide a mode of delivering non-money remedies which patients want, e.g. acknowledgements, apologies and assurances that steps have been taken to make sure that their accident will not happen again to someone else.

Expert meetings are likely to become more common and will change the face of litigation because people will not be able to bluff their way to the door of the court; the strengths and weaknesses of their case will become apparent much earlier.

APPENDICES

APPENDIX 1: LEGAL TERMS GLOSSARY

accepting service: a defendant's solicitor may accept service of a writ or other court process on behalf of his client.
action (civil): a *civil action* is brought to enforce a legal right e.g. pursuing an action to recover payment of an unpaid debt or an action for negligence.
administration (of deceased's estate): the granting of letters of administration occurs when a person dies without making a will.
affidavit: this is a sworn written statement. The person must swear or affirm that the contents are true before a solicitor, commissioner for oaths or a court official.
allegation: an assertion or statement in a pleading, affidavit or indictment which the party making the allegation intends to prove by providing evidence at trial.
appeal: an application to a higher court to examine the decision of an inferior court e.g. appeals about a decision made in the County Court or High Court are heard by the Court of Appeal.
assault: this is an "intentional or reckless act" that causes the subject to believe they are in imminent danger of physical harm but not necessarily involving any physical contact. Assault is often used to include the term battery, which is intentional or reckless physical contact without that person's consent.
automatic directions: directions of the court which provide a timetable for the various preparatory stages leading up to the trial of an action for personal injury, that take effect automatically following close of pleadings.
barrister: a lawyer who specialises in advocacy (speaking on behalf of or in support of), providing independent advice (*opinions*) and assisting with preparations for trial. With certain exceptions, barristers must be instructed by a solicitor rather than directly by the client.
bill of costs: a solicitor's bill in respect of legal services rendered to her client.

Calderbank letter: a letter sent to the other party in an action offering to settle the matter on terms other than damages, which cannot be referred to at trial.
case law: law that has developed as a result of decisions made by courts (*judicial decisions*) in previous cases.
causation: for a medical negligence claim to be successful, a causal link has to be established between the act of negligence and the injury for which the plaintiff is claiming compensation. This is referred to as causation.
cause of action: the grounds on which a person in entitled to sue.
chambers: the term used both to describe the offices occupied by a barrister or group of barristers and to describe a group of barristers practising from a set of chambers. The private office of judges, registrars and masters is also referred to as chambers.
claimant: see plaintiff.
class action: see multi party action.
circuit judge: these are judges who sit in the County Courts (and Crown Court) who are barristers of not less than ten years' standing or solicitors who have been recorders for at least three years.
civil court: a court which deals with civil matters as opposed to criminal e.g. County Court and High Court.
close of pleadings: 14 days after the defence has been served on the plaintiff, the pleadings are deemed to be closed. The plaintiff's solicitor must now prepare the case for trial.
conditional fee agreement: a written agreement between a legal practitioner and his client stating that the fees will only be payable under certain specified circumstances e.g. if the case is successful.
conference: a meeting between the barrister and solicitor to discuss the case which is usually held at the barrister's chambers and at which the client and experts advising on the case may also be present. (If the barrister is a QC, the conference may be referred to as a *consultation*.)
coroner: a barrister, solicitor or medical practitioner of not less than five years' standing appointed by the Crown to investigate deaths by ordering a post-mortem and if appropriate, conducting an inquest. Coroners also deal with treasure trove.
counsel: the term used for a barrister (or barristers).
counterclaim: a claim made by a defendant in response to a claim made by a plaintiff. The counterclaim is not part of the defence but has a separate cause of action.
County Court: the County Court has jurisdiction in civil claims to the value of £50,000. There are around 300 County Courts across the country.

court of first instance: the court where proceedings were initiated or the court where a case was tried as opposed to a subsequent appeal court.
Court of Protection: a court which looks after the affairs and property of someone incapable of managing his or her own affairs.
damages: the sum of money awarded by the court in respect of a claim for compensation.
defendant: the person or body against whom the claim is made.
dependant: a person who relies on someone else for financial support and maintenance e.g. dependant spouse or children.
discovery: discovery (and inspection) of documents involves obtaining a list from the other party containing details of documents which have been or are held in their possession which are relevant to the case and then subsequent inspection of the documents. There can also be discovery of facts by obtaining answers on oath to question asked by means of interrogatories.
dismissal of action: the termination of a claim in favour of the defendant either at the end of the trial or during the course of proceedings.
duty of care: a common law duty to exercise reasonable care to avoid causing damage. Negligence can only be established if it can be shown there was a duty of care. Doctors have a duty of care to their patients; solicitors have a duty of care to their clients.
endorsement of writ: the writ of summons must be endorsed with certain information. In other words, it must include such things as the plaintiff's name and address (and that of his or her solicitor), and at least general description of the type of claim being pursued.
entering judgment: a procedure by which a judgment made by a civil court is formally recorded.
examination: the process of questioning a witness under oath (or affirmation) during the trial. Examination-in-chief (questioning by the party that called them as a witness); cross examination (questioning by the opposing party) and re-examination (questioning on issues raised by the cross examination).
exchange of medical reports: medical reports which will be used at trial must be exchanged prior to the hearing.
executor: personal representative appointed by a will to administer the estate of the deceased.
exemplary damages: also known as punitive damages. These are damages awarded to punish the defendant as opposed to

compensating for injury caused. Exemplary damages are not usually awarded in medical negligence cases.

ex-gratia: a payment that is made 'as a matter of favour' rather than as a legal duty. Hospitals will sometimes make ex-gratia payments to patients but on the basis that they are not legally liable to compensate the person.

general damages: damages awarded for losses where it is not possible to estimate a precise financial loss e.g. pain and suffering, loss of amenity, psychiatric injury etc.

inquest: an inquiry conducted by a Coroner into a sudden death where the cause is unknown or suspicious, where the death occurred in prison or where the Coroner has reason to suspect that the cause of death was other than due to natural causes.

interim payment: payment made by a defendant to the plaintiff prior to the conclusion of the case to cover on-going care needs. This usually only occurs after liability has been admitted, or judgment has been made in the plaintiff's favour or where the total damages are substantial.

interlocutory proceedings: the stage between issue of the writ/summons and the trial.

interlocutory judgment: an interlocutory judgment is a decision made by the court prior to the trial and which only deals with part of the matter in dispute e.g. disputes over procedural issues, limitation, etc.

interrogatories: formal written questions submitted by one party to the other where the answer must be submitted on oath.

intestacy: describes the position when a person dies without having made a will to dispose of his property.

judicial review: a legal remedy for challenging decisions made by inferior courts, tribunals and administrative authorities e.g. the decision of a Coroner.

junior barrister: all barristers who are not Queen's Counsel (QC) are referred to as juniors. This does not mean that they lack expertise or experience.

Law Society: the solicitor's professional body.

leader: a Queen's Counsel or the senior barrister acting on the case.

leave: obtaining permission from the court to undertake a particular step during the course of legal proceedings.

letters of administration: if a person dies without leaving a will (intestate), authority can be granted by the court to an individual to act as an administrator of the deceased's estate. This is referred to as granting letters of administration.

limitation (of actions): statutory rules (statutes of limitation) which state the time limits within which civil actions must be brought.

litigant: a person who is involved in a court action. The litigant may represent himself or herself or may be represented by a solicitor or barrister.

locus standi: the right to bring an action before the courts.

Lord Chancellor: a government minister who is appointed by the Crown on the advice of the Prime Minister to head the judiciary (judges) and with wide ranging responsibilities including overseeing law reform, legal aid and administration of the courts.

Lord Chief Justice: second in rank to the Lord Chancellor and is the President of the Court of Appeal (Criminal Division).

loss of amenity: the inability to enjoy or perform activities formerly undertaken by the plaintiff as a result of physical or mental incapacity e.g. playing an instrument, playing sport etc. Damages may be claimed for loss of amenity.

McKenzie man (friend): a person who advises an unrepresented litigant in court.

Mental Health Review Tribunal: a person detained under the Mental Health Act can apply to a Mental Health Review Tribunal for discharge from hospital.

minor (infant): a child under the age of 18.

multi party action: an action where a group of people sue the same defendant and have a common cause of action e.g. a claim against a drug manufacturer. Also referred to as "class action" or "group action".

negligence: breach in a duty of care leading to injury and loss.

nervous shock: a recognisable psychiatric illness following a traumatic event for which damages can be claimed. It is necessary to establish that the illness caused by the traumatic incident was reasonably foreseeable.

next friend: an appropriate person who acts on behalf of a minor (a child under 18 years of age) or a person incapable of managing his or her own affairs in the conduct of legal proceedings.

notice of discontinuance: notice served by a plaintiff that he or she is withdrawing his or her claim (action).

Official Solicitor: an officer of the Supreme Court who acts as adviser for someone who is incapable of managing his or her own affairs and where there is no appropriate alternative next friend.

originating summons: a court document which commences an action in the court e.g. an action for pre-action discovery.
particulars: details of an allegation. If the other party requires more details of the allegation he or she can request 'further and better particulars'.
parties: the two (or more) persons involved in litigation e.g. plaintiff and defendant.
payment into court: a payment made by the defendant into an account held by the court as an offer of settlement of the claim. The plaintiff has 21 days to decide whether or not to accept the sum paid into court. If the plaintiff does not accept the sum and the case goes to trial, the plaintiff is at risk of being ordered to pay the costs from the date of the payment in if the judge awards an equal or lower amount of money in damages.
perjury: perjury is the giving of evidence under oath or affirmation which the witness knows to be false.
personal representative: a person entitled to administer the affairs of the deceased either as administrator or executor of a will.
perverting the course of justice: acting in an intentional way to obstruct the administration of public justice e.g. destroying evidence, or giving false statements.
plaintiff: the injured party who is seeking a remedy through the courts. In medical negligence, this would be the patient or in the event of death, the estate and/or the dependants (by executor/administrator). The plaintiff may also be referred to as a 'claimant'.
pleadings: formal written statements outlining the allegations which the parties intend to prove at trial e.g. "Statement of Claim" (plaintiff) or "defence" (defendant) and the remedy they are seeking.
precedent: a judgment or decision of a court used as an authority for deciding subsequent cases.
prima facie: translated from the Latin, this means, at first appearance or on the face of things.
prima facie case: a case where the available or preliminary evidence appears to be sufficient evidence to establish a claim unless and until further investigations prove otherwise.
prima evidence: the best evidence available e.g. the original of a document as opposed to a photocopy.
privilege(d): a document which is exempt from disclosure to the other party e.g. communication between a lawyer and his or her client about the case.

proof beyond reasonable doubt: the standard of proof required in a criminal case (and in disciplinary cases brought before professional bodies). In civil cases the standard is on the balance of probabilities.
proof of evidence: a proof contains only those matters which the client will be able to submit in evidence at trial as opposed to a statement which can contain matters which would not be admissible at trial e.g. opinion, hearsay etc.
provisional damages: if the plaintiff's future prognosis is not clear at the time of settlement of his or her claim but there is a reasonable risk of further injury arising, the plaintiff may request that the damages award should be 'provisional' and that he or she should be allowed to come back to the court within a specified time for a further award in the event that he or she does suffer further injury as a consequence of the risk specified.
punitive damages: see exemplary damages.
QC: Queen's Counsel – a senior barrister who has 'taken silk'.
Queen's Bench Division: the division of the High Court primarily concerned with the trial of civil actions which includes medical negligence actions.
recorder: a barrister or solicitor appointed to act as a part-time judge.
re-examination: questioning of a witness by the party which called him or her to testify following questioning by the opposing party (cross examination).
renewal of writ: an order made by the court to extend the validity of a writ for service beyond the normal four month period.
res ipsa loquitor: 'the matter speaks for itself'. If the plaintiff has been injured in a manner which would reasonably be associated with a negligent act then, even in the absence of evidence to prove that a particular act of negligence caused the injury, it may be presumed that the injury was caused by negligence e.g. if someone undergoes a knee operation but leaves the theatre with a broken arm then, even in the absence of records to demonstrate how the arm was broken, it could be assumed that negligence took place.
RSC: Rules of the Supreme Court.
setting aside: an order made by a court which cancels an order or judgment previously made.
setting down for trial: the stage in a court action where the plaintiff files the pleadings to be relied on at trial with the court and the case is then entered in the list of cases awaiting trial or a trial date is set.

small claim: a civil action where the plaintiff is only seeking a small sum in damages.

special damages: actual financial losses which the plaintiff has incurred as a result of the injury. See chapter 19.

split trial: a trial where issues of liability and damages are tried in two separate hearings.

statement of claim: the document (pleading) prepared by the plaintiff in a High Court action which contains his or her main allegations against the defendant and the remedy sought. This should normally be served on the defendant within 14 days of the defendants giving acknowledgement of service.

statute barred: a plaintiff will be prevented from pursuing an action if the time limit in which to bring such as action has expired. For example in a personal injury action the ordinary time limit is three years from the date the plaintiff knew he had a cause of action.

sub judice rule: rule against publication of information which might prejudice prior to legal proceedings.

substantive law: the part of the law which deals with legal principles as distinct from procedural matters.

sue: to commence a claim in the civil courts by issuing court proceedings.

summary judgment (Order 14): judgment entered at the interlocutory stage where cases are undefended or indefensible. The case will not then proceed to a full trial.

summons: a court order to an individual to appear in court e.g. in the County Court medical negligence claims are instituted by a summons. In the High Court "a summons for directions" means that the parties must attend to consider the future conduct of the case.

superior court: e.g. House of Lords, Court of Appeal, High Court. Decisions of these courts may be used as legal precedents.

taxation of costs: the process by which the costs payable by one party to another are assessed by an officer of the court.

taxing master: the officer of the court responsible for reviewing solicitors' bills and deciding which of the costs were reasonably incurred and therefore should be paid by the other party.

test case: a case brought to test a principle of law or to establish a legal right. If the test case is successful, it may create a legal precedent.

third party proceedings: if a defendant to an action believes that someone else was partly to blame for what happened, he or she can sue that other party. Rather than starting a separate action, he or she can bring third party proceedings, joining the third party to the existing action.

Tomlin order: a stay in the action where the terms of compromise involve more than simple payment of money. The terms of the stay will be set out in a schedule and there will be liberty to restore the action if necessary to carry the terms into effect.

tort: a wrongful act or omission committed by one party against another for which the injured party may claim damages in a civil court e.g. the tort of negligence.

ultra vires: 'beyond the powers'. This describes an act by a public body which falls outside the limits of the powers conferred upon them.

vexatious action (litigant): an action which is brought for the purpose of annoying the opposing party and which has no prospect of success. A vexatious litigant is a person who regularly makes unfounded legal claims.

vicarious liability: legal liability for the actions of an employee even though the employer made liable may not have been personally at fault.

volenti non fit injuria: a defence raised based upon the plaintiff's acceptance of the risks involved which precludes him or her from claiming damages should he or she be injured by such foreseen risks, for example an injury caused in a boxing match.

warned list: a number of actions which are likely to be heard in the High Court on the following day will be listed together and printed in the Daily Cause List under the title of the Warned List.

without prejudice: letters and documents headed with the phrase 'without prejudice' may not be produced in a court action without the consent of both parties. Parties wishing to negotiate a settlement of an action may do so 'without prejudice' indicating there is no admission of liability.

writ (or summons): a legal document by which an action is commenced in the High Court.

APPENDIX 2: MEDICAL ABBREVIATIONS

Medical records can be very difficult to decipher because they-often contain abbreviations and hieroglyphs. The following are some of the more commonly used abbreviations and hieroglyphs that are likely to be encountered in medical records:

Common hieroglyphs

+++	much/many
#	fracture
Δ	diagnosis
ΔΔ	differential diagnosis
℞	treatment
°	nil/nothing/no
↑	up, increasing
→	constant, normal or lateral shift (e.g. of apex of heart)
↓	down, decreasing
>	greater than
<	less than
⊥	central (of the trachea)
1/7	one day
2/52	two weeks
3/12	three months
$T38^6$	temperature 38.6
T-2/40 or T-2/52	term (i.e. date baby due) less 2 weeks
T+1/40 or 1/52	term plus 1 week
35^4	35 weeks and 4 days
37^3	37 weeks and 3 days
	period
’	done
?	query
??	query query

Common medical abbreviations

(these may be written in capitals or lowercase)

aa	of each (Greek)
Aal	anterior axillary line
ac	before food
ACTH	adrenocorticotrophic hormone
ad	up to or right ear (aurus dextra)
add.	adduction
ADH	antidiurectic hormone
adl	activities of daily living
ad lib	to the desired amount
ADP	adenosine diphosphate
A&E	accident and emergency
ae	air entry
AF	atrial fibrillation
AFB	acid fast bacillus (TB)
AFP	alpha-fetoprotein
AID	artificial insemination-donor
AIDS	acquired immune deficiency syndrome
AIH	artificial insemination – husband
aj	ankle jerk (reflex: see also BJ, KJ, SJ, TJ)
alt die	every other day
alt noct.	alternative nights
al s	alimentary system
AN	antenatal
ANS	autonomic nervous system
Anti-D	gamma globulin given by injection to Rhesus negative mother who delivers/aborts Rhesus positive child/foetus.
AP	artificial pneumothorax
Apgar	Apgar score: means of recording baby's condition at birth by observing and 'scoring' (0, 1 or 2) 5 parameters
APH	antepartum haemorrhage
applic.	applications
aq	water
ARC	aids related complex
ARDS	adult respiratory distress syndrome
ARM	artificial rupture of membrances
ASD	atrial septum defect
AST	aspartate transaminase
ATP	adenosine triphosphate
AU	both ears
aurist	ear drops
a/v	anteverted
A&W	alive and well
BaE	barium enema
BaM	barium meal
bd	both
b.d.	twice a day
BI	bone injury
bid	brought in dead
bj	biceps jerk (reflex: see AJ)
blood Sugar	normal 2.5 – 5.5 mmol/1
blood Urea	normal 2.5 – 6.6 mmol/1
BMR	basal metabolism rate
BNF (plus date)	British National Formulary
BO	bowels open
BP (plus date)	British Pharmacopoeia
BP	blood pressure
BS	(i) breath sounds (ii) bowel sounds (iii) blood sugar (iv) British Standard

BSE	bovine spongiform encephalopathy
BUN	blood urea nitrogen
c	with (Latin: cum)
C_2H_5OH	alcohol
Ca	(i) carcinoma/cancer (ii) calcium
CA	chronological age
Caps	capsules
CAT scan/CT	computed axial tomograph
CCF	congestive cardiac failure
CCU	coronary care unit
CDH	congenital dislocation of the hip
CHF	congestive heart failure
cp	compare
CIN	cervical intraepithelial neoplasia (cervical cancer)
CMV	cytomegalovirus
CNS	central nervous system
CO	complaining of or carbon monoxide
CO_2	carbon dioxide
COAD	chronic obstructive airways disease
COETT	cuffed oral endotracheal tube (see COT and ETT)
comp	compounded of
COT	cuffed oral tube
CPD	cephalo-pelvic disproportion (baby too big to fit through pelvis)
CPR	cardiopulmonary resuscitation
crem	cream
C & S	culture and sensitivity
CSF	cerebro-spinal fluid
CTG	cardiotocograph – electronic monitoring of fetal heart rate and uterine contractions during pregnancy and labour
CVA	cardiovascular accident (stroke)
CVP	central venous pressure
CVS	cardiovascular system or chorionic villus sampling
Cx	cervix
CXR	chest X-ray
D	diagnosis
D&C	dilatation and curettage
DIC	disseminated intravascular coagulation
dil	dilute
DNA	(i) did not attend (ii) deoxyribonucleic acid
D & V	diarrhoea and vomiting
DOA	dead on arrival
DOB	date of birth
DOPA	dopamine
DTs	delirium tremens
DU	duodenal ulcer
DVT	deep vein thrombosis
D/W	direct word
Dx	diagnosis
ECG	electrocardiogram
ECT	electroconvulsive therapy
EDD	expected date of delivery
EEG	electroencephalogram
EMG	electromyo/gram/graph
EMU	early morning urine
ENT	ear nose and throat
EOG	electro-oculogram
ER	external rotation
ERCP	endoscopic retrograde cholangio-pancreatography
ERPC	evacuation of retained products of conception
ERG	electroretinogram
ESN	educationally subnormal

ESR	erythrocyte sedimentation rate
EUA	examination under anaesthetic
Ex	extension
FB	finger's breadth or foreign body
FBC	full blood count
FB	fetal blood sampling (ob) or fasting blood sugar
FH	family history
FHH	fetal heart heard
FHHR	fetal heart heard regular
FHNH	fetal heart not heard
FHR	fetal heart rate
flex	flexion
FLK	funny looking kid
FMF	fetal movements felt
FSE	fetal scalp electrode
FSH	family/social history or follicle-stimulating hormone
GA	general anaesthetic
G & A	gas and air
garg	gargles
GLC	gas liquid chromatography
GCT	glucose tolerance test
GFR	glomerular filtration rate
GI	gastrointestinal (GIT – GI tract)
GOK	god only knows
GTT	glucose tolerance test
GU	gastric ulcer
GUT	genitourinary tract
Hb	haemoglobin
HCG	human chorionic gonadotrophin
hco	history of present complaint *or* HPC
HDL	high density lipoprotein
HDU	high dependency unit
HI	hypodermic injection
HRT	hormone replacement therapy
HS	heart sounds
HVS	high vaginal swab
Hx	history
ICF	intracellular fluid
ICS	intercostal space
ICU	intensive care unit
IDDM	insulin dependent diabetes mellitus
IgA, IgB, IgG, IgM	immunoglobulins
IJ	internal jugular vein
IM	intramuscular
Implant	implantation
In aq	in water
In d	daily
Inj	injections
IP	intraperitoneal or inpatient
IQ	intelligence quotient
IR	internal rotation
Irrig	irrigations
ISQ	in status quo (no change)
ITU	intensive therapy unit
IUCD	intra-uterine contraceptive device
IUD	intra-uterine death
IV	intravenous
IVF	in-vitro fertilisation
IVI	intravenous infusion
K	potassium
KJ	knee jerk
KPa	kilopascal, approx 7.5 mm Hg
L or l	litre
LA	local anaesthetic
LATS	long acting thyroid stimulator
LCS	left convergent squint
LDS	left divergent squint

LFT	liver function tests
LH	lutenizing hormone
LIF	left iliac fossa
LIH	left inguinal hernia
linc.	linctus
liq.	solutions
LMP	last menstrual period
LN	lymph node
LOA	left occiput anterior
LOC	loss of consciousness
LOL	left occiput lateral
LOP	left occiput posterior
LRTI	lower respiratory tract infection
LSCS	lower segment caesarean section
LSK	liver, spleen, kidneys
m	mix
MA	mental age
mane	in the morning
MAOI	monoamine oxidase inhibitors (type of antidepressant drug)
mcg	microgram
MC&S	microscopy culture and sensitivity
MCH	mean corpuscular haemoglobin (MCV – MC volume)
MCL	mid clavicular line
mg	milligram
mmttg	mm of mercury unit of pressure
ml	millilitres
MRSA	methicillin/multiple resistant staphylococcus
MRI	magnetic resonance imaging
MSH	melanophore stimulating hormone
N & V	nausea and vomiting
nad	nothing abnormal detected
NAI	non-accidental injury
NBI	no bone injury
NBM	nil by mouth
ND	normal delivery
Neb	nebuliser (a spray)
ng	nanogram
NG	neoplastic growth/new growth
NIDDM	non-insulin dependent diabetes mellitus
NMCS	no malignant cells seen
nocte	night
NOAD	no other abnormality detected
NOF	neck of femur
NP	proper name
N/S	normal size
NSAID	non-steroidal anti-inflammatory drug
O_2	oxygen
OA	occipito-anterior or on arrival or osteoarthritis
occ or oc	for the eyes
OD	outside diameter or right eye
OE	on examination
om	every morning
oe	every evening
OP	occipito-posterior or outpatient
P	pulse rate
pa	to the affected part
Pa	Pascal
PAS	periodic acid – Schiff reaction
pc	after meals
PCB	post-coital bleeding
PCO	patient complains of
PCV	packed cell volume

PERLA	pupils are equal and react to light and accommodation
PE	pulmonary embolism
pes	pessaries
PET	pre-eclampsia toxaemia
pH	acidity/alkalinity scale
PH	past history
PID	pelvic inflammatory disease; or prolapsed intravertebral disc
PMB	post-menopausal bleeding
PMH	past medical history
PMS	premenstrual syndrome
PN	post-natal
PN(R)	percussion note (resonant)
PND	post nasal drip
PNS	peripheral nervous system
PO	per or – by mouth
POP	plaster of paris
PP	placenta praevia or private patient
PPH	post-partum haemorrhage
PR	per rectum
PRN	as required/as occasion arises
PUO	pyrexia of unknown origin
PV	per vagina
qds	four times daily
RA	rheumatoid arthritis
RBC	red blood cells/red blood count
RCS	right convergent squint
RDS	respiratory distress syndrome
REM	rapid eye movements
rep	to be repeated
RIA	radio immune assay
RIH	right inguinal hernia
ROA	right occiput anterior
ROL	right occiput lateral
ROM	range of movement
RPF	renal plasma flow
RQ	respiratory quotient
RS	respiratory system
RSI	repetitive strain injury
RT	reaction time
RTA	road traffic accident
RTI	respiratory tract infection
SAD	seasonal affective disorder
SAH	subarachnoid haemorrhage
SB	stillbirth
S/B	seen by
SCAN	suspected child abuse or neglect
SCBU	special care baby unit
S/D	systolic/diastolic
SEM	scanning electron microscope
SI	sexual intercourse
SIDS	sudden infant death syndrome
SH	social history
SJ	supinator jerk
SMI	school medical inspection
SOA	swelling of ankles
SOB	shortness of breath
SOL	space occupying lesion
SROM	spontaneous rupture of membranes
stat	at once
SVC	superior vena cava
SVD	spontaneous vaginal delivery
Ts & As	tonsillectomy & adenoidectomy
TATT	tired all the time
TCA	to come again
TCI 3/52	to come (in three weeks' time)
TCRE	transcervical endometrial resection

tds	three times daily
TGH	to go home
THR	total hip replacement
TIA	transient ischaemic attack
TID	three times a day
TJ	triceps jerk
TLE	temporal lobe epilepsy
TLC	tender loving care
TOP	termination of pregnancy
TPR	temperature, pulse and respiration
TSH	thyroid stimulating hormone
TTA	to take away
U & E	urea and electrolytes
ung.	ointments
UG	urinogenital system
URTI	upper respiratory tract infection
USS	ultrasound scan
VA	visual acuity
vap	vapour
VE	vaginal examination
VF	ventricular fibrillation
VI	virgo intacta
VT	ventricular tachycardia
V/V	vulva and vagina
Vx	vertex
WBC	white blood count

APPENDIX 3: MEDICAL PERSONNEL

The hospital hierarchy: doctors

Pre-registration house officer (houseman): this is the first appointment of any newly qualified doctor having passed a qualifying examination in medicine and attained provisional registration with the GMC. House officers must complete two approved resident hospital posts, usually of six months' duration each, in medicine and surgery. On satisfactory completion of this pre-registration year, they can qualify for full registration with the GMC.

Senior House Officer (SHO): SHO posts normally have a tenure of six months although some posts are linked to a rotation so that the doctor may move through a number of different specialities. SHOs may do routine operations under the supervision of a more senior member of the 'firm'. SHOs will be deciding their future speciality.

Registrar: a doctor who is acquiring specialist experience in a particular field of medicine and holds a registrar post in a hospital speciality e.g. obstetrics, surgery etc. A registrar will perform operations without supervision unless a difficult procedure is involved. After two or three years at this grade, a doctor would normally be looking to apply for a senior registrar's post.

Senior Registrar: a doctor would normally spend three or four years at the senior registrar grade to complete his/her specialist training and in preparation for applying for a consultant's post. Clinically, a senior registrar can be equally as competent as a consultant but may merely be awaiting one of the rare vacancies for a consultant's post to become available.

Specialist Registrar: as from the 1st April 1996, the posts of registrar and senior registrar are being phased out to be replaced by a unified training grade of specialist registrar. The period of training should be completed within seven years, certificates of completion of specialist training (CCST) to be awarded by the Specialist Training Authority, and be ready to apply for a consultant's post.

Consultant: this is the senior specialist in a particular field of medicine. Most consultants act as the head of a team or 'firm' of junior doctors or 'doctors in training' (i.e. registrars, senior house officers, clinical assistants etc.) Consultants undertake full responsibility for the clinical care of patients.

Staff Grade: doctors who will not be taking up a consultant's post can be employed in a non-training staff grade post.

Other medical posts within hospital include associate specialists, hospital practitioners (GPs) and clinical assistants.

University Medical School Hierarchy

Professor and Senior Lecturer: equivalent status to Consultant.
Lecturer: equivalent grade to senior registrar, occasionally to registrar.

Hospital hierarchy: Nursing staff

(1) Senior Sister
(2) Sister or Charge Nurse (male equivalent)
(3) Staff Nurse (qualified nurse):
 a. Registered Nurse Level 1: RGN
 b. Registered Nurse Level II: EN(G) – Enrolled nurse
(4) Final year RGN student nurse.
(5) Second year RGN student nurse.
(6) First year RGN student nurse.

(Note: The 'Nurse in Charge' is the person responsible for the patients, nursing and other staff on a particular ward.)

Nurse training. There are three routes for nurse training: Project 2000, nursing degree course and traditional ward/nursing school training. The latter has gradually been phased out to be replaced by Project 2000, a more theoretical training although practical ward experience is still an important part of the training. Degree course training has the highest theoretical content with less practical experience.

Other qualifications

(1) Registered mental nurse (RMN): qualified to work in mental health but not general nursing.
(2) Registered midwife (RM): most midwives have completed nurse training and have then undergone specialist training in midwifery. Midwives are known as student midwives when qualifying and registered midwives when qualified. There are a few colleges that now provide direct entry training in midwifery without requiring a nursing qualification.

Nursing assistants and auxiliaries

(1) Healthcare support workers: these replaced the service contribution of student nurses following the introduction of Project 2000 but are now being phased out.
(2) Nursing auxiliary: provide basic care such as bathing and distributing meals but do not have specific training. Being phased out.
(3) Health care assistants (HCA):
(a) NVQ Level II Care Assistant: one year training, able to take blood pressure, pulse and temperature.
(b) Health Care Assistant: receive six months in-house training. Can take blood pressure, pulse and temperature.

Guide to the common medical specialities

Anaesthesia: administration of anaesthetics, intensive care, pain relief etc. (anaesthetist).
Cardiology: diagnosis and treatment of diseases of the heart and blood vessels (cardiologist, cardiothoracic surgeon, cardiovascular surgeon).
Dermatology: diagnosis and treatment of skin conditions (dermatologist).
Endocrinology: diagnosis and treatment of disorders of the endocrine glands e.g. thyroid, adrenals etc.
ENT: diseases of the ear nose and throat also known as **Otorhinolaryngology.**

Gastroenterology: digestive system (gastroenterologist, colorectal/anorectal surgeon).
General Surgery: non-specialist surgery covering a wide range of surgical procedures e.g. appendix, gallbladder, varicose veins etc.
Genitourinary: diseases of the urinary system of both sexes and male reproductive system.
Gerontology/geriatrics: diseases of old age (geriatrician).
Gynaecology: female reproductive system (gynaecologist).
Haematology: blood and its disorders (haemotologist).
Immunology: diagnosis and treatment of disorders of the immune system.
Microbiology: detection and treatment of infection. May be clinical i.e. qualified doctor, or a medical laboratory scientific officer.
Neonatology: care and treatment of the newborn.
Nephrology: diseases of the kidney (nephrologist).
Neurology: diagnosis and treatment of disorders of the nervous system (neurologist, neurosurgeon, neuroradiologist).
Obstetrics: care of mother and fetus during pregnancy and childbirth (obstetrician).
Oncology: treatment of cancer (oncologist).
Ophthalmology: diagnosis and treatment of eye disease/injury (ophthalmologist/ophthalmic surgeon).
Orthopaedics: bones and joints (orthopaedic surgeon, rheumatologist).
Paediatrics: infants and children up to 14 years (paediatricians).
Pathology: diagnosis of disease, study of diseased tissue, post mortems.
Pharmacology: drug therapeutics (clinical pharmacologist).
Physician: treatment of medical conditions as opposed to surgical. Physicians may specialise e.g. chest physician, cardiologist etc.
Plastic Surgery: surgical repair of damaged or defective tissue.
Psychiatry: diseases of the mind (psychiatrist, clinical psychologist).
Radiology: diagnostic and therapeutic art of X-ray.
Radiotherapy: radiotherapy treatment (radiotherapist).
Rheumatologist: connective tissues disorders.
Surgery: surgical treatment as opposed to medical.
Urology: diagnosis and treatment of diseases of the genitourinary system.
Venerology: sexually transmitted diseases.
Virology: diagnosis and treatment of viruses.

Non-medical specialities

Audiometrist: hearing test (audiometrist).

Chiropodist: foot disorders.

Dietitian: ensuring patient has appropriate nutrition and devising specialised diets.

Occupational therapists: rehabilitation and treatment through specific activities.

Orthoptists: investigation and treatment of eye disorders e.g. as squints.

Ophthalmic opticians: prescription of spectacles and contact lenses. Dispensing opticians supply spectacles but do not perform eye tests.

Physiotherapist: following disease or injury will by physical manipulation attempt to restore function.

Psychologist (clinical): behavioural treatments, trauma counselling, etc.

Speech therapy: treatment of disorders of speech.

Radiographer: X-ray technician.

Technicians: there are a number of technical or paramedical staff who carry out physiological measurements including technicians in audiology, cardiology, neurophysiology, physics, vascular system etc.

Theatre technicians: assist in operating theatres e.g. scrubbing, sterile equipment etc.

Primary healthcare team

A number of different professionals from the primary healthcare team within the community, the first point of contact for most patients, including:

(a) general practitioners.

(b) practice nurses: RGN or EN employed by a GP's practice;
(c) health visitors: RGN with a specialist qualification in health visiting;
(d) district nurses: RGN with a specialist qualification for providing care in the home;
(e) midwives; and
(f) counsellors.

There is a range of other specialists who will liaise with the community team e.g. chiropodists, specialist nurses (incontinence advisers, etc), occupational therapists, social workers etc.

Medical qualifications for doctors

Qualifying degrees in medicine

MBBS	Bachelor of Medicine and Bachelor of Surgery awarded by most universities. Some universities are different – BM ChB, BM BCh, BM BS.
MRCS LRCP	Awarded by the Conjoint Board of the Royal College of Surgeons and Licentiate of the Royal College of Physicians. The same status as MBBS but not awarded by a university.

Research degrees

MD or MS, occasionally MChir and at Oxford DM. These have roughly the same status as PhD or DPhil and will vary according to university.

Specialist medical/dental qualifications

BAc	Bachelor of Acupuncture
BAO	Bachelor of the Art of Obstetrics
BC/BCh	Bachelor of Surgery
BChir	Bachelor of Surgery
BDS	Bachelor of Dental Surgery
BDSc/BDS	Bachelor of Dental Science
BChD	Bachelor of Dental Science

BChir	Bachelor of Surgery
BHy	Bachelor of Hygiene
BM	Bachelor of Medicine
ChB	Bachelor of Surgery
ChM/CM	Master of Surgery
DA	Diploma in Anaesthetics
DCH	Diploma in Childhealth
DCP	Diploma in Clinical Pathology
DDerm	Diploma in Dermatology
DDO	Diploma in Dental Orthopaedics
DDS	Doctor of Dental Surgery
DDR	Diploma in Diagnostic Radiology
DLO	Diploma in Laryngology and Otology
DO	Diploma in Ophthalmology
DObst	Diploma in Obstetrics
DRCOG	Diploma in Obstetrics and Gynaecology
FFARCS	Fellow of the Faculty of Anaesthetists of the Royal College of Surgeons
FFCM	Faculty of Community Medicine
FRCA	Fellow of the Royal College of Anaesthetists
FRCGP	Fellow of the Royal College of General Practitioners (by election etc.)
FRCOG	Fellow of the Royal College of Obstetricians & Gynaecologists (by election etc.)
FRCOphth	Fellow of the Royal College of Ophthalmologists (highest qualification)
FRCP	Fellow of the Royal College of Physicians (by election etc.)
FRCPath	Fellow of the Royal College of Pathologists
FRCPsych	Fellow of the Royal College of Psychiatrists (highest qualification)
FRCR	Fellow of the Royal College of Radiologists (highest qualification)
FRCS	Fellow of the Royal College of Surgeons (highest qualification)
MB	Bachelor of Medicine
MB BS	Bachelor of Medicine and Bachelor of Surgery
MB ChB	Bachelor of Medicine and Bachelor of Surgery
MCD	Master of Clinical Dentistry
MCh/MChir	Master of Surgery
MChirOrth	Master of Orthopaedic Surgery
MD	Doctor of Medicine (research degree)

MDS	Master of Dental Surgery
MRCGP	Member of the Royal College of General Practitioners (higher diploma)
MRCOG	Member of the Royal College of Obstetricians & Gynaecologists (highest qualification)
MRCOphth	Member of the Royal College of Ophthalmologists (qualifying diploma)
MRCP	Member of the Royal College of Physicians (by examination)
MRCPath	Member of the Royal College of Pathologists (by examination)
MRCPsych	Member of the Royal College of Psychiatrists (qualifying diploma)
MRCS	Member of the Royal College of Surgeons (by examination)

APPENDIX 4: GENERAL MEDICAL COUNCIL – THE SYSTEM OF REGISTRATION FOR DOCTORS

Before someone can practise as a doctor within the United Kingdom, they must first be registered with the General Medical Council. The system of registration is governed by the Medical Act 1983. To achieve registration, they must satisfy the educational requirements laid down by the Council.

There are three Registers held by the GMC:

- the Register of Medical Practitioners;
- the Specialist Register; and
- the Register of Medical Practitioners with Limited Registration.

The Register of Medical Practitioners

The Register of Medical Practitioners contains the names of those individuals holding full or provisional registration and is divided into four lists as follows:

(1) The Principal List: the main list of qualified doctors practising in the United Kingdom
(2) The Overseas List: doctors who are resident outside the United Kingdom and EEA
(3) The Visiting Overseas Doctors List: overseas qualified doctors who are temporarily working in the United Kingdom and who have been granted 'temporary full registration' to provide specialist medical services
(4) The Visiting EEA Practitioners List: EEA doctors temporarily providing medical services within the United Kingdom

The Principal List

Provisional Registration

Doctors who have qualified in the UK are entitled on application to be granted provisional registration on graduation from University and must then satisfactorily complete a year of general clinical training as a resident house officer in an approved hospital or institution before they are eligible for full registration. This is referred to as the pre-registration year. In the published register, doctors with provisional registration are identified with an asterisk.

Doctors who have qualified outside the United Kingdom and hold recognised qualifications can also be granted provisional registration, but at the GMC's discretion. They must demonstrate that they have the necessary knowledge of English and that they are of good character.

Full Registration

Once doctors have completed general clinical training and have been certified as having done so by their examining bodies they are entitled on application to full registration. This enables doctors to engage in any form of professional medical practice in the UK.

Registration of EEA doctors

Nationals of member states of the EEA who hold a recognised EEA qualification and have an unrestricted licence to practise medicine in their own member state are eligible for full registration as above. Further details can be obtained from the General Medical Council.

Registration of non-EEA qualified doctors

Doctors who have qualified outside the UK and hold recognised overseas qualifications can be granted full registration but at the GMC's discretion. They must show that they have the experience required for full registration, have the necessary knowledge of English, and that they are of good character.

Doctors who hold overseas qualifications and are nationals of another member state of the EEA are in a similar category to the previous one except that they do not have to demonstrate a knowledge of English.

Details held on the register

The 'Medical Register' contains details of the doctors name, registered address, sex and registration number, registered qualifications and dates of provisional and full registration. The registered qualifications include the 'primary' qualifications which enabled the doctor to qualify for registration e.g. MB BS, MRCS, LRCP. The Medical Register is quite separate from the 'Medical Directory' in that the Directory only gives details of doctors on the 'principal list' and inclusion is optional although most practitioners will opt to be included. The Medical Directory is published by FT Healthcare not the GMC.

Conditions placed on Registration

A doctor with full registration may have specific conditions (restrictions) attached to their registration, in particular, where the doctor has been subject to fitness to practice procedures. The sort of conditions that might be imposed could include a doctor not being allowed to practise in specified branches of medical practice, only being able to practise in certain types of post or under supervision, not being able to prescribe or possess controlled drugs, having to undergo retraining etc.

The Specialist Register

The European Specialist Medical Qualifications Order – which first came into effect on 12 January 1996 – requires the GMC to keep and publish a specialist register. From 1 January 1997 it is a legal requirement that only those doctors whose names are included in the specialist register may take up a consultant post in the NHS (except in the case of doctors who held a consultant post as an oral and maxillo-facial surgery immediately before 1 January 1997).

In order to qualify for admission to the specialist register, a doctor must obtain a Certificate of Completion of Specialist Training (CCST) in the relevant speciality awarded by the Specialist Training Authority (STA) of the Royal Colleges. There are transitional arrangements for existing specialists.

Other doctors eligible for inclusion on the specialist register include:

- nationals of member states of the EEA who hold specialist qualifications awarded by other member states which are recognised under the European Medical Directive
- overseas trained specialists whose training is assessed by the STA as equivalent to CCST standard
- those in academic or research medicine whose level of knowledge and skill is assessed by the STA as consistent with practice as a consultant in the NHS

Before the introduction of the specialist register, specialist training was indicated with a 'T'. The 'T' indicator continues to be used at the doctor's written request to signify specialist training in the case of general practitioners (GPs) who are not included in the specialist register.

The Register of Medical Practitioners with Limited Registration

This applies to doctors who qualified outside the EEA whose qualifications do not entitle them to full registration but would entitle them to limited registration. The GMC now accepts primary medical qualifications listed by the WHO Directory of Medical Schools for limited registration. In order to be eligible to apply for limited registration a doctor should normally have completed at least 12 months clinical experience in a teaching hospital approved for internship training and thereafter have passed, or gained exemption from the test of professional knowledge and competence in English known as the PLAB test. A doctor must have passed the International Language Testing System before sitting the PLAB test. Doctors with limited registration can only work in supervised posts in hospitals which provide an approved standard of training. A doctor may only remain on the limited registration list for a maximum of five years. A doctor who can demonstrate they have acquired appropriate skill and professional experience may apply for full registration after limited registration.

APPENDIX 5: VACCINE DAMAGE PAYMENTS ACT 1979

Anyone who has been severely disabled as a result of a vaccination or as a result of contact with a person who has been vaccinated (with oral vaccine for polio), can claim a one-off payment of £30,000 tax free under the Vaccine Damage Payments Act 1979. A claim can also be made where a person has been disabled as a result of his or her mother being vaccinated during pregnancy.

A claim can be made for severe disability caused by any of the following vaccinations:

(a) diphtheria;
(b) tetanus;
(c) whooping cough (pertussis);
(d) poliomyelitis;
(e) measles;
(f) rubella (German measles);
(g) tuberculosis;
(h) mumps;
(i) Hib (Haemophilus Influenzae type b);
(j) any other disease which is specified by the Secretary of State.

The vaccines covered by the Act also include the combined vaccines such as the MMR (measles, mumps, rubella).

Criteria for receiving a payment under the Act

(1) The person must have suffered 80% disability or more; this could be a mental or physical disability.
(2) The child must be two or more years old before a claim can be made.
(3) The vaccination must have been carried out in the United Kingdom or Isle of Man; the main exception is if the vaccination took place overseas but was given as part of the armed services medical facilities.
(4) With the exception of rubella and poliomyelitis, the vaccination must have been carried out before the age of 18 (unless the vaccination took place during an outbreak of the disease).

Time limit for claims under the Act

A claim for payment under the Act must be made:

(1) within six years of the date of the vaccination; or
(2) within six years of the child reaching the age of two (if administered before two years of age)

Making a claim under the Act

Parents/claimants should usually contact the Vaccine Damage Payment Unit (VDPU) for a copy of the claim form (currently VAD 1A/leaflet HB3) which must be completed and returned to the Unit. The address of the VDPU is:

The Vaccine Damage Payment Unit
Palatine House
Lancaster Road
Preston
Lancs PR1 1HB
Tel:01253 856123
Fax:01772 899257

Parents would be advised to seek advice.

How claims are assessed

Claims will initially be considered by the VDPU (on behalf of the Secretary of State). The claimant will be informed in writing of the decision. If a claim is turned down either because it is not considered that the vaccine caused the disability or because the person is less than 80% disabled, the claimant can appeal to an independent medical tribunal. The tribunal panel consists of a legal chairman and two members, usually a consultant paediatrician and a neurologist. The child can be represented by a solicitor.

Payment under the Act

Successful claimants under the Act receive a one-off lump sum payment of £30,000 for claims made on or after 15th April 1991. (When the Act first came into force, the payment was £10,000; this was increased in July 1985 to £20,000, and then further increased in 1991 to the present sum of £30,000.)

Legal Action

In addition to the statutory payment of £30,000, if a child has been damaged, for example, as a result of negligence on the part of the manufacturer of a vaccine or the person who administered the vaccine, then the child may have grounds for a legal claim. Such claims are extremely difficult to prove but there are a number of solicitors who are currently specialising in investigating such claims, particularly in respect of the whooping cough vaccine and the MMR vaccine. For further information contact AVMA, the Law Society or the organisations listed below.

Support Groups

The Association of Parents of Vaccine Damaged Children
2 Church Street
Shipston-on-Stour
Warwickshire CV36 4AP
Tel: 01608 661595

JABS (Justice Awareness and Basic Support)
1 Gawsworth Road
Golborne
Warrington
Cheshire WA3 3RF
Tel: 01942 713565 Fax: 01942 715251

APPENDIX 6: SUMMARY OF THE ACCESS TO HEALTH RECORDS ACT 1990

Section 1 defines a 'health record' as information relating to the physical or mental health of an individual made by a healthcare professional.

Section 2 defines 'healthcare professional' as a medical practitioner, dentist, optician, chemist, nurse, midwife, health visitor, chiropodist, dietician, occupational therapist, orthoptist, physiotherapist, psychologist, psychotherapist, speech therapist, an art or music therapist or a scientist employed by a Health Authority.

Section 3 allows an application for access to a health record to be made by a patient (including parent, guardian or personal representative) or someone authorised in writing on his behalf. 'Access' means allowing the applicant to inspect the record or extract the record. It also allows the applicant to be supplied with a copy of the record or extract. Where the record is expressed in terms which are not intelligible without explanation, an explanation of those terms shall be provided, by the record holder.

A fee not exceeding £10 (as set down by the Data Protection Act 1984 Section 21) is payable. In addition the holder is entitled to charge 'a fee not exceeding the cost of making the copy and posting it to the applicant'.

Disclosure must be given within 21 days.

Section 4 sets out when the right of access may be wholly excluded as follows:

- where the application is by a child and the holder of the record is satisfied that the child does not understand the application, or that proper consent has been obtained, or that disclosure would not be in his best interests;
- where the patient had died and there is a note on the record at the patient's request that he did not wish access to be given on the application by his personal representatives.

Section 5 sets out the position where a right of access may be partially excluded as follows:–

- where the record would disclose information likely to cause serious harm (physical or mental) to the patient or any other individual;
- where the record could disclose information about another independent individual who has not consented to the application;
- where in the case of a child, mental patient or deceased the information was given in the expectation that it would not be shown to the applicant;
- where the patient has deceased and the record is not relevant to any claim which may arise out of the death (relevance is determined by the record holder).

Section 6 allows for the correction of inaccurate records where a person considers that the Health Record is inaccurate and may apply to the holder of the record for a correction to be made. Inaccurate means 'incorrect, misleading or incomplete'.

APPENDIX 7: USEFUL ADDRESSES

Advice agencies and self-help groups

Community Health Councils (CHCs)

These are the community's watchdogs for health services. There is a community health council covering every Health Authority. They can offer free confidential help and advice to patients on making a complaint and, if needed, can write letters on behalf of complainants, attend meetings and in some cases, can act as the patient's representative at hearings. Details of the nearest CHC should be available in the local telephone directory, in the front of the Thomsons directory, in libraries, hospitals and GP surgeries.

Health & Social Services Councils in Northern Ireland

This is the Northern Ireland equivalent of the Community Health Council and can assist patients with making complaints about health care. There are four Councils covering the four main health regions.

Advice and Information for patients

Health Information Services
Freephone: 0800 665544
National helpline for information on all issues to do with health.

Medical Advisory Service
P.O. Box 3087
London
W4 4ZP
Tel: 0181 995 8503

Patients Association
P.O. Box 935
Harrow
Middlesex
HA1 3XS
0181 423 8999

Children's Health/Disability

BLISS/BLISSLINK
(Baby Life Support Systems)
17–21 Emerald Street
London
WC1N 3QL
0171 831 9393
Freecall helpline for parents with sick newborn & premature babies: 0500 151617 (Mon Fri)

Contact-a-Family
170 Tottenham Court Road
London
W1P OHA
Tel: 0171 383 3555
Families with disabled children.

Erb's Palsy Group
2 Willoughby Close
Coventry
CV3 2GJ
Tel: 01203 452321
Self-help group.

Meningitis Research (England)
13 High Street
Thornbury
Bristol
BS12 2AE
Helpline: 01454 413344
Meningitis & septicaemia.

National Meningitis Trust
Fern House
Bath Road
Stroud
Gloucestershire GL5 3TJ
Voice & Minicom: 01453 751738
24hr Support Line: 0345 538118

SCOPE (formerly, The Spastics Society)
12 Park Crescent
London W1N 4EQ
0171 636 5020
Cerebral Palsy
Helpline: 0800 626216

Toxoplasmosis Trust
61–71 Collier Street
London N1 9BE
Information, Advice, Helpline
Helpline: 0171 713 0599

Pregnancy and childbirth

AIMS : The Association for
Improvement in Maternity Services
40 Kingswood Avenue
London NW6 6LS
Tel: 0181 960 5585
Support & advice, a pressure group campaigning for improvements in maternity services.

Association for Post-Natal Illness
25 Jerdan Place
Fulham
London
SW6 1BE
Tel: 0171 386 0868

ISSUE (The National Fertility
Association) Ltd
509 Aldridge Road
Great Barr
Birmingham
West Midlands B44 8NA
Tel: 01922 722888
Self-help organisation.

Miscarriage Association
c/o Clayton Hospital
Northgate
Wakefield
West Yorkshire WF1 3JS
Tel: 01924 200799 (24hr)
Miscarriage & ectopic pregnancy.

National Association of Premenstrual Syndrome
P.O. Box 72
Sevenoaks
Kent TN13 1XQ
Tel: 01732 741709

National Childbirth Trust
Alexandra House
Oldham Terrace
Acton
London W3 6NH
Tel: 0181 992 8637

Pre-Eclampsia Society (PETS),
Eaton Lodge
8 Southend Road
Hockley
Essex SS5 4QQ
Tel: 01702 205088
Self-help & support group.

SAFTA (Support after Termination for
Abnormality)
73 Charlotte Street
London W1P 1LB
Tel: 0171 631 0285
Information & support.

Medical Conditions/Disability

Action for ME & Chronic Fatigue
P.O. Box 1302
Wells
Somerset
BA5 2WE
Tel: 01749 670799
Helpline: 0891 122976

Arachnoiditis Self-help Group
PO Box 27
Stoneycroft
Liverpool
Merseyside L13 5RS
Tel: 0151 259 0222
Self-help Group, advice and support.

Breakthrough Breast Cancer
7th Floor, Kingsway House
103 Kingsway
London
WC2B 6QX
Tel: 0171 405 5111

British Tinnitus Association
4th Floor, White Building
Fitzalan Square
Sheffield
South Yorkshire
S1 2AZ
Tel: 0114 279 6600
Information, self-help groups and counselling.

CAMPAIN
St. Thomas' Hospital
PO Box 4700
London
SE1 7YB
Tel: 0171 922 8304
Information and helpline service, records on chronic pain support groups.

Cancerlink
11–21 Northdown Street
London N1 9BN
Freephone helpline: 0800 132905
Macline for young people: 0800 591028

Disability Information Database
Admin Tel: 01306 742282
Service database: 01306 742130
Database register of 3000+ disability organisations.

HEADWAY National Head Injuries Association
7 King Edward Court
King Edward Street
Nottingham
Nottinghamshire
NG1 1EW
Tel: 0115 924 0800
Local support groups, day centres, information and publications.

Menopause & Pre-Menstrual Syndrome Group
2nd Floor, Alderney Building
Mile End Hospital
Bancroft Road
London E1
Tel: 0171 377 7044/7898
Self-help group.

National Back Pain Association
16 Elmtree Road
Teddington
Middlesex TW11 8ST
Helpline: 0181 977 5474

Pain Society
9 Bedford Square
London
WC1B 3RA
Tel: 0171 636 2750
Information about pain clinics and pain management programmes, newsletter.

Pain Concern UK
PO Box 318
Canterbury
Kent
CT2 0GP
Helpline: 01277 264677

Advice and support following a death

Child Bereavement Trust
1 Millside
Riversdale
Bourne End
Buckinghamshire
SL8 5EB

Compassionate Friends
National Office
53 North Street
Bristol
BS3 1EN
Helpline: 0117 953 9639
Bereaved parents

CRUSE – Bereavement Care
126 Sheen Road
Richmond
Surrey
TW9 1UR
Helpline: 0181 332 7227
Head Office Tel: 0181 940 4818

Foundation for the Study of Infant Deaths
14 Halkin Street
London
SW1X 7DP
Cot death helpline: 0171 235 1721

Inquest
Ground Flr, Alexandria National Hse
330 Seven Sisters Road
Finsbury Park
London
N4 2PJ
Tel: 0181 802 7430/7450
Deaths in controversial situations: advice, legal representation, information and publicity.

SANDS (Stillbirth & Neonatal Death Society)
28 Portland Place
London W1N 4DE
Helpline: 0171 436 5881
Self-help, support groups, counselling, advice, helpline, information.

Counselling/Mental Health

Anxiety Care
112 Cranley Drive
Ilford
Essex IG2 6AJ
Tel: 0181 554 0711
Tel: 0181 478 3400
Phobias.

British Association for Counselling
1 Regent Place
Rugby
Warwickshire
CV21 2PJ
Tel: 01788 578328
Provides a list on request of counsellors in a given area.

British Association of Psychotherapists
37 Mapesbury Road
London
NW2 4HJ
Tel: 0181 452 9823
Help in finding a psychotherapist.

ECT Anonymous
14 Western Avenue
Riddlesden
Keighley
West Yorkshire
BD20 5DJ
Tel: 01535 661493
Self-help group.

MIND (National Association for Mental Health)
Granta House
15/19 Broadway, Stratford
London E15 4BQ
Tel: 0181 519 2122
Information, advice, magazine, newsheet, meetings.

National Schizophrenia Fellowship
28 Castle Street
Kingston-upon-Thames
Surrey KT1 1SS
Advice line: 0181 974 6814

POPAN – The Prevention of Professional Abuse Network
3rd Floor
1 Wyvil Court
Wyvil Road
London
SW8 2TG
Tel: 0171 622 6334

Samaritans
10 The Grove
Slough
Berkshire
SL1 1QP
Tel: 01753 532713
Tel: 0345 909090
Crisis emotional support.

SANE (Schizophrenia : A National Emergency)
199–205 Old Marylebone Road
London NW1 5QP
Support and Information
Tel: 0345 678000

Traumatic Stress Clinic
73 Charlotte Street
London W1P 1LB
Tel: 0171 530 3666
Treatment for PTSD by GP referal

The Trauma After-Care Trust
Buttfields
The Farthings
Withington
Glos. GL54 4DF
PTSD 24hr Helpline: 01242 890306

Drug damage and damage caused by other medical products

The Association of Parents of Vaccine Damaged Children
2 Church Street
Shipston-on-Stour
Warwickshire CV36 4AP
Tel: 01608 661595

Council for Involuntary Tranquillizer Addiction
Cavendish House
Brighton Road
Waterloo
Liverpool
Merseyside
L22 5NG
Helpline: 0151 949 0102

Debendox Action Group
21 Corden Avenue
Mickleover
Derby
Derbyshire
DE3 5AQ
01332 517896
Information and advice on drugs given in pregnancy.

DES (Diethylstilboestrol) Action Group
c/o Women's Health
52–54 Featherstone Street
London
EC1Y 8RT
0171 251 6580
DES (Diethylstilboestrol)
Advice and information.

GASP (Group Against Steroid Prescription)
72 Costa Street
South Bank
Middlesbrough
Cleveland
TS6 6EU
Tel: 01642 465118 (Mon-Fri 2–4pm)
Self-help.

JABS (Justice Awareness and Basic Support)
1 Gawsworth Road
Golborne
Warrington
Cheshire
WA3 3RF
Tel: 01942 713565
Children's vaccinations; self-help group.

Radiotherapy Action Group Exposure
(RAGE)
24 Lockett Gardens
Trinity
Salford
Greater Manchester M3 6BJ
0161 839 2927
Support group, information and advice.

Silicone Support U.K.
3 Cherrybank Road
Merrylee
Glasgow
Scotland G43 2PQ
Tel: 0141 637 8450
Breast implants and silicone injections.

Steroid Aid Group
PO Box 220
London
E17 3JR
Self-help group.

Thalidomide Society
19 Central Avenue
Pinner
Middlesex HA5 5BT
Tel: 0181 868 5309

Statutory and professional bodies

Office for the Supervision of Solicitors
Victoria Court
8 Dormer Place
Leamington Spa
Warwickshire CV32 5AE
Helpline: 01926 822007/8/9
Complaints about solicitors

Law Society
113 Chancery Lane
London WC2A 1PL
Tel: 0171 242 1222
Solicitors' professional body

General Council of the Bar
3 Bedford Row
London WC1R 4DB
Tel: 0171 242 0082
Fax: 0171 831 9217
Barristers' professional body

Office of the Legal Services
Ombudsman
22 Oxford Court
Oxford Street
Manchester M2 3WQ
Tel: 0161 236 9532
Fax: 0161 236 2651

Human Fertilization & Embryology
Authority (HFEA)
Paxton House
30 Artillery Lane
London
E1 7LS
Tel: 0171 377 5077

Useful telephone numbers

Action for ME & Chronic Fatigue: 0891 122976
Action for Victims of Medical Accidents: 0181 686 8333
Action on Elder Abuse: 0181 679 7074 (based at Age Concern)
Age Concern: 0181 679 8000
Association for Spina Bifida and Hydrocephalus: 01733 555988
British Colostomy Association: 0118 939 1537
British Epilepsy Association: 0800 309030
Counsel and Care for the Elderly: 0171 485 1566
Down's Syndrome Association: 0181 682 4001
Mencap: 0171 454 0454
Myalgic Encephalomyelitis Association: 01375 361013
Royal National Institute for the Blind: 0171 388 1266
Royal National Institute for the Deaf: 0171 813 2480
Soldiers' Sailors' & Airmen's Families Association: 0171 403 8783
Spinal Injuries Association: 0181 444 2121

INDEX